Trade Liberalisation and Poverty in South Asia

The link between trade liberalisation and poverty has arguably been one of the most discussed topics in development policy debate. Existing studies on the subject have primarily used multi-country cross-sectional data, and there is a growing concern about the limitations of this approach in providing a sound empirical basis for informing the policy debate. These limitations point to the need for undertaking in-depth analyses within individual countries over time.

In order to examine the connection between trade liberalisation and poverty, this book provides case studies of trade policy reforms and poverty reduction outcomes of seven countries in South Asia – Bangladesh, Bhutan, India, Maldives, Nepal, Pakistan and Sri Lanka. The South Asia region allows for an excellent comparative study given the widespread emphasis on liberalisation reforms in the region over the past two decades, as well as highlighting significant inter-country differences in terms of the timing and comprehensiveness of reforms, and the heavy concentration of world poverty in the region. This book is a useful contribution to studies on South Asia, as well as International Trade and Development Economics.

Jayatilleke S. Bandara is an Associate Professor at the Department of Accounting, Finance and Economics, Griffith University, Australia. He has published extensively in the areas of trade, development and economic modelling, particularly focusing on South Asian countries.

Prema-chandra Athukorala is Professor of Economics, Crawford School of Economics and Government, College of Asia and the Pacific, Australian National University and Fellow of the Academy of the Social Sciences in Australia. He has published numerous books and articles on international trade and economic development.

Saman Kelegama is the Executive Director of the Institute of Policy Studies of Sri Lanka and a Fellow of the National Academy of Sciences in Sri Lanka. He has written a number of books on Sri Lankan economy and South Asian economic issues.

Routledge Studies in the Growth Economies of Asia

Trade Liberalisation and Poverty in South Asia

Edited by
Jayatilleke S. Bandara,
Prema-chandra Athukorala and
Saman Kelegama

Routledge
Taylor & Francis Group

LONDON AND NEW YORK

First published 2011
by Routledge
2 Park Square, Milton Park, Abingdon, Oxfordshire OX14 4RN

Simultaneously published in the USA and Canada
by Routledge
711 Third Avenue, New York, NY 10017

First issued in paperback 2015

Routledge is an imprint of the Taylor & Francis Group, an informa business

British Library Cataloguing in Publication Data
A catalogue record for this book is available from the British Library

Library of Congress Cataloging in Publication Data
    Trade liberalisation and poverty in South Asia / edited by Prema-chandra
Athukorala, Jayatilleke S. Bandara and Saman Kelegam.
        p. cm. – (Routledge studies in the growth economies of Asia ; 105)
    Includes bibliographical references and index.
    1. South Asia–Commercial policy. 2. South Asia–Economic policy. 3.
Free trade–South Asia. 4. Poverty–South Asia. 5. Economic development–
South Asia. I. Athukorala, Prema-chandra. II. Bandara, Jayatilleke S. III.
Kelegama, Saman.
    HF1586.5.T73 2011
    382'.30954–dc22
            2010052900

ISBN 13: 978-1-138-94823-5 (pbk)
ISBN 13: 978-0-415-56175-4 (hbk)

Typeset in Times New Roman
by Taylor & Francis Books

Contents

Illustrations

Acknowledgements

The idea of preparing this volume was mooted in 2006, and the attempt came to fruition in 2008 when the Friedrich Ebert Stiftung (FES)-Colombo agreed to sponsor a conference on 'Trade–Poverty Nexus in South Asia' based on a concept paper prepared by the Institute of Policy Studies of Sri Lanka (IPS). We are very grateful to Joachim Schluetter, Resident Director, FES-Colombo, for the financial support and Rohini Peiris, FES-Colombo, for logistical support for organising the conference where individual South Asian country papers were presented. The revised papers of this conference constitute this book.

We are grateful to Muchkund Dubey, Co-Chairman, South Asia Centre for Policy Studies (SACEPS), for agreeing to be the Chief Guest, and Ravi Ratnayake, Director, Poverty and Development Division and Coordinator, Poverty Theme Group, UN-ESCAP, for being the Guest of Honour at the conference, which took place in May 2008 in Colombo. Our thanks also go to all the Chairpersons (Akmal Hussain, PIDE; Ibrahim Zaki, Government of Maldives; T. Palanivel, UNDP-RCC; Dushni Weerakoon, IPS; Sridhar Khatri, SACEPS; and Farooq Sobhan, BEI) and Discussants (Sunil Chandrasiri, University of Colombo; Selim Raihan, SANEM; Ramani Gunatilake; I.N. Mukherjee, JNU; Shiva Sharma, NLA-Nepal; Deshal de Mel, IPS; Ananya Raihan, D.Net; and Biplove Choudhary, UNDP-RCC) at the conference for their valuable comments on the papers presented.

Our thanks go to Ganga Tilakaratna and her team at the Poverty and Social Welfare Unit of the IPS for preparing the concept paper and the terms of reference for the paper writers, Deshal de Mel and his team at the International Economics Policy Unit of the IPS for organising the conference. We are grateful to all the paper-writers for revising their original paper taking into account the comments made at the conference and the book referees. Our thanks also go to D.D.M. Waidyasekera for editing the preliminary version of the manuscript and Pabasara Jayathilaka and Ruwan Jayathilaka for formatting the manuscript.

Last but not least, our thanks go to Sharmini de Silva for taking the lead role in organising the conference and for help with preparing the manuscript for publication.

The editors
July 2010

List of contributors

Prema-chandra Athukorala Professor of Economics, Crawford School of Economics and Government, Australian National University, College of Asia and the Pacific, Australia.

Jayatilleke S. Bandara Associate Professor, Department of Accounting, Finance and Economics, Griffith Business School, Griffith University, Australia.

Rashmi Banga Economist, United Nations Conference on Trade and Development, India.

Deshal de Mel Research Economist, Institute of Policy Studies of Sri Lanka, Colombo, Sri Lanka.

Jagath Dissanayake Research Officer, Institute of Policy Studies of Sri Lanka, Colombo, Sri Lanka (currently a PhD student at the Australian National University in Australia).

Chencho Dorji Head, Money and Banking Sector, Royal Monetary Authority of Bhutan, Thimpu, Bhutan.

Suwendrani Jayaratne Research Assistant, Institute of Policy Studies of Sri Lanka, Colombo, Sri Lanka.

Ruwan Jayathilaka Research Officer, Institute of Policy Studies of Sri Lanka, Colombo, Sri Lanka (currently a PhD student at Griffith University in Australia).

Saman Kelegama Executive Director and Fellow, Institute of Policy Studies of Sri Lanka, Colombo, Sri Lanka.

Yuba Raj Khatiwada Governor, Rastra Bank, Nepal.

Selim Raihan Associate Professor, Department of Economics, University of Dhaka, Dhaka, Bangladesh.

Shruti Sharma Consultant, United Nations Conference on Trade and Development – India Project, India.

Rehana Siddiqui Senior Research Economist, Pakistan Institute of Development Economics, Islamabad, Pakistan.

Acronyms and abbreviations

ADB	Asian Development Bank
AGE	Applied General Equilibrium
AMDP	Accelerated Mahaweli Development Project
APTA	Asia-Pacific Trade Agreement
ASI	Annual Survey of Industries
BaU	Business as Usual
BEI	Bangladesh Enterprise Institute
BIMSTEC	Bengal Initiative for Multi-Sectoral Technical and Economic Cooperation
BLSS	Bhutan Living Standard Survey
BMR	Balancing, Modernisation and Replacement
BOP	Balance of Payments
BST	Bhutan Sales Tax
CBS	Central Bureau of Statistics
CES	Constant Elasticity of Substitution
CET	Constant Elasticity of Transformation
CGE	Computable General Equilibrium
CIA	Central Intelligence Agency
CIF	Cost Insurance and Freight
CMI	Census of Manufacturing Industries
CMIE	Centre for Monitoring Indian Economy
COTI	Countries Other Than India
CSO	Central Statistical Office
DCS	Department of Census and Statistics
DGCI&S	Directorate General of Commercial Intelligence and Statistics
DPD	Dynamic Panel Data
EDB	Export Development Board
EOBI	Employees' Old-Age Benefits Institution
EPZ	Export Processing Zone
ESAF	Enhanced Structural Adjustment Facility
ESCAP	Economic and Social Commission for Asia and the Pacific
EU	European Union
EV	Equivalent Variation

FCBU	Foreign Currency Banking Units
FDI	Foreign Direct Investment
FISB	Foreign Investment Services Bureau
FL	Full Liberalisation
FOB	Free on Board
FTA	Free Trade Agreement
FTZ	Free Trade Zone
GATS	General Agreement on Trade in Services
GATT	General Agreement on Tariff and Trade
GCEC	Greater Colombo Economic Commission
GDP	Gross Domestic Product
GMM	Generalised Method of Moments
GSP	Generalised System of Preferences
GTAP	Global Trade Analysis Project
HCR	Head Count Ratio
HDI	Human Development Index
HIES	Household Income and Expenditure Survey
HO	Hechscher–Ohlin
HS	Harmonised Commodity Description and Coding System
IDRC	International Development Research Centre
IDSC	Infrastructure Development Surcharge
IFPRI	International Food Policy Research Institute
IGC	Integrated Gewog Centres
IMF	International Monetary Fund
IPO	Import Policy Order
IPS	Institute of Policy Studies of Sri Lanka
IS	Import Substitution
ISIC	International Standard Industrial Classification
ISO	International Organisation for Standardisation
JNU	Jawahalal Nehru University
JVP	Janatha Vimukthi Peramuna
LC	Letter of Credit
LDC	Least Developed Country
LES	Linear Expenditure System
LKR	Lanka Rupees
LSSP	Lanka Sama Samaja Party
MDG	Millennium Development Goal
MFA	Multi-Fibre Arrangement
MFN	Most Favoured Nation
MIMAP	Micro Impact of Macroeconomic Adjustment Policies
MMA	Maldives Monetary Authority
MPND	Ministry of Plain and National Development
MRP	Mixed Recall Period

NCEUS	National Commission for Enterprises in the Unorganised Sector
NFYP	Ninth Five Year Plan
NIC	National Industrial Classification
NLA	National Labour Academy
NSSO	National Sample Survey Organisation
NWFP	Non-wood Forest Products
OGL	Open General Licence
OTRI	Overall Trade Restrictiveness Index
PAM	Production, Access and Market
PAR	Poverty Analysis Report
PDS	Pakistan Development Studies
PIDE	Pakistan Institute of Development Economics
PL	Partial Liberalisation
PTC	Presidential Tariff Commission
QR	Quantitative Restrictions
R&D	Research and Development
REER	Real Effective Exchange Rate
RGOB	Royal Government of Bhutan
RMG	Ready-Made Garments
RNR	Renewable Natural Resource
SAARC	South Asian Association of Regional Cooperation
SAF	Structural Adjustment Facility
SAFTA	South Asian Free Trade Agreement
SAM	Social Accounting Matrix
SANEM	South Asia Network of Economic Modelling
SAP	Structural Adjustment Programme
SAPTA	South Asian Preferential Trade Area
SD	Supplementary Duties
SDG	SAARC Development Goals
SEZs	Special Economic Zones
SIE	Small Island Economy
SLFP	Sri Lanka Freedom Party
SPS	Sanitary and Phytosanitary Measures
SS	Stolper–Samuelson
TBT	Technical Barriers to Trade
TFYP	Tenth Five Year Plan
TOT	Terms of Trade
TTRI	Trade and Tariff Restrictiveness Index
UAE	United Arab Emirates
UN	United Nations
UNCTAD	United Nations Conference on Trade and Development
UNDP	United Nations Development Programme
UNDP-RCC	United Nations Development Programme: Regional Centre Colombo

UNESCAP	United Nations Economic and Social Commission for Asia and the Pacific
UNP	United National Party
URP	Uniform Recall Period
VAT	Value Added Tax
WTO	World Trade Organisation

1 Trade liberalisation and poverty in South Asia

Reforms, stylised facts and preview

Prema-chandra Athukorala,
Jayatilleke S. Bandara and
Saman Kelegama

The role of trade policy[1] in economic development and poverty reduction in developing countries has remained at the centre of the debate on economic policy making in developing countries. Trade policy, through its influence on the levels and composition of imports and exports, impacts on the structure of production and pattern of development of all economies. The emphasis placed on trade policy is usually very high in developing countries for reasons associated with their shared economic backwardness. The typical developing country adopts its development strategy from an initial position characterised by limited capacity to produce manufactures and dependence of domestic firms on imported inputs and technology for their ability to produce output. Therefore the nature of the trade regime, in particular the mechanism used to repress import demand, could have important implications for resource allocation, efficiency and income distribution in the economy.

In the 1950s and 1960s there was a broad consensus in the economics profession that the basic strategy for development should be based on 'import substitution' (IS) – the promotion of industries oriented towards the domestic market by using import restrictions, or even import prohibition, to encourage the replacement of imported manufactures by domestic products. The case for the import-substitution strategy was so widely accepted at the time that 'developing-country exemptions' were even incorporated into the General Agreement on Tariff and Trade (GATT),[2] enabling developing countries to pursue protectionist policies at a time when developed countries were removing their tariffs to increase the openness of their economies. Moreover, the two Bretton Woods institutions (the International Monetary Fund and the World Bank) and other international organisations with commitment to economic development in developing countries generally supported the basic thrust of the import-substitution policy (Krueger 1997).

The period from about the late 1960s has witnessed a decisive shift in development thinking and policy away from the entrenched import-substituting views and in favour of outward-orientated (export-oriented) trade strategy. The case for this policy was based on a number of multi-country studies of the contrasting experiences of developing countries under alternative trade policy regimes.[3] Policy advocacy based on this 'neo-classical revival in the applied trade and development literature' (Diaz-Alejandro 1975: 94) soon became an integral part of aid conditionality of the World Bank and the International Monetary Fund (IMF) and the major bilateral donors. Reflecting this new ideological orientation (popularly known as 'the Washington Consensus'), coupled with the influence of aid conditionality, trade liberalisation became the linchpin of policy reforms in many countries around the world. The new orthodoxy in favour of trade liberalisation also provided the setting for dismantling of trade concessions for developing countries under the trade policy reforms in the Uruguay Round.

The past two decades have seen the emergence of a strong revisionist school of thought in response to the lacklustre outcome of policy reforms in many countries. The revisionists do accept that the old-style import-substitution strategy bordering on autarchy has outlived its usefulness and that growth prospects for developing countries can be greatly enhanced through integration into the global economy. But they argue that trade can help achieve self-sustained growth with poverty alleviation only through cautious liberalisation combined with the right kind of government action to make 'openness work'.[4]

Most, if not all, of the empirical evidence used by the revisionists is derived from aggregate multi-country (cross-section or pooled time series) regression analyses. Quite apart from general methodological flaws relating to model specification and econometric procedure (Levine and Renelt 1992; Srinivasan and Bhagwati 2001; Athukorala 2011), there are two fundamental limitations that make results from any cross-country study on this subject rather dubious. First, cross-country regression analysis is based on the implicit assumption of 'homogeneity' in the observed relationship across countries. This is a very restrictive assumption. It is common knowledge that there are considerable variations among developing countries in relation to various structural features and institutional aspects that have a direct bearing upon the reform outcome. Second, given vast differences among countries with respect to the nature and quality of data, cross-country comparison is fraught with danger because attempts to characterise the 'average' developing country in terms of a cross-country regression are unlikely to yield sensible results. Comparison of results from various studies is also complicated by the absence of a unique measure of trade openness. Even if these limitations are ignored, cross-sectional studies are only a means of testing the validity of generalisations. Such tests are of obvious importance for broadening our understanding of economic phenomena. But in order to inform the policy debate, it is necessary to go beyond the general picture and obtain a comprehensive account of the underlying growth process and related social, political and institutional aspects.

These considerations point to the need for undertaking in-depth analyses within individual countries, by appropriately combining quantitative analysis with qualitative analysis in its own historical context, in order to build a sound empirical foundation for the debate on policy reforms in developing countries. This is the motivation behind the production of this volume. It brings together case studies of trade policy reforms and poverty reduction outcomes of seven countries in South Asia – Bangladesh, Bhutan, India, Maldives, Nepal, Pakistan and Sri Lanka.[5] South Asia provides an ideal laboratory for studying the subject at hand for the following reasons. All countries in the region have undergone notable shifts in trade policy regimes with a clear shift towards greater outward orientation over the past two decades, and the timing of reforms and the degree of trade opening achieved varied notably among the countries. Second, the overall growth trajectory, poverty incidence and the success of poverty reduction effort have also varied among the countries, providing rich material for a comparative study. Third, over 40 per cent of the total world poverty headcount population living are in South Asia, with India alone accounting for a third. An understanding of the South Asian experience is therefore vital for the contemporary policy debate on the role of policy reforms in poverty reduction. Fourth, after almost two decades of reforms, there has been a growing concern among policy circles in almost all countries in the region that the economic outcome of liberalisation reforms has fallen well short of the initial expectations. Consequently, the political climate has become more receptive to calls for more 'nationalistic' and protectionist policies and there are signs of a mounting policy backlash that can perpetuate and aggravate, rather than redress, current problems. In this context, it is vital to assess systematically the achievements of liberalisation reforms and the causes of their failure to match expectations.

The remainder of this chapter is organised as follows. The next section provides a historical overview of policy reforms in South Asia. The section following provides stylised facts on economic performance and the incidence of poverty. The final section provides a preview of the structure, content and key policy lessons of the case studies presented in the ensuing chapters.

Trade policy reforms: an overview

During the first four decades of the post-World War II period, import substitution was the basic tenet of development strategy in all South Asian countries.[6] This policy choice was much in line with the climate of 'development' opinion at the time – there was a broad consensus in the economics profession that the basic strategy for development should be based on 'import substitution'. Apart from the ideological consensus of the day, import substitution also had a natural appeal to the strong nationalistic and anti-colonial sentiments that naturally accompanied the attainment of independence. There was a strong perception that the ex-colonial powers had enforced the primary commodity-dependent status on the developing countries and thereby had become economically stronger.

The policy regimes during the period were characterised by stringent trade barriers to international trade with high tariffs and quantitative restrictions

(QRs), restriction on foreign investment, industrial licensing aimed at governing sectoral priorities of private sector participation in line with the objectives of central planning, and direct pervasive state participation in the economy through setting up of public enterprises.

In the 1960s and 1970s there were episodes of partial liberalisation in some countries driven principally by donors' initiatives, but they were rather short-lived. Sri Lanka led the way in breaking away from the protectionist past by embarking on a decisive process of economic opening in 1977. The other countries embarked on significant liberalisation reforms from the late 1980s. While there are vast inter-country differences in terms of the degree of liberalisation achieved during the ensuing years and comprehensiveness of reforms, by the mid-1990s all seven countries seemed to have moved into a seemingly irreversible process of economic liberalisation. Table 1.1 provides a chronology of policy shifts.

After the separation from Pakistan in 1971, Bangladesh adopted a protectionist trade regime until the mid-1980s. Under structural adjustment

Table 1.1 A chronology of trade policy shifts in South Asia

Bangladesh

1971–9	Tightening trade restrictions
1980	Import duty reduction began
1985	Reduction in QRs began
1986	Simplification of tariff began
1991 onwards	Movement towards a uniform tariff structure with low tariff rate
1994	Achieved Article VIII status of the IMF

Bhutan

Until 1960s	Virtually a closed economy
1960s	Began gradual integration into the world economy
Early 1970s	The customs tariff was reduced
Early 1990s	Replacement of quantitative trade restrictions by tariffs, setting the stage for further tariff cuts in the ensuing years.
1999	Negotiation for WTO accessions commenced

India

1947–52	Liberal trade regime
1952–65	Consolidation of the control regime
1966–71	Reduction of some tariffs and introduction of some export subsidies
1972–4	Tightening of import controls in response to the first oil shock
1975–9	Selective liberalisation of investment good imports
1980–2	Tightening of import controls in response to the second oil shock
1983–90	Liberalisation of some investment and intermediate imports
1991 onwards	Policy reforms from mid-1991 involved significant trade liberalisation with simplification and unification of tariff, while retaining most consumer good imports under strict control. Most of the latter restrictions are to be removed by early 2000.
1994	Achieved Article VIII status of the IMF

Table 1.1 (continued)

Maldives	
Until 1989	Restricted trade regime
1989	Trade liberalisation began
1998 onwards	Elimination of quantitative import restrictions followed by tariff cuts at successive stages

Nepal	
1935–55	Liberal trade regime
1956–62	Tightening import control
1962–74	Export promotion via export incentives
1975–85	Tightening of import controls further
1985–91	Gradual and slow place of trade liberalisation
1992 onwards	Further progress of trade liberalisation
1994	Achieved Article VIII status of the IMF

Pakistan	
1947–52	Liberal trade regime
1952–9	Tightening import controls in response to balance of payments crisis
1959–65	Partial import liberalisation and selective export incentives
1966–71	Tightening import controls
1972–5	Partial import liberalisation
1974	Achieved Article VIII status of the IMF
1977–88	Tightening import controls and introduction of new export incentives
1988 onwards	Gradual move towards a liberal trade regime

Sri Lanka	
1948–55	Liberal trade regime
1956–67	Consolidation of trade controls
1968–9	Partial import liberalisation with export incentives
1970–7	Reversing liberalisation and tightening controls
1977–89	First phase of trade liberalisation – elimination of QRs and gradual reduction of tariff, with new export incentive
1989 onwards	Second phase of liberalisation – further tariff cuts, elimination of export duties, combined with other market-oriented reforms
1994	Achieved Article VIII status of the IMF

Sources: Athukorala and Rajapatirana (2000); Bandara and McGillivray (1998); Dean *et al.* (1994); Dowlah (1999); Joshi and Little (1996); Guisinger and Scully (1991); Raihan (2007); and country studies in this volume.

programmes, the Bangladesh government began moderate trade policy reforms in 1980 and introduced substantial changes to the trade policy regime in 1984 by abolishing the import licensing system. Further comprehensive trade policy reforms were introduced in the 1990s. These reforms included removal of QRs, significant reductions in tariffs and moving from multiple to a unified and flexible exchange rate.

Bhutan embarked on trade policy reforms as part of a structural reform package in the early 1990s. Currently, Bhutan is in the process of obtaining WTO membership. Although Bhutan was virtually a closed economy in the

1960s it has now become a small open economy, as indicated by the trade integration index (118.8). More than 80 per cent of Bhutan's trade has been carried out under free trade agreements with India and Bangladesh. The Bhutanese government has given priority to gradual integration into the world economy as part of the developmental priorities of its ninth five year plan (2002–7) and its draft tenth five year plan (2008–13).

In India, up to about the late 1950s, the role of the government in the economy remained largely indicative and trade protection remained modest. From then until the early 1980s, there was a palpable shift in policy towards greater direct government intervention in the economy with a view to achieving rapid industrialisation through import substitution. The liberalisation of commodity markets started with partial dismantling of trade barriers in the mid-1980s, but followed a tortuous route in the late 1980s. In 1991, India initiated a decisive break away from the strong inward-oriented policy regime, following a massive balance of payments crisis, which severely constrained its ability to continue with past policies. Trade liberalisation process was supported by the simplification of FDI rules. In addition, the government introduced reforms in infrastructure, deregulation and restructuring of the financial and services sectors as complementary measures to trade reforms.

Maldives had a protectionist trade regime until the late 1980s. It maintained significantly high tariffs and import restrictions for the purpose of raising government revenue and protecting government trading corporations. Maldives began its policy shift towards outward-oriented, private sector-led growth strategy in 1989. It became a member of the WTO and notified its trade policy commitments to the WTO in 1995.

The history of Nepal's trade regimes has three distinctive episodes. The trade regime remained highly liberal with only modest revenue-raising import duties until 1956, when there was a decisive policy shift towards import-substitution development strategy as in the other South Asian countries. Gradual dismantling of trade barriers began in 1985. Nepal implemented a series of trade- and market-oriented reforms in the 1990s as part of the process leading to becoming a member of the WTO in 2004.

Pakistan has a chequered history of trade liberalisation. As Guisinger and Scully (1991: 205) put it, 'compared with most developing countries that have undergone trade liberalisation, Pakistan is a tortoise rather than a hare'. Following some trade liberalisation attempts in the 1960s, Pakistan qualified for Article VIII status at the IMF in 1970. But even by the mid-1980s there was still a long way to go in lifting QRs and reducing tariffs. However, the years from 1989 have seen substantial tariff reductions and the dismantling of quantitative restrictions. However, the trade liberalisation process was hampered by serious macroeconomic instability culminating in the implementation of an IMF rescue package in 2008.

During the first decade after independence in 1948, Sri Lanka continued with a liberal trade regime until growing balance of payments problems induced a policy shift towards protectionist import substitution policies from the early 1960s. By the mid-1970s the Sri Lankan economy had become one of the most inward-oriented and regulated outside the group of centrally planned economies. In 1977, Sri Lanka responded to the dismal economic outcome of the closed-economy era by embarking on an extensive economic liberalisation process, becoming the first country in the South Asian region to do so. By the mid-1990s Sri Lanka had become one of the most open economies in the developing world, notwithstanding some high tariffs and some quantitative restrictions on agricultural imports (World Bank 2004b). Despite some policy backsliding in recent years amidst major macroeconomic problems and political turmoil, trade and foreign investment regimes have continued to remain highly liberal by regional standards.

Table 1.2 summarises the main features of current trade policy regimes in South Asian countries. In the early 1990s, the simple average Most Favoured Nation (MFN) tariff rate in South Asia was the highest (around 25 per cent) among all the regions in the world (Islam and Zanini 2008). By 2007, this had come down to about 13 per cent. The rates of individual South Asian countries varied in the range of 11.4 per cent (Sri Lanka) to 21.9 per cent (Bhutan). Quantitative import restrictions have virtually disappeared in all countries.

In addition to unilateral trade liberalisation, the countries in the region have attempted to increase cooperation and trade among themselves by signing regional and bilateral trade agreements. In 1993, members of the South Asian Association of Regional Cooperation (SAARC) – Bangladesh, Bhutan, India, Maldives, Nepal, Pakistan and Sri Lanka – signed the SAARC Preferential Trading Arrangement (SAPTA), which became operational in December 1995. SAPTA became SAFTA (South Asian Free Trade Agreement) in 2006. Because of the poor performance of SAPTA, a number of bilateral free trade agreements (FTAs) have been signed between countries in the region such as the Indo-Sri Lanka FTA and the Pakistan–Sri Lanka FTA (see Ahmed and Ghani 2007; Bandara 2004, 2010; Bandara and Yu 2003; Kelegama 1996, 1999).

Economic performance and poverty: some stylised facts

Basic indicators of economic performance and poverty incidence in South Asian economies in the overall global context are given in Tables 1.3 and 1.4. During the period 1960–80, the average growth rate of countries in South Asia was a modest 3.6 per cent compared to a growth rate of 4.7 per cent in world output. The South Asian growth rate was lowest among the major regions in the world, including Sub-Saharan Africa during the 1960s and 1970s. There has been a notable improvement in growth performance during the past three decades, notably from the mid-1990s. The average growth rate of countries in the region increased to 5.4 per cent during 1980–2000 and to 6.7 per cent during 2000–8. Growth rates vary across South Asian countries, and economic growth between 1960 and 2008 varied considerably across

Table 1.2 A summary of trade regimes in South Asian countries circa 2007

Policies	Bangladesh	Bhutan	India	Maldives	Nepal	Pakistan	Sri Lanka
Exchange rate	Unified	Unified	Unified	Unified	Unified	Unified	Unified
Exchange rate determination	Free float	Peg to Indian rupee	Free float	Fixed parity against US$	Peg to Indian rupee	Managed float	Managed float
Payment convertibility							
Current account	Yes, some limit	Yes	Yes	Yes	Yes	Yes	Yes
Capital account	No	No	Yes, limited	Yes	No	No	Yes, limited
Import restrictions	No	n/a	No	Yes	Yes, limited	No	Yes, limited
Import licensing	Yes, limited	n/a	No	Yes, minor	Yes, minor	No, minor	Yes, minor
QRs on imports	Yes	n/a	Yes	Yes	Yes	Yes	Yes
State monopolies							
Trade and Tariff Restrictiveness Index (TTRI)	11.3	n/a	14.5	n/a	16.4	12.2	6.8
TTRI with preferences	10.6	n/a	14.4	n/a	16.4	12.2	6.2
Overall Trade Restrictiveness Index (OTRI)	20.6	n/a	20.7	n/a	n/a	n/a	6.3
MFN tariff, simple average	14.6	21.9	14.1	20.2	12.6	13.5	11.4
Applied tariff trade weighted	13.2	14.8	7.8	20.5	14.6	14.7	9.5
ROW applied tariff trade weighted	4.5	0.6	4.8	3.7	2.8	6.8	5.3
Binding coverage at WTO	15.5	No	73.8	97.1	99.4	98.7	37.8
Average of bound tariff rates	169.2	n/a	50.2	36.9	26.0	59.9	30.3
Export policies	Yes	n/a	Yes	Yes	Yes	No	No
Some export QRs	Yes	n/a	Yes	Yes (on only one)	Yes	Yes	No
Some export taxes	No	n/a	Yes	No	No	No	Yes
Some direct export subsidies	Yes	n/a	Yes	Yes	Yes	Yes	Yes
Indirect export subsidies							
Openness to trade (trade as % of GDP)	56.5	84	54.8	187.1	58.9	41.8	62.3

Source: Islam and Zanini (2008).
Notes: OTRI is calculated as the TTRI, but including non-tariff measures. Expressed as percentage (as if it were a tariff rate). n/a denotes not available.

Table 1.3 An overview of economic performance of South Asian countries in the global context

Regions	Average annual GDP growth rate			Per capita income in 2008		Povertyheadcount index[1] in 2005		
	1960–80	1980–2000	2000–8	Dollars	PPP	Headcount index	Number of poor (million)	% of total world poor
East Asia and Pacific	5.6	7.9	8.7	2,952	5,030	16.8	316.2	23.0
South Asia	**3.6**	**5.4**	**6.7**	**951**	**2,484**	**40.3**	**595.6**	**43.3**
Bangladesh	2.6	4.0	5.8	497	1,233	50.5	77.4	5.6
Bhutan	n/a	7.2	8.9	1,869	4,395	26.8	0.2	0.0
India	3.4	5.7	7.1	1,017	2,721	41.6	455.8	33.2
Maldives	n/a	n/a	6.6	4,135	5,169	n.a	n.a	n.a
Nepal	2.6	4.5	3.9	438	1,020	54.7	14.8	1.1
Pakistan	5.8	2.7	4.8	991	2,344	22.6	35.2	2.6
Sri Lanka	4.4	4.7	5.2	2,013	4,215	103	2.0	0.1
Middle East and North Africa	6.6	3.3	4.5	3,303	6,710	3.6	11.0	0.8
Sub-Saharan Africa	4.3	2.2	4.9	1,194	1,899	51.2	390.6	28.3
Latin America and Caribbean	5.5	2.4	3.6	7,448	9,758	8.4	46.1	3.3
Europe and Central Asia	n/a	n/a	5.8	8,736	11,205	3.7	17.3	1.3
High income countries	4.6	2.8	2.3	40,525	34,362	n/a	n/a	n/a
World	4.7	2.9	3.0	9,042	9,602	n/a	1,376.8	100.0

Source: World development indicators; Chen and Ravallion (2008); Ravallion and Chen (2009); http://econ.worldbank.org/povcalnet
Notes:
[1] Percentage of people living below poverty line and number of poor (millions) based on poverty line of US$ 1.25.
n/a denotes not available.

Table 1.4 Headcount poverty in South Asian countries (the US$1.25 poverty line): 1981–2005

Country	1981	1984	1987	1990	1993	1996	1999	2002	2005
Bangladesh	44.18	46.1	47.85	49.6	51.01	49.95	54.7	52.85	50.47
Bhutan	47.35	45.2	43.61	51.01	47.69	47.69	29.88	26.23	26.79
India	59.8	55.5	53.6	51.3	49.4	46.6	44.8	43.9	41.6
Rural	60.92	57.78	55.6	53.92	52.46	49.41	47.43	46.40	43.83
Urban	51	48.25	47.5	43.51	40.77	38.78	37.74	37.54	36.16
Nepal	n/a	n/a	80.62	77.03	73.81	68.44	61.82	56.44	54.7
Pakistan	72.9	68.25	66.46	58.47	23.87	48.14	29.56	35.87	22.59
Sri Lanka	31.01	19.96	18.01	15.01	14.7	16.32	16.05	13.95	10.33
South Asia	**59.4**	**55.6**	**54.1**	**51.1**	**46.1**	**46.9**	**44.1**	**43.8**	**40.3**

Source: Chen and Ravallion (2008); http://econ.worldbank.org/povcalnet
Note: n/a denotes not available

countries in the region. However, all South Asian countries have recorded improvement in growth performance, with Nepal and Pakistan recording relatively low growth rates reflecting economic disruption caused by domestic political instability. India has been the fastest growing country (with the exception of Bhutan) in the region from the late 1990s in a significant departure from 'the Hindu Equilibrium' (Lal 2005) maintained during the first four decades of the post-independent era. Sri Lanka's growth performance has continued to remain impressive during this period, notwithstanding economic disruption caused by the separatist conflict.

Poverty is a multi-dimensional phenomenon with longstanding controversial complexities related to its measurement. However, absolute poverty (headcount index) has now become a widely accepted yardstick for assessing the overall performance of poverty reduction in developing economies (Chen and Ravallion 2007: 2). Because of these complexities and measurement problems, different estimates are available in the literature. Data on absolute poverty have always been questionable. There are two ways of measuring absolute poverty: using either national accounts data or data from national surveys. Various studies provided different estimates of poverty incidence using different methods (see Kaplinsky 2005 for a comparison). In this chapter, internally consistent estimates of a time series (for nine 'reference years') based on survey data for regions developed by Chen and Ravallion (2007, 2008) are used to explain the stylised facts related to South Asia in comparison with other regions in the world. The main poverty line used in the discussion is the $1.25 a day poverty line since it is more realistic and 'consistent with the definition of poverty underlying prior international poverty lines used by the World Bank' (Chen and Ravallion 2008: 18).

Poverty incidence in South Asia is compared with that in the other major regions in the world in Figures 1.1 and 1.2. Data on poverty trends in the individual South Asian countries are given in Tables 1.3 and 1.4.

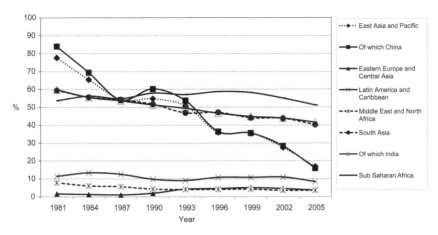

Figure 1.1 Percentage of poor living below US$1.25 a day by region
Source: Chen Ravallion (2008)

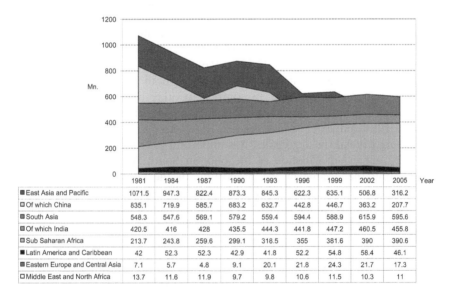

	1981	1984	1987	1990	1993	1996	1999	2002	2005	Year
■ East Asia and Pacific	1071.5	947.3	822.4	873.3	845.3	622.3	635.1	506.8	316.2	
▫ Of which China	835.1	719.9	585.7	683.2	632.7	442.8	446.7	363.2	207.7	
▨ South Asia	548.3	547.6	569.1	579.2	559.4	594.4	588.9	615.9	595.6	
▫ Of which India	420.5	416	428	435.5	444.3	441.8	447.2	460.5	455.8	
▥ Sub Saharan Africa	213.7	243.8	259.6	299.1	318.5	355	381.6	390	390.6	
■ Latin America and Caribbean	42	52.3	52.3	42.9	41.8	52.2	54.8	58.4	46.1	
▨ Eastern Europe and Central Asia	7.1	5.7	4.8	9.1	20.1	21.8	24.3	21.7	17.3	
▫ Middle East and North Africa	13.7	11.6	11.9	9.7	9.8	10.6	11.5	10.3	11	

Figure 1.2 Number of people living below US$1.25 a day by region
Source: Chen and Ravallion (2008)

Poverty in South Asia has always been consistently high compared with other regions in the world except Sub-Saharan Africa. South Asia is home to the largest proportion of the poor in the world (43.3 per cent), with India alone accounting for 456 million poor people (35 per cent of the world total). Although the aggregate poverty rate in the region has fallen from about 59.4 per cent to 40.3 per cent over the period of 1981–2005, this has had little impact on the relative poverty of the region in the global context. The number of poor people in the region has increased by about 47 million between 1981 and 2005, while the number of world poor fell significantly by around 519.5 million during the same period. There has been a startling contrast between South Asia and East Asia in terms of the poverty reduction outcome of economic performance. Between 1981 and 2005, the proportion of world poor living in South Asia increased from 28.9 per cent in 1981 to 43.3 per cent, whereas its proportion fell from 56.5 per cent to 22.9 per cent in East Asia (including China).

Chen and Ravallion (2007: 10) compare the poverty incidences in countries between 1981 and 2004 using 'US\$ 1-a-day" and 'US\$ 2-a-day' poverty lines. According to this comparison, South Asia's progress in poverty reduction is much slower in terms of the latter criterion compared to the former. This comparison suggests an increase in the number of people who are living between \$1 and \$2 in South Asia. In other words, those people who escape poverty in terms of the US\$ 1-a-day have failed to improve their economic status further during this period.

At the individual country level, the poverty headcount index has fallen significantly in Bhutan, India, Nepal, Pakistan and Sri Lanka (Table 1.4). Interestingly, Pakistan and Sri Lanka have been the most successful countries in the region in reducing poverty: between 1981 and 2005, the poverty head-count index fell from 72.9 to 22.59 in Pakistan and from 31.01 to 10.33 in Sri Lanka. The headcount index has fallen in both rural and urban areas in India, but at a slower rate. In contrast to other countries in the region, Bangladesh's poverty rate has increased from 44 per cent to 50 per cent between 1981 and 2005.

Looking beyond the aggregates, it is important to examine the composition and geographical distribution of the poor in South Asian countries. While appreciating the decline in the proportion of the poor in these countries over the last two decades, some observers have raised concerns on rising inequalities among different segments in these countries. For example, observing the recent Indian experience, Rajan (2006: 55) notes that 'rising inequality between rural and urban areas, fast-growing and slow-growing states, forward castes and backward castes' has been a major concern in India. A recent World Bank (2006a: 9) study has further emphasised this point, stating that 'poverty in South Asia will increasingly be concentrated in lagging regions, stagnant sectors, disadvantaged ethnic and caste groups and vulnerable populations'.

Poverty in rural areas has long been a concern in these countries. The poverty ratio in the rural sector is higher than that of the urban sector India (Table 1.3). Further, the number of people living in rural poverty has increased over time, compared with the falling trend in East Asia, particularly in China. According to the estimates of Ravallion *et al.* (2007), the number of poor living in the rural sector increased from 384.99 million to 407.03 million between 1993 and 2002 in the region. According to their estimates, South Asia is also one of the two regions with the highest urban poverty across regions, with approximately 46 per cent of the total world urban poor (in terms of the US$ 1-a-day poverty line) living in the region.

There is a huge variation in the poverty ratio across states or provinces in these countries. For example, five poor states in India (Bihar, Uttar Pradesh, Madhya Pradesh, Orissa and Rajasthan) are lagging behind states in south and west India; creating regional disparities (see Datt and Ravallion 2002; World Bank 2006a). Similarly, Balochistan and the North West Frontier province are poorer than the rich Punjab province in Pakistan. In Sri Lanka, Southern, Northern, Eastern, Sabaragamuwa and Uva provinces are lagging behind the Western province and the process of poverty reduction in the estate (plantation) sector has been far slower than that in urban and rural sectors (see World Bank 2007c; IPS 2010). In all of these countries, poverty is a major problem in poor states and provinces.

The above stylised facts reflect that poverty still remains a serious concern in South Asia despite some decline in the poverty incidence over the past two decades. What are the prospects of achieving the millennium development goal (MDG) of halving the proportion of people in extreme poverty between 1990 and 2015 in South Asia? Conflicting evidence is emerging from different values of poverty lines. For example, as suggested by Chen and Ravallion (2008: 22), if the current trend were to continue until 2015, the poverty rate would fall to 32.5 per cent in terms of the poverty line of $1.25 per day. In other words, South Asia cannot achieve MDG (reducing 51.7 per cent of poverty rate in 1990 by half by 2015) without a higher trend rate of poverty reduction. However, as Chen and Ravallion (2008: 22) further point out, the poverty rate would fall to 15.7 per cent by 2015 and South Asia is on track to achieve MDG in terms of a lower poverty line of $1.00 per day at 2005 prices.

Preview

The overview of reforms and economic performance in South Asia in the previous sections suggest that greater outward orientation of policy regimes have generally been accompanied by a reduction in poverty across the countries in South Asia (even though the poverty incidence in all countries remains high compared to that in East Asia). However, *coexistence* does not necessarily imply *causation*; the timing and intensity of reforms have varied notably across countries and factors other than those impacting on growth performance and poverty deduction have been at work. Therefore a closer look at the reform process and economic performance in each individual country is needed to arrive at meaningful inferences and policy lessons relating to the trade–growth–poverty nexus. This is the purpose of the ensuing country case studies in this volume.

The next chapter provides a comprehensive review of the literature on trade policy reforms and poverty in order to provide the context for the case studies. The ensuing seven chapters (arranged in alphabetical order of the country name) examine the reform process and economic performance of each country with a focus on the reform–growth–poverty nexus. Each country study contains a historical narrative of policy shifts built around the central questions of how and why things happened and what were the economic outcomes.

Each country's experience is of interest in its own right in informing the policy debate in that country. But taken together, the country case studies offer some lessons of general relevance for the contemporary debate on the implications of trade policy reforms for economic performance and poverty reduction.

Trade liberalisation generally helps poverty reduction, both through faster growth, which provides new income-generating opportunities in an expanding economy, and through structural shifts in production towards labour-intensive production. However, the new outcome depends crucially on the nature of the overall policy reform package; the poor are more likely to share in gains from liberalisation when appropriate complementary policies are in place. The evidence from India (Chapter 5) suggests that reforms would have benefited the poor more if the trade reforms had been implemented in conjunction with policies aimed at redressing labour market rigidities. The Pakistan study shows that the impact of trade liberalisation on poverty reduction has not been uniform across the regions and the quality of institutions and transmission channels is important in these differences. Political instability and policy uncertainly have also seriously impeded reaping gains from trade openness.

In Sri Lanka, significant expansion in labour-intensive manufacturing following the liberalisation reforms in the late 1970s was the joint outcome of trade liberalisation, which increased the potential returns to investments capitalising on the country's comparative advantage, and investment liberalisation, which permitted the entry of international firms with the capacity to take advantage of such profit opportunities. Despite political risk and policy uncertainty, rapid export growth was consistent with this policy configuration as it ensured a handsome profit in labour-intensive export production, which is usually characterised by a short payback period in a labour-abundant economy. Interestingly, the Sri Lankan (Chapter 9) experience over the past two decades has clearly demonstrated that an outward-oriented policy regime can yield a superior industrial outcome compared to a closed-economy regime, even under severe strains of political and macroeconomic instability. In Bangladesh (Chapter 3) too, rapid expansion of the export-oriented garment industry, which provided employment opportunities for over a million women from low-income families, was aided by trade liberalisation combined with selective liberalisation of foreign direct investment.

The abundance of surplus labour in the pre-reform economy does not necessarily lead to poverty reduction through employment generation during the post-reform era. This depends crucially on the degree to which the population is well integrated within the income-generating process of the economy. Impediments to labour mobility between sectors and among the regions in the country also have a direct impact on this outcome. As has been inferred in the case studies of India (Chapter 5), Sri Lanka (Chapter 9), Bangladesh (Chapter 3) and Maldives (Chapter 6), there is a clear case for devising mechanisms for income transfers to those segments of the population which for various reasons are not participating in the income-generating process, in order to make the reform outcome equitable and also to make the reform process politically palatable.

The Indian case study (Chapter 5) contains a unique analysis of the impact of trade reforms on wages and employment of unskilled workers in manufacturing. The analysis, which is based on a new data set painstakingly put together from numerous sources, finds that export expansion had a significantly positive impact on the wages and employment of unskilled workers. There is also no evidence of wage suppression or employment losses resulting from import penetration. These results are consistent with the predictions of the standard trade theory.

The case studies of Nepal (Chapter 7) and Bhutan (Chapter 4) serve to bring into sharp relief unique issues surrounding the growth and poverty implications of trade policy reforms in poor landlocked economies. The study of Maldives provides insights into unique problems faced by a micro state. In these countries, trade liberalisation is unlikely to yield the anticipated outcome unless reforms are appropriately combined with systematic efforts to address issues relating to trade-related logistics and infrastructure bottlenecks.

Bhutan is unique among the South Asia countries: it is a low-income country but its comparative advantage lies not in labour-intensive production but in relatively capital-intensive, source-based activities (predominantly mining and hydro-electricity generation). Unemployment and the incidence of poverty is high in the country in spite of rapid economic growth because the skill mismatch and the ample availability of cheap labour from the Indian hinterland. In this context, the Bhutan study has convincingly argued that economic expansion through economic opening would not yield the expected outcome of poverty reduction through domestic employment creation unless concrete attempts are made to improve the quality of the domestic labour force. The Maldivian case study also finds the low skill levels of domestic workers an impediment to the realisation of poverty reduction effect emanating from domestic employment expansion in the liberalised economy.

Notes

1 'Trade policy' encompasses various policies that governments adopt towards international trade. Tariffs, import quotas and subsidies are the obvious examples of trade policy instruments in most developing countries. Policies towards foreign direct investment can also be considered as part of trade policy as these policies have become key instruments of export promotion and import substitution beyond the levels dictated by market forces in many countries. Some authors treat exchange rate policy as part of trade policy (Diaz-Alejandro 1975: 93; Thomas and Nash 1991: 1–2), but the standard practice is to consider it as part of macroeconomic policy.

2 The Article XVIIII(B) of GATT explicitly exempted the developing countries from the 'obligations' of industrial countries, explicitly permitting them to adopt tariffs and quantitative restrictions as policy tools (Krueger 1995: 38).

3 The chief studies were directed by Little *et al.* (1970) at the Organisation for Economic Cooperation and Development (OECD), Balassa (1971 and 1982) and Lal and Mynt (1996) at the World Bank, Bhagwati (1978) and Krueger (1978) at the National Bureau of Economic Research and Donges (1976) at the Kiel Institute of World Economics.

4 For a comprehensive survey of the revisionist literature see Thirlwall and Pacheco-Lopez (2009).

5 Afghanistan is not covered because of dearth of material.

6 The literature is too numerous to list here. See Athukorala (2002), Panagariya (2002) and Parikh (2006) for useful surveys.

2 Trade and poverty

Theory, evidence and policy issues

Jayatilleke S. Bandara

The link between trade liberalisation and poverty has been a hotly debated topic in international trade and development in recent years, for a number of reasons. First, poverty reduction has become a main priority of national governments and global institutions such as the United Nations (UN) and the World Bank since the setting of millennium development goals (MDGs) by the UN. According to MDG 1 (the poverty goal), the world needs to reduce absolute poverty by half between 1990 and 2015 on the basis of the international poverty line (using a US$ 1-a-day poverty line). Second, poverty has become an important issue as a result of the social and political consequences of rapid globalisation (UNCTAD 2004: 68). In a recent report, UNCTAD (2004: 67) argue that trade can play an important role in reducing poverty in both least developed and developing countries, although the link between trade and poverty is not clear and automatic. Finally, recent food price rises and the global financial crisis have made achieving MDG 1 even more challenging for policy makers in developing countries and international organisations.

The literature on the link between poverty and either trade liberalisation or globalisation has grown rapidly over the last few years. The purpose of this chapter is to survey the literature with a specific focus on studies of the South Asia experience in order to set the context for the country case studies in the ensuing chapters. In order to achieve this objective, the chapter begins with a brief overview on the main channels through which trade liberalisation affects poverty in the next section. It then focuses on some empirical studies carried out so far on the trade–poverty link related to South Asian countries in Section 3. Lessons from other developing countries are considered in Section 4 to examine whether there is a general agreement on the topic. The final section of the chapter provides concluding remarks.

The trade–poverty nexus: an overview

As noted previously, poverty is heterogeneous with many dimensions and there are many reasons which contribute to poverty. Therefore it is difficult to define and measure such a complex and multidimensional concept, as is acknowledged in some recent excellent surveys (for example, Goldberg and Pavcnik 2004; Winters *et al.* 2004; Aisbett 2007). Measuring the effects of trade liberalisation on poverty is complex because of the indirectiveness of the different mechanisms through which trade liberalisation affects poverty. For instance, trade liberalisation affects both relative prices of goods and services and factors of production and, in turn, both aggregate income of household and investment and saving decisions, creating inter-temporal effects. It may also alter government income and expenditure. The effects of trade liberalisation also depend on rural infrastructure and market structures (see Coxhead 2003). Because of all of these complexities, there is a heated debate over the trade–poverty link in the literature. As reviewed by many authors, establishing the trade and poverty nexus is an even more difficult task. As Goldberg and Pavcnik (2004: 250) note: 'perhaps a more manageable approach is to relate changes in trade policy to particular phenomena that are highly correlated with poverty. To this end, it is instructive to first understand through which channels poverty can be affected.'

Following the conceptual framework in decomposing the trade and poverty links provided a few years ago by Winters and his colleagues (see for example, Winters 2000a, 2000b, 2002; Winters *et al.* 2004), a number of researchers have identified the channels through which trade liberalisation affects poverty (for example, Bannister and Thugge 2001; Hertel and Reimer 2002; UNCTAD 2004; Goldberg and Pavcnik 2007; Nissanke and Thorbecke 2007). To my knowledge, different authors have identified these channels in different ways following the introduction of the main conceptual framework by Winters and his co-authors. For example, Goldberg and Pavcnik (2004: 250) have identified three main channels: 'the participation and earning of household members in labour markets, household consumption, and household production'. Bannister and Thugge (2001) have identified five main trade–poverty channels, while Nissanke and Thorbecke have identified seven channels focusing on globalisation. Rather than repeating what has already been covered in the above studies, this section provides a brief overview of these channels in order to set a background for the remaining sections of this chapter. In general, the literature identifies the following main channels through which trade liberalisation affects poverty (see details in Bannister and Thugge 2001: 5–14; Nissanke and Thorbecke 2007).

- *Prices of tradable goods*: Trade liberalisation leads to a change in prices of imports and exports. These price changes affect the poor.
- *Factor prices, income and employment*: Trade liberalisation gives rise to a change in the relative prices of factors of production such as skilled and unskilled labour and capital. These changes affect the income and the employment of the poor.
- *Government income and expenditure:* Trade liberalisation may lead to a decline in government revenue affecting government expenditure, with direct transfers to the poor.

- *Incentives for investment and innovation:* Trade liberalisation can affect the long-run economic growth through its incentive effect.
- *External shocks:* Integration through trade liberalisation makes an economy vulnerable to external shocks which will have an impact on the poor.
- *Short-run risk and adjustment costs:* During the liberalisation process economies face certain adjustment costs which will create effects on the poor.
- *Flow of information:* Trade liberalisation facilitates the flow of information and knowledge globally, impacting on the poor.
- *Institutions:* Institutions at global, national, regional and local levels mediate various channels and mechanisms linking liberalisation and poverty, creating effects on the poor.

As Nissanke and Thorbecke (2007: 23–4) note:

> these channels can be compared to rivers and canals flowing into a common sea or a lake. Some of the rivers may be muddy and even polluted, while others may be crystal clear. The resulting quality of the lake or sea water depends on how these various flows combine, and similarly, the ultimate net effects of the different globalisation–poverty channels depend on their combined individual effects.

It is, however, difficult to examine the combined effects of trade liberalisation on poverty under all the above channels in a single empirical study. Therefore, many studies covered in recent surveys have focused on only one or a few of these channels while ignoring others. Since the first two channels through which trade liberalisation affects poverty are the most important, many empirical studies have focused on them. Many analysts have used household survey data to examine the effects of the changes in prices of tradables.

Any empirical analysis of the impacts of trade liberalisation on poverty involves two major steps. In the first step, trade liberalisation is linked to the price changes faced by the household. In the second step, the price changes are linked to household choices and characteristics (Porto 2007: 1436). Similarly, there are attempts to establish the links between trade liberalisation, factor markets and factor income. Emphasising the role of adjustment to trade liberalisation Porto (2007: 1432) further points out that 'after trade reform, consumers may switch to cheaper goods; producers may shift to more profitable activities; firms may expand employment; individuals may increase their labour supply'. This reinforces the observation that the first two channels of the above list are important when examining the trade–poverty link.

The income effects of trade liberalisation play an important role in the trade–poverty debate. Some researchers have attempted to study links between trade liberalisation, labour market and factor income (see Goldberg and Pavcnik 2004). The well-known Hechscher–Ohlin (HO) and Stolper–Samuelson (SS) theorems have provided the theoretical bases for the pro-poor trade liberalisation argument. According to the HO model, countries have comparative advantage in producing goods that intensive in the relatively abundant factors of production since they are relatively cheaper. Therefore, countries with abundant capital have comparative advantage in producing capital-intensive goods and countries with abundant labour have comparative advantage in producing labour-intensive goods. On the basis of this model, developing countries gain from trade by specialising in labour-intensive goods since they are labour-abundant countries. With the theoretical foundation of the HO model, the SS model establishes the link between free trade and income distribution among the factors of production, suggesting that real income of the abundant factor increases when a country liberalises trade. Since unskilled labour is the abundant factor in many developing countries, the poor in developing countries gain when developing countries liberalise their trade regimes, according to the SS model. The HO and SS models indicate that structural changes take place in favour of labour-abundant industries when developing countries open their economies. As a result, the demand for unskilled labour will increase, leading to an increase in real income. Many economists have used this theoretical base to argue that trade liberalisation is good for the poor (for example, Krueger 1983; Bhagwati and Srinivasan 2002). There have been many empirical studies covering labour market and wages channels which link trade liberalisation and poverty. The next section deals with a selected list of empirical studies related to South Asia.

The trade–poverty nexus in South Asia

Different analysts have used a number of different empirical methods to capture the combined effects of different channels through which trade liberalisation affects poverty. Following recent surveys by Hertel and Reimer (2002, 2005), Goldberg and Pavcnik (2004) and Aisbett (2007: 38–9), all the methods employed in empirical studies can be categorised under the following six categories.

- *Cross-country regression analyses* (using aggregate data sets) which examine the link between trade, growth, income, poverty and inequality measured at the national level.
- *General equilibrium studies* using single-country computable general equilibrium (CGE) or applied general equilibrium (AGE) models and global CGE models.
- *Micro–macro simulation studies* (known as 'micro–macro synthesis') combining CGE modelling and micro simulation models.
- *Partial equilibrium/cost-of-living analyses* based on household expenditure data which focus on commodity markets and their role in determining the effects on poverty.
- *A macro–meso–micro approach* in analysing the impact of a particular value chain on poverty.

- *Micro-economic studies* that analyse micro-level data from household or plant-level surveys and other micro-level studies linking trade liberalisation and poverty.

Although a great deal of empirical work has been carried out in other parts of the world, such as Latin America and Sub-Saharan Africa, to examine the link between trade and poverty, the empirical work focusing on the South Asian region or individual countries in the region is limited. This section will undertake a survey on the available evidence. First, this chapter brings together results specifically relating to South Asia from cross-country studies. This is followed by a detailed discussion on South Asian country studies.

Cross-country studies

The analysis of the link between trade and poverty is based on 'a two-step argument: that trade enhances growth, and that growth reduces poverty' (Bhagwati 2004: 53). A number of cross-country or multi-country studies have been carried out to examine this two-step link between trade liberalisation, growth and poverty. The early studies of Dollar and Kraay (2002, 2004) have established the positive link between trade and poverty by relating trade liberalisation with growth and growth with poverty. South Asian countries are included in this analysis and therefore the findings of these studies are relevant to South Asian countries as well. Their main conclusion is that 'The increase in growth rates leads on average to proportionate increases in incomes of the poor. The evidence from individual cases and cross-country analysis supports the view that globalisation leads to faster growth and poverty reduction in poor countries' (Dollar and Kraay 2004: 22).

According to their findings, trade liberalisation is good for the poor: trade liberalisation in countries around the world including South Asia leads to a reduction in poverty. However, their published studies and findings attracted criticisms from different directions (for example, Rodrik 2000). Much has been written in the literature on this debate: unnecessary repetition is avoided in this section. A brief summary of the main problems of these studies is given below using recent literature. Ravallion (2001: 1803) argues that 'cross-country correlations are clouded in data problems, and undoubtedly hide welfare impacts; they can be deceptive for development policy'. Very often, there has been broad generalisation that trade leads to growth and growth leads to a reduction in poverty. Harrison (2007b: 15) and Nissanke and Thorbecke (2007: 5) point out that the evaluation of the trade and poverty nexus using cross-country studies remains problematic for the following reasons:

- finding precise measurements for globalisation;
- problems associated with definitions of globalisation and poverty;

- difficulty in finding appropriate instruments for trade policy at the country level and adequately controlling other changes that are occurring at the same time;
- technical problems associated with econometric techniques used in these studies;
- the quality of data on the incomes of the poor;
- growth potentially leading to unequal gains across different income levels even if cross-country studies establish a positive link between trade and growth; and
- the heterogeneity across different segments of the population including spatial dimensions.

Harrison (2007b) has revisited the evidence on the link between trade and growth and highlights the problems of previous multi-country regression analysis. She finds that 'there is no evidence in the *aggregate* data that trade reforms are good or bad for the poor' (Harrison 2007b: 13). Rather than focusing on trade only (as an approximation to openness), Heshmati (2007) has recently developed two composite indices of globalisation – the Kearny index and author's own index with four components (economic integration, personal contact, technology and political engagement) – to indicate the level of globalisation of 62 countries including some South Asian countries. Using these indices the author has undertaken a multi-country regression analysis to examine the impact of globalisation on poverty. In this study, which also included South Asia as a region, Heshmati (2007) finds a weak link between globalisation and poverty. Ravallion (2007) has also attempted to contribute to the debate using a multi-country database ('macro lens'). He finds that 'based on cross-country comparisons, it is hard to maintain the view that expanding external trade is, in general, a powerful force for poverty reduction in developing countries' (Ravallion 2007: 138). All the other cross-country studies demonstrate that there is no clear and strong evidence to suggest that trade liberalisation reduces poverty in South Asia.

As a result of recent dissatisfaction with using cross-country studies to evaluate the trade and poverty link, some policy analysts have emphasised the need for case studies. For example, Ravallion (2004) emphasises the need for more detailed and deeper micro-empirical research in the area. Echoing similar sentiments, Nissanke and Thorbecke (2007: 5) note that:

> while a number of studies have been conducted to investigate the globalisation–poverty relationship through cross-country regressions, a deeper insight into this critical nexus cannot be obtained by regression studies alone, as it requires detailed empirical research in a country and region-specific context.

This claim has been supported by a number of recent studies and surveys (for example, Hertel and Winters 2006; Harrison 2007a).

CGE and macro–micro simulation studies

Chen and Ravallion (2004a: 31) observe that 'although partial equilibrium analysis requires little or no aggregation of the primary household data, it misses potentially important indirect effects of prices and wages'. Similarly, after evaluating a number of studies presented to a recent conference, Coxhead (2003: 1308) comments that 'a complete picture of poverty changes can only be obtained in [a] general equilibrium context; partial equilibrium estimates (based only on output prices, for example) will be misleading'. Some analysts argue that a general equilibrium approach is more suitable for capturing economy-wide effects of trade liberalisation on poverty. This view has given rise to a number of CGE studies on trade and poverty in South Asia. Many trade and poverty analysts have used both global and single-country CGE models to examine the link between trade and poverty. What do these studies tell us? Not all of them demonstrate that trade liberalisation reduces poverty; some even show a negative relationship between trade and poverty. In this section, a survey of a selected number of studies is presented.

In recent years, the global CGE modelling technique (particularly using the Global Trade Analysis Project (GTAP) database and the modelling framework) has been used to estimate the effects of global trade liberalisation on poverty in different regions and individual countries, since these models are capable of capturing poverty channels of product and factor price changes. A summary of the results of a few selected studies is given in Table 2.1.

Anderson *et al.* (2006) have found that, for poverty reduction, full merchandise trade liberalisation with domestic reforms (increasing productivity) is more effective than trade liberalisation under the Doha Round, although in

Table 2.1 Empirical estimates of global CGE studies: change in poverty

Study	South Asia (change in millions)	Bangladesh (change in millions)	India (change in millions)	Sri Lanka (change in millions)
Anderson et al. (2006)				
Full Doha simulation (with productivity effects)	−2.6			
Full liberalisation (with dynamic effects)	−12.5			
UNESCAP (2008)				
Under Doha reforms (short run)		0.4	5.9 (rural) 1.3 (urban)	0.0
Under Doha reforms (long run)		0.3	5.9 (rural) 1.3 (urban)	0.0
Under comprehensive agricultural reform (short run)		−2.5	−10.2 (rural) −2.2 (urban)	0.1
Under comprehensive agricultural reform (long run)		−2.4	−10.0 (rural) −2.1 (urban)	0.1

Source: Author's compilation based on studies surveyed in this chapter.

both cases trade liberalisation reduces poverty in South Asia, according to that study. UNESCAP (2008) has also attempted to evaluate the effects of trade liberalisation on poverty, finding that poverty in countries in South Asia is projected to increase under the Doha scenario in the short run as well as in the long run. However, the UNESCAP study suggests that comprehensive agricultural trade liberalisation may reduce poverty in Bangladesh and India, but not in Sri Lanka in either the short or the long run (see Table 2.1). These multi-country CGE studies, therefore, do not provide a clear view on the trade–poverty nexus in South Asia: their results provide some inconclusive mixed messages.

In addition to the poverty impact of trade liberalisation obtained from global CGE studies for the South Asia region and for some individual countries in the region, there have been a number of attempts to undertake single-country CGE studies in relation to all five large South Asian countries. A summary of these studies is presented in Table 2.2. Some of the early CGE studies carried out related to Bangladesh, India and Pakistan under the Micro Impact of Macroeconomic Adjustment Policies (MIMAP) project funded by the International Development Research Centre (IDRC). Iqbal and Siddiqui (2001) have surveyed these studies. The general message emerging from these country studies is that trade liberalisation favours high-income groups compared to low-income groups. To avoid repetition, these early studies are not included in this survey.

Other South Asian CGE studies on the trade and poverty link found in the literature were carried out as components of recent multi-country research projects on trade liberalisation (or globalisation) and poverty. The results of four of these studies (case studies of Bangladesh, India, Pakistan and Sri Lanka) have been summarised by Round and Whalley (2006). The main features and a summary of the results of selected studies, including the studies covered in Round and Whalley (2006), are shown in Table 2.2.

The results of four CGE applications applied to Bangladesh are summarised in this table. The first three of these four studies were undertaken by a small group of researchers as components of multi-country trade–poverty related projects. These three studies show some mixed results. The authors of these studies find that trade liberalisation plays a minor role in reducing poverty in Bangladesh and that unskilled rural workers do not benefit. They also observe that domestic trade liberalisation and migrant remittances are powerful tools in reducing poverty in Bangladesh. The fourth Bangladeshi case study focuses on the impact of trade liberalisation on income distribution rather than on poverty itself. The results of this study also indicate that urban educated skilled labourers benefit more from trade liberalisation than do rural unskilled labourers.

Using the same CGE methodology applied in the first Bangladesh case study as a part of a multi-country study, Pradhan (2002) has attempted to examine the link between trade liberalisation and poverty in India. He finds that trade liberalisation has only a minor impact on poverty in India.

Table 2.2 Recent numerical evaluations on trade and poverty nexus in South Asia

Author(s)	Country	Type of model	Type and source of data	Main findings
Mujeri and Khondker (2002)	Bangladesh	Static 2-sector Ricardo–Viner type model	Double calibration to 1985 and 1996 data	Trade plays a minor role in changing poverty. Technical and endowment changes are the main drivers of changing poverty.
Khondker and Mujeri (2006)	Bangladesh	CGE model with 25 sectors, 7 factors of production (including 6 labour categories) and 7 types of households	Calibrated to a SAM for 1995/6 and double calibration to 1985 and 1996	Trade reforms have neither readily nor necessarily benefited the poor in Bangladesh. Few skilled categories of workers are benefited, while the rural unskilled are not benefited.
Annabi et al. (2006)	Bangladesh	Sequential dynamic CGE model with 15 sectors, 4 factors of production and 9 household groups	Calibrated to a SAM for 1999/2000 and used data from the 2000 household survey	The Doha scenario has negative welfare and poverty impacts. Free world trade scenario has similar but larger welfare and poverty impacts. Domestic trade liberalisation produces positive welfare and poverty effects in the long run even though it produces some negative effects in the short run. Domestic liberalisation effects far outweigh those of free world trade when free world trade is combined with domestic trade liberalisation. Remittances are a powerful tool in reducing poverty.
Hoque (2006)	Bangladesh	Comparative-static CGE model of the ORANI tradition with 86 industries/sectors, 94 commodities and 3 factors of production (including 8 types of labour) and 9 household groups	Used input–output tables for 1999–2000 plus household survey data	Urban high-educated households are mostly benefited from trade liberalisation in terms of real consumption. Urban skilled labour benefits from trade liberalisation.

(Continued on next page)

Table 2.2 (continued)

Author(s)	Country	Type of model	Type and source of data	Main findings
Pradhan (2002)	India	Static 13-sector Ricardo-Viner type model	Single calibration to data for 1994 and forward projections	Trade liberalisation has a minor impact on poverty.
Cockburn (2006)	Nepal	CGE-micro-simulation model with 15 sectors, 5 factors of production and 3 regions	Model is based on a previously developed CGE model and the Nepalese 1995 Living Standards Survey (NLSS)	Trade liberalisation favours urban households as opposed to Terai (fertile plains) and hills/mountain households. The impacts of trade liberalisation on income distribution appear to be small. Urban poverty falls and rural poverty increases.
Siddiqui and Kemal (2002a)	Pakistan	Static 11-sector Ricardo-Viner type model	Single calibration to data for 1989–90 and forward projections	Simulations with and without remittances produce different results on poverty. Non-globalisation variables are key in understanding the link between trade and poverty.
Butt and Bandara (2009)	Pakistan	'Top-down' regional CGE model with 4 regions and 38 sectors.	Calibrated to data for the year 1991	While large regions are benefited from trade liberalisation, small regions are affected.
Weerahewa (2002)	Sri Lanka	Static 2-sector Ricardo-Viner type model	Double calibration to pairs of years (1977, 1994, 2000)	Trade liberalisation does not essentially affect poverty; technical changes and endowment changes are the main drivers in changing poverty.

Table 2.2 (continued)

Author(s)	Country	Type of model	Type and source of data	Main findings
Weerahewa (2006)	Sri Lanka	A comparative static CGE model with 5 sectors, 2 factors and 8 provinces	Single calibration to input–output data for 2000	Import ban on rice reduces household income and welfare. Removal of tariff on rice along with removals of the import tariff on fertiliser and or/ subsidy payments on other agricultural sectors would improve economic welfare and household efficiency across provinces. The key channel of transmission of trade shock to households appears to be through government transfer payments that are influenced by change in government expenditures on subsidy payments.
Naranpanawa (2005)	Sri Lanka	Poverty focused ORANI type CGE model with 8 types of labour and 5 types of household sectors. Poverty has been linked with the model indirectly with FGT measures	Single calibration to SAM data for 1995	In the short run, the effects of overall trade liberalisation on low-income groups are insignificant. This situation would change in the long run. Compared with agricultural trade liberalisation, liberalisation of the manufacturing sector is pro-poor. Reduction in tariff revenue plays an important part.

Cockburn (2006) has used a more sophisticated CGE study to examine the trade–poverty nexus in Nepal. Although many CGE models contain representative households, this study has attempted to replace the conventional CGE modelling approach of representative households by a sample of actual households (3,373) and to incorporate them into a CGE micro-simulation model. The results of this study demonstrate that trade liberalisation favours urban households in Nepal. According to this study, trade liberalisation leads to a fall in urban poverty and a rise in rural poverty in Nepal.

There have been some attempts to examine the trade and poverty link in Pakistan using CGE models, after the early attempts under the MIMAP project, covered in the survey by Iqbal and Siddiqui (2001). Siddiqui and Kemal (2002a) have shown that non-globalisation variables are important to understanding how globalisation affects poverty. They have also shown the positive role that remittances play in reducing poverty. In a recent study, Butt and Bandara (2009) have examined the link between trade and poverty within a regional context using a regional CGE model. This study finds that while large states benefit from trade liberalisation, small states are affected by trade liberalisation, which allows room for regional conflicts.

The last three studies summarised in Table 2.2 are Sri Lankan CGE case studies. Weerahewa (2002) attempted to examine the link between trade and poverty using a very simple CGE model. The results of this study show that trade does not play a role in explaining poverty changes and that technical changes and endowments are the main drivers of poverty changes. Weerahewa (2006) attempted to examine the effects of the removal of the import ban on rice and of its related subsidies in agriculture. This study finds that liberalisation in the rice sector improves household welfare. Government transfer payments play an important role in reducing poverty. Naranpanawa (2005) has developed a poverty-focused CGE model to examine the trade–poverty link in Sri Lanka. This study observes that the effects of trade liberalisation on low-income groups are insignificant in the short run, but that the situation would change in the long run.

Micro–macro simulation models are extensions of standard CGE models. Apart from Cockburn's (2006) study considered previously in this sub-section, there have not been, to the author's knowledge, attempts to examine the trade–poverty link under the category of micro–macro simulation models in South Asia. In fact, one of the most advanced and sophisticated ways of capturing the effects of trade liberalisation on poverty has been the combination of CGE and micro-simulations models. Unfortunately, it is difficult to find such a study for South Asian countries.

It is clear from the above discussion that many analysts prefer to use a CGE modelling framework to examine the effects of trade liberalisation on poverty. Recently it has become one of the most popular empirical methods of investigating the trade-poverty link. This has also attracted a number of criticisms in using trade policy analysis in recent years. Some recent critics have raised concerns over general equilibrium effects by highlighting limitations of the technique (see, for example, Ackerman 2005; Charlton and Stiglitz 2005; and Taylor and von Arnim 2007). Therefore, it is important to note some of the criticisms directed towards CGE applications to highlight why further refinements are necessary in examining the trade–poverty link using CGE models.

According to these critics, the results derived from CGE models are subject to a number of limitations. First, these models are based on a set of restrictive assumptions such as the utility-maximising and profit-maximising behaviour of consumers and producers, perfect competition in factor and commodity markets, and perfect capital mobility. Taylor and von Arnim (2007: 2) have demonstrated that the results obtained from CGE models such as GTAP are highly problematic and that these models are based on 'implausible assumptions about elasticities, the exchange rate and macro causality'. They argue that one of the main problems of these models is that they assume that central macroeconomic indicators such as trade deficits and foreign debt, which are important to developing countries, do not change as a response to any trade policy change. They are further critical of using the well-known 'Armington' specification incorrectly. Some even find that the assumptions used in these models are so rigid that the models tend to provide pre-determined answers.

Assumptions made on important parameter values such as export demand elasticities, substitution elasticities between labour and capital, and imported goods and locally produced goods (the so-called Armington elasticity) play an important part in the results generated by CGE models. Recently Dixon (2009) illustrated how a report prepared by a group of researchers at the Australian Productivity Commission has generated implausible welfare benefits (about A\$500 million) using a CGE model related to an experiment on the effects of a tariff cut in the Australian automotive industry. He further demonstrates that the welfare gains from the above experiment are smaller (even negative) by reworking the same experiment with more realistic parameter values. This is an eye-opener for other CGE modellers and users.

Second, they are basically comparative–static models and do not incorporate second or third-generation effects of trade liberalisation. So far, all CGE studies undertaken to examine the effects of trade liberalisation in South Asia have been the 'first generation' of standard static GTAP model or single-country CGE models which assume perfect competition, constant returns to scale and so on. This ignores scale and variety effects as well as dynamic effects of trade liberalisation. In order to capture these effects, it is necessary to use 'second generation' CGE models (which allow for increasing returns and imperfect competition in some industries) and 'third generation' CGE models (which incorporate dynamic accumulation effects) to evaluate the effects of trade liberalisation on poverty in South Asian countries (see Baldwin and Venables 1995 for details of these models). When the modellers add features such as increasing returns to scale, the effects of trade liberalisation tend to be larger.

Third, the labour market is not properly modelled in the standard CGE models. As Kurzweil (2002: 2) noted, 'besides a split-up of the working force in skilled and unskilled labor, there are neither labor market policies nor other employment specified characteristics implemented' in the standard GTAP model. Charlton and Stiglitz (2005) have noted that CGE models do not account for unemployment, which is an important feature in developing countries. Therefore, the impact of trade liberalisation on poverty via labour market channels cannot be fully captured in these standard models.

Finally, data problems and interpreting the results generated from large and complex global and single-country CGE models have become major issues. In other words, the modellers have very often not been able to present the results in a convincing way to explain 'where the results come from'. Therefore, some label such models as giant 'black boxes'. Recently, Adams (2005) has articulated the way in which the results from CGE models like GTAP can be presented and interpreted.

Although CGE models are subject to the above criticism, they are still useful tools in evaluating trade policy issues if the modellers attempt to improve the techniques and data. Taylor and von Arnim (2007: 3) have put forward this idea clearly:

> CGE models can be useful quantitative supplements to experimental thinking about the importance of different potential linkages among economic variables at the country or world level. However, mechanically churning out 'projections' of welfare gains or any other indicator subject to one single set of causal assumptions and parameter values is a fundamental misuse of a sometimes helpful tool.

After surveying CGE studies on the trade–poverty link in South Asia and highlighting their limitations, this sub-section can be concluded by using a quotation from Charlton and Stiglitz (2005: 297): 'we do not place much faith in the actual values derived from CGE analysis, but they do highlight many interesting general equilibrium effects and enable us to draw inferences from comparisons across alternative scenarios'.

Partial equilibrium studies – cost-of-living and micro-economic analyses

Hertel and Reimer (2002, 2005) identify that these studies focus on only one or a limited number of markets using mainly survey data. Their survey covered a number of such studies related to several South Asian countries including India and Bangladesh. These studies have focused on different channels (previously listed) through which trade liberalisation affects poverty. For example, Ravallion (1990), in examining the welfare effects of food price changes in Bangladesh, finds that while an increase in the price of rice will be likely to have adverse effects on rural households in the short run, the poor households are likely to benefit from such price changes in the long run.

Using expenditure data from the 1987–8 and 1993–4 Indian national sample surveys, Deaton and Tarozzi (2000) have examined the link between price and poverty, focusing mainly on the price indices and poverty lines. In their study they find that, although there are problems with the current procedure in calculating official poverty lines, their results agree with the trends in official price indices over the time.

A large number of studies have also attempted to examine the link between trade and poverty by focusing on different poverty channels using partial equilibrium approaches. For example, Dorosh and Valdes (1990) have studied the link between farm gate prices and trade policy reforms. They observe that farm gate prices received by farmers have increased significantly in Pakistan because of trade reform. Similarly, Gisselquist and Grether (2000) show that trade liberalisation creates benefits to agricultural producers in Bangladesh as a result of increased availability of inputs. Consumers are also benefited from the increased availability of goods. Ninno *et al.* (2001) have demonstrated how trade liberalisation assisted in mitigating the post-flood food crisis in Bangladesh in 1998, with private imports of rice stabilising market prices and increasing supply. Kabeer (2000) has shown how trade liberalisation has assisted in creating jobs for women in the clothing industry in Bangladesh.

Krishna (2004) has undertaken a micro-level study focusing on 35 North Indian villages using household surveys. According to this study, while members of 11.1 per cent of 6,376 households in these villages have escaped from poverty, 7.9 per cent have fallen into the poverty trap in the last 25 years. He finds that different sets of factors are associated with escaping poverty and falling into poverty. Therefore, distinct sets of policies are advocated to promote poverty reduction and to arrest falling into poverty.

Topalova (2007) has undertaken a study to examine the impact of trade liberalisation on poverty and inequality in Indian districts using a regression analysis. Using household survey data before and after trade policy reforms in India, Topalova suggests that the poor in rural areas gained less from trade liberalisation than other income groups or the urban poor. Further, she demonstrates that the progress in poverty reduction in rural areas has been slow. According to her study, Indian states with more flexible labour laws have been able to minimise or eliminate adverse effects of trade liberalisation on the poor. In a previous study, Topalova (2004) also finds that the factor mobility is extremely limited in India because of inflexible labour laws. Sharma *et al.* (2000) examine the link between liberalisation and productivity in the manufacturing sector in Nepal and they argue that the effect of liberalisation on productivity is small because the lack of complementary policies such as policies on investment in infrastructure.

Macro–meso–micro studies

There are some studies carried out to examine the impact of a global value chain on poverty in developing countries. Recently, Jenkins (2007) has used this macro–meso–micro approach to examine the impact of globalisation (not only trade liberalisation) on poverty. Bangladesh has been included in his study. Jenkins (2007) finds that the growth of labour-intensive exports of manufactures such as ready-made garments, which has resulted from globalisation, has provided employment to low-income rural women. This has established a positive link between globalisation and poverty in Bangladesh. Thus, in contrast to the CGE studies related to Bangladesh, this study finds some positive effects of trade liberalisation on unskilled labour.

What are the messages that emerge from the studies surveyed in this section? Although the studies are not comparable and the link between trade and poverty is complex, some broad findings are emerging. First, the empirical evidence from South Asia on the trade–poverty link shows some mixed results. Some of these results indicate that trade liberalisation is not good for the poor. For example, the results of a number of multi-country and single-country CGE models indicate that the poor in Bangladesh are affected by trade liberalisation. In contrast, two other studies (partial equilibrium and micro–meso–macro) show that trade liberalisation provides opportunities for the rural women in Bangladesh and therefore trade liberalisation is good for the poor. Second, some studies demonstrate that trade liberalisation is not the only reason for the fall in poverty in South Asian countries. They find that the increase in remittances has played a major role in reducing poverty in some of these countries, like Bangladesh, Pakistan and Sri Lanka. Third, the evidence shows that different segments and geographical locations have not benefited from trade liberalisations. For example, the rural poor and poor provinces with poor infrastructure are lagging behind the rich provinces and the urban rich. Finally, it is clear from the empirical evidence that countries in the region need to implement complementary policies with trade liberalisation to reduce poverty in these countries.

Lessons from other countries

Although there have been a limited number of empirical studies focusing on the trade liberalisation and poverty link using the South Asian experience, a large number of empirical studies have been carried out to investigate this link using many other countries. The findings of these studies have been summarised and reviewed by a number of recent surveys.

Berg and Krueger (2003) have focused on the micro-evidence from a large number of individual trade liberalisation episodes in many developing countries and they find that there are no systematic effects of trade on the poor beyond its overall effects on the poor. After surveying large number of studies, they observe that trade policy is not a 'magic bullet' of growth and poverty reduction – rather, it is only one of many determinants. They further emphasise that there is little evidence that there are other reforms that must precede trade reforms, although there are many reforms that are complementary.

One of the most prominent surveys on trade liberalisation and poverty has been Winters *et al.* (2004). This comprehensive study has reported the findings of many studies of *ex post* data related to actual episodes of trade liberalisation, and surveys the evidence on trade liberalisation and poverty under four headings (covering many trade–poverty channels): macroeconomic aspects; households and markets; wages and employment; and government revenue and expenditure. Winters *et al.* (2004) offer the following conclusions after surveying the large amount of empirical evidence.

- There is no evidence to reject the traditional view that 'growth, on average, benefits the poor'.
- The recent evidence suggests that openness and trade liberalisation have strong positive impacts on productivity and its rate of change.
- There is plenty of evidence to suggest that households respond to the impact of trade liberalisation as consumers or producers, to take advantage of or protect themselves from the adverse effects of trade liberalisation. However, the ability to respond varies across households, and supplementary policies are needed to make sure both the poor and the rich take advantage of the opportunities created by trade liberalisation.
- There is little evidence to establish a direct link between trade liberalisation and vulnerability at the household level.
- There is no simple general conclusion on the direct link between trade liberalisation and poverty.
- There is no empirical evidence to support the view that trade liberalisation has an adverse impact on poverty.
- The impact of trade liberalisation on poverty depends on the environment in which it is implemented.
- Trade liberalisation is not the only instrument available to address the issue of poverty. However, it is the easiest one to change.
- Trade liberalisation can be an important ingredient of a 'pro-poor' development strategy.

Goldberg and Pavcnik (2004) have surveyed the evidence on the trade–inequality–poverty link focusing on the Latin American experience. They have focused mainly on country studies that used micro-level or firm-level data, with poverty impacts via changes in wages and labour markets their particular focus. Their survey summarises a number of findings, as follows:

- In developing countries, the most heavily protected industries tend to employ a large proportion of unskilled labour. Therefore, trade liberalisation can have negative impacts on unskilled workers and their income in the short and medium run.
- The documented empirical literature related to developing countries using the experience of the 1980s and 1990s suggests that there is a lack of major labour reallocation across sectors.

- According to some evidence, trade liberalisation leads to a decrease in industry wage premiums in those sectors that experience the largest tariff cuts.
- The price and wage response to trade liberalisation is more significant that the quantity response, reflecting market rigidities in developing countries in the short run.
- Some firm-level empirical evidence suggests that productivity increases in those industries that experience more liberalisation because there is significant reallocation of output towards more productive firms within an industry.
- Establishing the link between trade liberalisation and absolute poverty is a difficult task in rural areas. However, it is relatively promising in documenting correlation between trade liberalisation and certain indicators of urban poverty.
- Trade liberalisation affects poverty through relative price changes and their effects on consumption.

Goldberg and Pavcnik (2004: 257) indicate that the existing empirical evidence does not provide a clear message on the trade–poverty link and 'a direct connection to an increase – or reduction – in poverty is naturally even more tenuous'.

Hertel and Winters (2006), in their edited volume, summarise some empirical evidence from a number of country case studies that are based on a multi-country research project conducted on the link between the Doha Round trade liberalisation and poverty. This project has covered some countries in Asia, Africa, Latin America and Russia. The country case studies have been carried out using a standard methodology (CGE models). The summary of their results indicates that the poverty impacts of trade liberalisation are mixed, with negative impacts on poverty in some countries and positive impacts on poverty in other countries. In general, the case studies in this research project suggest that, in terms of poverty reduction, countries exporting agricultural products (e.g., Brazil) are benefited and net food importers like Bangladesh are affected under the Doha trade liberalisation. The most important message emerging from this project is that complementary domestic reforms enhance the impact of trade liberalisation on poverty (positively), and such reforms provide opportunities for households to take market advantages created by agricultural trade liberalisation.

Harrison (2007b) has summarised the main findings of another research volume involving cross-country studies as well as country case studies, concluding that 'there is no evidence in aggregate data that trade reforms are good or bad for the poor' Harrison (2007b: 13). This volume suggests that the poor in countries with abundant unskilled labour are not always benefited by trade liberalisation as predicted in HO and SS models, but are benefited by trade liberalisation when there are complementary policies in place. Case studies of India and Colombia in this volume clearly demonstrate the need for such complementary policies with trade liberalisation to reduce poverty. Further, the evidence in Mexico, India, Zambia, Colombia and Poland demonstrates that export growth and inward FDI flows are associated with poverty reduction. According to different countries' experiences, while poor wage-earners in export sectors and sectors associated with FDI gain from trade, the poor farmers and workers in protected sectors that are exposed to import competition lose from trade liberalisation. Further, the Mexican case study in this volume shows that trade liberalisation produces opposite effects on two set of farmers within a single region.

Recently Porto (2007) has attempted to examine some channels and evidence on trade and poverty using the Latin American experience (particularly using Guatemala and Argentina). This study shows that higher export prices resulting from trade liberalisation make food items expensive while creating higher wage income and labour demand to reduce poverty. In this analysis, the positive income effect is higher than the negative consumption effect on poverty. The case studies in this paper further demonstrate that the impacts on poverty are heterogeneous and that different countries and different households are affected by trade liberalisation in different ways.

In addition to the above major studies, several recent studies have concluded that the poor are more likely to gain from trade when complementary policies are implemented together with trade liberalisation. Nissanke and Thorbecke (2007: 45) argue that agrarian economies during transformation should provide a flow of resources to agriculture continuously, in terms of irrigation, inputs, research and credit, drawing lessons from Korea and Taiwan. The key role of agriculture in reducing poverty has also been highlighted by Ravallion and Chen (2004: 31), who argue that the bulk of poverty in China declined before the 1980s as a result of decollectivisation in agriculture: 'While the country's success in trade reforms may well bring longer term gains to the poor ... the experience of 1981–2001 does not provide support for the view that China's periods of expanding external trade brought more rapid poverty reduction.'

The overall message emerging from the empirical studies covering cross-country and single-country studies reviewed in this and the previous section is that the effects of trade liberalisation on poverty vary widely from country to country and region to region, depending on domestic economic structure, flexibility of resource mobility, domestic infrastructure and complementary policy reforms.

Concluding remarks

This chapter has provided an interpretive survey of the literature on the relationship between trade liberalisation and poverty with emphasis on the South Asian experience. A number of inferences have emerged from the survey. First, the relationship between trade policy and poverty is rather complex and difficult to delineate empirically. This is because the outcome of policy reforms depends crucially on the structural peculiarities of the countries and the complementary policies in place. Therefore, finding accurate empirical answers to the question of whether trade liberalisation reduces poverty in the South Asian region has proved elusive. Second, different empirical studies provide contradictory results (or mixed results), with some studies demonstrating that trade liberalisation reduces poverty and others showing that trade liberalisation increases poverty. Third, there are some winners in countries in the region: some segments and regions have managed to reduce poverty. Finally, in the region there are losers among the poor from trade liberalisation: for example, a case study of India demonstrated that trade liberalisation has been associated with a rise in poverty in regions where inflexible labour laws exist.

Similar to previous surveys on the topic, this survey suggests that trade liberalisation is not a 'magic bullet' in reducing poverty; it is important to have complementary policies to reduce poverty while implementing trade policy reforms. As a recent UNCTAD report lucidly summed up: '[T]he controversy about the effects of openness has now see-sawed between "it is good" and "it is bad" to reach the more nuanced position that "it is good if the right complementary policies are adopted"' (UNCTAD 2004: 70). The evidence reviewed in this chapter also supports this view. In order to evaluate the link between trade liberalisation and poverty and the need for complementary policies in South Asian countries, more systematic detailed country studies are needed. The next seven chapters of this volume attempt to undertake such case studies related to South Asia.

3 Bangladesh

Selim Raihan

For over one and a half decades following independence in 1971, Bangladesh pursued an import-substitution industrialisation strategy. The trade policy regime was characterised by high tariffs and non-tariff barriers to trade and an overvalued exchange rate system. This policy was pursued with the aim of improving the balance of payments position of the country and creating a protected domestic market for manufacturing industries (Bhuyan and Rashid 1993). The government embarked on a gradual process of dismantling trade barriers in the mid-1980s. The reform process gathered momentum in the early 1990s. Since then, successive governments have reaffirmed their commitment to the development of a more liberal trade regime.

There are intense debates among economists and policy makers on the extent of trade liberalisation. The World Bank and IMF have claimed that the pace and extent of liberalisation in Bangladesh in the 1990s has not been as rapid as in other developing countries (World Bank 1999). However, this is not endorsed by economists and private industrial entrepreneurs in Bangladesh, who argue that a much slower pace of liberalisation is warranted (Mahmud 1998). It has also been pointed out that the views of the stakeholders have not been taken into consideration in the framing and implementation of trade liberalisation policies.

In fact, there have been concerns over whether the impact of trade liberalisation has been favourable to the domestic economy. There is a lack of consensus on the issue as well (World Bank 1999). There is also debate over the future direction of trade liberalisation in Bangladesh. Questions have been raised over whether Bangladesh ought to undertake further drastic wholesale liberalisation of trade or adopt a more gradual approach. Against this backdrop, the chapter attempts to examine the link between trade liberalisation, growth and poverty in Bangladesh.

Overview of trade liberalisation in Bangladesh

Similar to other countries in the Indian sub-continent, Bangladesh pursued an import-substituting industrialisation strategy in the 1970s immediately after its independence. The key objectives of this strategy were to: (1) safeguard the country's infant industries, (2) reduce the balance of payments (BOP) deficit, (3) use the scarce foreign exchange efficiently, (4) ward off international capital market and exchange rate shocks, (5) lessen fiscal imbalance, and (6) achieve higher economic growth and self-sufficiency of the nation.

The basic policy tools used under this policy regime included high import tariffs, quantitative restrictions, foreign exchange rationing and an overvalued exchange rate. However, in the face of failure of such inward-looking strategies to deliver the desired outcomes, along with rising internal and external imbalances, trade policy reforms were introduced in the early 1980s. Since then, trade liberalisation has become an integral part of Bangladesh's trade policy.

Trade policy during 1972–80 consisted of significant import controls. The major administrative instruments employed to implement the import policy during this period were the foreign exchange allocation system and the Import Policy Orders (IPOs). Under the IPOs, it was specified whether items could be imported, were prohibited or required special authorisation. With the exception of a few cases, licences were required for all other imports. The argument behind the import-licensing system was that it would ensure the allocation of foreign exchange to priority areas and protect vulnerable local industries from import competition. However, the system was criticised for not being sufficiently flexible to ensure its smooth functioning under changing circumstances. Moreover, it was characterised by complexity, deficiency in administration, cumbersome foreign exchange budgeting procedures, poor inter-agency coordination, rigid allocation of licences and time-consuming procedures (Bhuyan and Rashid 1993).

Trade liberalisation has been one of the major policy reforms in Bangladesh. It has been implemented as part of the overall economic reform programme, namely the structural adjustment programme (SAP) which was initiated in 1987 and formed the component of the 'structural adjustment facility' (SAF) and 'enhanced structural adjustment facility' (ESAF) of the IMF and World Bank. This adjustment programme put forward a wide range of policy reforms including trade policy, industrial policy, monetary policy, fiscal policy and exchange rate policy, privatisation of state-owned enterprises and promotion of foreign direct investment.

During the 1980s, a moderate import liberalisation took place. In 1984, a significant change was made in the import policy regime with the abolition of the import-licensing system, and imports were permitted against letters of credit (LC). Since 1986, there have been significant changes in the import procedures and IPOs with respect to their contents and structure. Whereas, prior to 1986, the IPOs contained a lengthy *Positive List* of importables, in 1986 it was replaced by two lists, namely the *Negative List* (for banned items) and the *Restricted List* (for items importable on fulfilment of certain prescribed conditions). Import of any items outside the lists were allowed. These changes may be considered as significant moves towards import liberalisation, since no restrictions were imposed on the import of items that did not appear in the IPOs. With the aim of increasing the elements of stability and certainty of trade policy, IPOs with relatively longer periods replaced the previous practice of framing annual import policies. Since 1990, the Negative and Restricted Lists of importables were consolidated into one list, namely the 'Consolidated List' (Ahmed 2001).

Table 3.1 suggests that at the HS-4 digit level, the range of products subject to import ban or restriction has been curtailed substantially from as high as 752 in 1985–6 to only 63 in 2003–6. Import restrictions have been imposed on two grounds: either for trade-related reasons (i.e., to provide protection to domestic industries) or for non-trade reasons (e.g., to protect environment, public health and safety, and security). Therefore, only the trade-related restrictions should be of interest to policy reforms and liberalisation. Table 3.1 shows that over the past two decades the number of trade-related banned items has declined from 275 to five. In a similar fashion, other restricted and mixed (a combination of ban and restriction) import categories have fallen quite rapidly. In 1987–8, about 40 per cent of all import lines at the HS-4 digit level were subject to trade-related quantitative restrictions (QRs), but these restrictions had been drastically reduced to less than 2 per cent.

From the late 1980s, the tariff regime has become increasingly liberalised. Between 1991–2 and 2004–5 the unweighted average rate of tariff fell from 70 per cent to 13.5 per cent (Table 3.2). Much of this reduced protection was achieved through the reduction in the maximum rate. Table 3.2 suggests that in 1991–2 the maximum tariff rate was 350 per cent, which came down to only 25 per cent in 2004–5. The number of tariff bands was 24 in the 1980s, 18 in the early 1990s and only four at present. The percentage of duty-free tariff lines more than doubled between 1992–3 and 1999–2000 (from 3.4 per

Table 3.1 Removal of QRs at the four-digit HS classification level

Year	Total	Restricted for trade reasons			Restricted for non-trade reasons
		Banned	Restricted	Mixed	
1985–6	478	275	138	16	49
1986–7	550	252	151	86	61
1987–8	529	257	133	79	60
1988-89	433	165	89	101	78
1989–90	315	135	66	52	62
1990–1	239	93	47	39	60
1991–2	193	78	34	25	56
1992–3	93	13	12	14	54
1993–4	109	7	19	14	69
1994–5	114	5	6	12	92
1995–7	120	5	6	16	93
1997–2002	122	5	6	16	95
2003–6	63	5	8	10	40

Source: Compiled from different sources (Bayes *et al.* 1995; Yilmaz and Varma 1995; Taslim 2004). Figures for 2003–6 are derived from the Import Policy Orders 2003–6.

Table 3.2 Tariff structure in Bangladesh

Fiscal year	Number of tariffbands	Maximum rate(%)	Unweighted tariff rate (%)	Import-weighted average tariff
1990–1				42.1
1991–2	18	350.0	70.0	24.1
1992–3	15	300.0	47.4	n/a
1993–4	12	300.0	36.0	n/a
1994–5	6	60.0	25.9	20.9
1995–6	7	50.0	22.3	n/a
1996–7	7	45.0	21.5	n/a
1997–8	7	42.5	20.7	n/a
1998–9	7	40.0	20.3	14.7
1999–2000	5	37.5	19.5	13.8
2000–1	5	37.5	18.6	15.1
2001–2	5	37.5	17.1	9.73
2002–3	5	32.5	16.5	12.45
2003–4	5	30.0	15.6	11.48
2004–5	4	25.0	13.5	n/a

Source: Ministry of Finance (2004).

cent to 8.4 per cent). Bangladesh has no tariff quotas, seasonal tariffs and variable import levies (WTO 2000a). All these measures have greatly simplified the tariff regime and helped streamline customs administration procedures.

A drastic reduction in unweighted tariff rates during the 1990s also resulted in the fall in import-weighted tariff rates. Table 3.2 also demonstrates that the import-weighted average tariff rate declined from 42.1 per cent in 1990–1 to 13.8 per cent in 1999–2000, and further to 11.48 per cent in 2003–4.

One important aspect of the tariff structure in Bangladesh relates to the use of import taxes (also known as para-tariffs) over and above customs duties (World Bank 2004b). These taxes include the infrastructure development surcharge (IDSC), supplementary duties (SD), and regulatory duties. Although these taxes have been primarily imposed to generate additional revenues, in the absence of equivalent taxes on domestic production, they have provided extra protection to local industries. Similarly, while the value-added tax (VAT) is supposed to be trade-neutral, exemptions for specified domestic products have also resulted in it having some protective content. Some of these para-tariffs, such as the IDSC, are applied across the board to all or practically all imports, and can be considered as general or normally applied protective tax which affect all or nearly all tariff lines. Others are selective protective taxes in that they are only applied to selected products, for example the 'supplementary' duties. The para-tariffs employed during the 1990s and early 2000s in Bangladesh are summarised in Table 3.3. It appears that, despite the lowering of customs duty, the presence of para-tariffs did not significantly lower the total protection rate.

Table 3.3 Average customs duties and para-tariffs in Bangladesh

Year	All tariff lines			Industrial tariff lines			Agriculture tariff lines		
	Customs duties	Para-tariffs	Total protection rate	Customs duties	Para-tariffs	Total protection rate	Customs duties	Para-tariffs	Total protection rate
1991–2	70.64	2.98	73.62	69.72	3.44	73.16	76.64	−0.01	76.63
1992–3	57.93	2.59	60.52	57.34	2.99	60.33	61.83	−0.03	61.80
1993–4	43.47	2.43	45.90	43.13	2.84	45.97	45.58	−0.17	45.41
1994–5	34.24	3.30	37.55	33.52	3.54	37.06	37.49	2.23	39.72
1995–6	28.70	3.26	31.96	28.40	3.47	31.87	30.07	2.28	32.36
1996–7	28.24	3.38	31.61	27.79	3.58	31.37	30.25	2.48	32.73
1997–8	27.27	5.88	33.15	26.80	5.98	32.78	29.42	5.42	34.83
1998–9	26.59	5.82	32.41	26.23	5.92	32.15	28.19	5.37	33.56
1999–2000	22.40	6.99	29.39	21.86	7.33	29.19	24.87	5.41	30.28
2000–1	21.10	7.43	28.54	20.39	7.84	28.23	24.53	5.46	30.00
2001–2	21.02	8.41	29.43	20.28	8.47	28.75	24.60	8.15	32.74
2002–3	19.91	6.51	26.42	19.08	6.74	25.82	23.85	5.44	29.29
2003–4	18.82	10.29	29.11	18.02	8.81	26.82	22.56	17.22	39.77

Source: World Bank (2004b).

Until the mid-1980s, Bangladesh followed a strategy of import-substitution. The regime was also characterised by a high degree of anti-export bias. However, since 1985 export policy reforms have been implemented, which have included trade, exchange rate, and monetary and fiscal policy incentives, aimed at increasing effective assistance to exports. A few sectors, especially the ready-made garments (RMG), have been among the beneficiaries of these reforms. The reforms have also provided exporters with unrestricted and duty-free access to imported inputs, financial incentives in the form of easy access to credit and credit subsidies, and fiscal incentives such as rebates on income taxes and concessionary duties on imported capital machinery. They were also aimed at strengthening the institutional framework for export promotion (Rahman 2001).

Impacts of trade liberalisation on economic growth in Bangladesh

Following the rapid liberalisation programme during the past few decades, the rate at which the economy grew was commendable. Above all, the fall in the incidence of poverty is also impressive. Therefore, poverty impact of trade liberalisation is a very interesting area of research. But there is no *ex post* econometric study on Bangladesh that analyses the link between trade policy and poverty. The main bar is the unavailability of data as poverty estimates are only available intermittently. Apart from the scarcity of detailed household data, it is indeed very tricky to measure the direct impact of trade liberalisation on poverty. In other words, it is often difficult to disentangle the impact of trade reform from those of other reforms, events and shocks that affect household poverty dynamics. All these have prevented economists from undertaking sophisticated econometric exercises to investigate the relationship between openness and poverty. However, there have been a number of studies, based on time series data, testing the relationship between trade and economic growth in the context of Bangladesh.

A study by Begum and Shamsuddin (1998) investigated the effect of export growth in Bangladesh for the period 1961–92. The authors concluded that the growth of exports has a significant and positive impact on economic growth through an increase in the total factor productivity of the economy. However, the study can be criticised for its weak methodology, as it considered only the short-run impact of export growth. On the other hand, using updated and revised data for the period 1980–2000 and examining the long-run impact of export on economic growth, Razzaque *et al.* (2003a) found no evidence of a long-term relationship between exports and economic growth in the context of the Bangladesh economy.

Ahmed and Sattar (2004) demonstrated that the higher average growth of Bangladesh in the 1990s over that of the 1980s should be attributed to the success of trade liberalisation. This simple approach is, however, seriously flawed as it does not take into account various other events that occurred simultaneously during that period. Therefore, it is not clear whether, after controlling for traditional sources of growth, liberalisation would have any distinct impact on growth. In the absence of such analysis, sceptics, taking an extreme view, could argue that the increased rate of growth in the post-liberalisation period arose despite rather than because of liberalisation.

To overcome the above problems, Razzaque *et al.* (2003b) and Raihan (2007) have employed regression methods to explain the output/growth performance using time-varying indicators of trade liberalisation measures and controlling for factors of production. In the first study, Razzaque *et al.* (2003b) extended the traditional neo-classical and endogenous growth models by incorporating three widely accepted trade liberalisation measures: trade–GDP ratio, ratio of consumers' goods import to GDP and the implicit nominal tariff rate. While the estimated model turned out to be satisfactory, none of the indicators of trade liberalisation, quite surprisingly, achieved statistical significance in any of the regression results (Part A of Table 3.4). The same study also did not find any significant effect of trade liberalisation on the export–growth relationship.

Raihan (2007) examined the impact of trade liberalisation on manufacturing sector growth in Bangladesh employing the production function framework. The study used a panel database for the manufacturing sector at the three-digit ISIC code level for 27 sectors with a time span of 22 years (1977–98). Five indicators of trade liberalisation were used: the import penetration of consumer goods, the implicit nominal tariff rate, the sectoral import penetration ratio, the sectoral export–orientation ratio, and a year dummy variable. The regression results failed to detect a statistically significant positive relationship between trade liberalisation and manufacturing growth (Part B of Table 3.4).

It appears from the aforementioned analysis that the econometric investigations using historical data fail to depict a conclusive relationship between trade liberalisation and growth in the context of the Bangladesh economy. There are studies that have undertaken simulation exercises based on applied general equilibrium models to find out *ex ante* positive effects of further liberalisation. Khondker and Raihan (2004), in a static CGE framework, examined the impact of different policy reforms in Bangladesh in a general equilibrium framework, and found that full trade liberalisation would generate negative consequences for the macro economy as well as for the welfare and poverty status of the households. The most influential study in this regard is the one by Annabi *et al.* (2006). Working with a dynamic sequential CGE model, the authors found that if all tariffs of Bangladesh are set to zero (i.e., the case when all policy-induced *ex ante* bias is removed), the effect on GDP is actually negative in the short run, which is defined to be one–two years, but positive over a long-run horizon of 15 years. Interestingly, however, the long run positive impact is found to be just 1.4 per cent higher than the base scenario. This suggests that the growth dividend from further liberalisation of tariffs is very low.

Table 3.4 The results of two econometric studies on trade liberalisation and growth

Part A: Trade liberalisation measures in growth models: A time series economic exercise

Explanatory variable	Coeff (s.e.)	Coeff (s.e.)	Coeff (s.e.)	Coeff (s.e.)	Coeff (s.e.)	Coeff (s.e.)
Constant	6.08*** (1.61)	6.35*** (0.61)	6.23*** (0.69)	3.53*** (0.43)	3.40*** (0.28)	3.31*** (0.39)
Ln (Capital stock)	0.23** (0.08)	0.22** (0.09)	0.23** (0.09)	0.50*** (0.07)	0.53*** (0.05)	0.53*** (0.08)
Ln (Labour)	1.13** (0.15)	1.15*** (0.18)	1.12*** (0.18)			
Ln (Human capital)				0.90*** (0.19)	0.80*** (0.19)	0.84*** (0.22)
Ln (Trade–GDP ratio)	−0.014 (0.012)			0.008 (0.02)		
Ln (Consumers' goods–GDP ratio)		0.008 (0.01)			0.005 (0.01)	
Ln (Import duties/Imports)			0.006 (0.01)			−0.001 (0.02)

Part B: Trade liberalization measures in panel data models of manufacturing output

Explanatory Variables	Coeff (s.e.)	Coeff (s.e.)	Coeff (s.e.)	Coeff (s.e.)	Coeff (s.e.)
Ln (Capital)	0.356*** (0.074)	0.339*** (0.07)	0.286*** (0.06)	0.362*** (0.074)	0.359*** (0.07)
Ln (labour)	0.492*** (0.05)	0.493*** (0.05)	0.498*** (0.04)	0.488*** (0.05)	0.491*** (0.05)
Ln (Import penetration ratio of Consumers' goods)	−0.041* (0.015)				
Ln (Implicit nominal tariff rate)		−0.1465 (0.28)			
Ln (Sectoral import penetration ratio)			−0.129*** (0.04)		
Ln (Sectoral export–orientation Ratio)				0.086 (−0.124)	
Liberalization year dummy					−0.105** (−0.05)
R^2	0.64	0.74	0.77	0.75	0.63
Observations	594	594	594	594	594

Source: Raihan (2007); Razzaque et al. (2003b).

Trade liberalisation and employment

In order to investigate the employment impact of trade liberalisation, a sectoral analysis has been undertaken in this study. We had disaggregated data on output, employment, total wage and sectoral export and import. We have estimated labour demand functions for each industry and augmented the trade liberalisation measure into the function to study the impact of trade liberalisation on demand for labour in each sector. Before running the formal regressions, the time series properties of the variable have been checked to avoid the problem of spurious regression. All variables were found to be integrated in their levels and stationary with their first difference. The summary of the regression results are provided in Table 3.5, and the detailed regression results are reported in Appendix 1.

Table 3.5 Trade liberalisation and employment: Empirical findings

Part A: Summary result from estimated labour demand function –industries which are cointegrated with sectoral export-output ratio as the explanatory variable

2-digit ISIC code	Name of the industry	Impact on the employment
02	Beverage industry	Positive significant
05	Wearing apparel	Positive significant
14	Petroleum refining	Positive significant
15	Miscellaneous petroleum products	Positive significant
17	Plastic products	Positive significant
07	Footwear except rubber	Positive significant
10	Paper and its product	Negative significant
04	Textile industry	Negative significant
03	Tobacco manufacturing	Negative insignificant
11	Printing and publishing	Negative insignificant
21	Iron and steel basic industries	Negative insignificant
24	Non-electrical machinery	Negative insignificant
26	Transport machinery	Negative insignificant
06	Leather and its product	Positive insignificant
09	Furniture manufacturing	Positive insignificant
12	Drugs and pharmaceuticals and other chemicals	Positive insignificant
13	Industrial chemicals	Positive insignificant
16	Rubber products	Positive insignificant
18	pottery and chinaware	Positive insignificant
19	glass and its products	Positive insignificant
20	Non-metallic mineral products	Positive insignificant
23	Fabricated metal products	Positive insignificant
08	Wood and cork products	Positive insignificant
27	Scientific, precision etc+ photographic, optical goods	Positive insignificant

Part B: Summary result from estimated labour demand function –industries which are cointegrated with sectoral import-output ratio as the explanatory variable

2-digit ISIC code	Name of the industry	Impact on the employment
06	Leather and its products	Positive significant
12	Drugs and pharmaceuticals and other chemicals	Negative significant
15	Miscellaneous petroleum products	Negative significant
24	Non-electrical machinery	Negative significant
25	Electrical machinery	Negative significant

Part B: Summary result from estimated labour demand function –industries which are cointegrated with sectoral import-output ratio as the explanatory variable

02	Beverage industry	Negative insignificant
01	Food manufacturing	Negative insignificant
10	Paper and its product	Negative insignificant
11	Printing and publishing	Negative insignificant
14	Petroleum refining	Negative insignificant
19	Glass and its products	Negative insignificant
20	Non-metallic mineral products	Negative insignificant
22	Non-ferrous metal industry	Negative insignificant
23	Fabricated metal products	Negative insignificant
05	Wearing apparel	Negative insignificant
13	Industrial chemicals	Positive insignificant
16	Rubber products	Positive insignificant
17	Plastic products	Positive insignificant
18	Pottery and chinaware	Positive Insignificant
21	Iron and steel basic industries	Positive Insignificant
03	Tobacco manufacturing	Positive Insignificant
09	Furniture manufacturing	Positive insignificant

Note: Data are derived from the Census of Manufacturing Industries (CMI) and they are from 1978 to 2000.

It is, however, important to note that trade openness is difficult to measure and the outcome variables like export–output ratio and import–output ratio are not without flaws. In this analysis, we have used the sectoral export–output ratio and sectoral import–output ratio as the imperfect proxy of trade liberalisation.

The industries have been categorised into two groups: Industries in which the labour demand functions are co-integrated when the labour demand function is augmented with the sectoral export–output ratio and industries in which the labour demand functions are co-integrated when the labour demand function is augmented with the sectoral import–output ratio.

The labour demand function is co-integrated when the export–output ratio is added as the explanatory variable for the following industries (Part A of Table 3.5): the beverage industry, tobacco manufacturing, wearing apparel, leather and its products, furniture manufacturing, paper and its products, printing and publishing, drugs and pharmaceuticals and other chemical products, industrial chemical products, petroleum refining, miscellaneous petroleum products, rubber products, plastic products, pottery and chinaware, glass and its products, non-metallic mineral products, iron and steel basic industries, fabricated metal products, non-electrical machinery, the textile industry, footwear except rubber, the wood and cork industry, transport machinery, and scientific, precision, etc., and photographic and optical goods. Among these industries, trade openness (as defined by sectoral export–output ratio) has proved to be helpful in boosting employment for the following industries: the beverage industry, wearing apparel, petroleum refining, miscellaneous petroleum products, plastic products, footwear except rubber. On the other hand, there was decreased demand for labour in the textile and paper industry when export–output ratio is taken as the proxy of trade openness. For the rest of the industries, there is no significant impact on employment due to trade liberalisation.

Trade liberalisation and poverty: a computable general equilibrium analysis

A dynamic computable general equilibrium (CGE) model for the Bangladesh economy has been applied in this section to examining the macroeconomic, poverty and welfare impacts of domestic trade liberalisation in the context of the economy of Bangladesh. The CGE analysis is widely used for the *ex ante* analysis of the economic consequences of comprehensive trade agreements whether multilateral or bilateral in nature (Francois and Shiells 1994). It has the advantage of delineation economy-wide implications of trade policy reforms while appropriately controlling for other factors impacting on the performance of the economy.

The model is calibrated with a Social Accounting Matrix (SAM) of Bangladesh for the year 2005. The model adopts the representative household approach, and the poverty and welfare effects of different policy shocks are estimated using the Bangladesh Household Income and Expenditure Survey (HIES), 2005. A 2005 Social Accounting Matrix (SAM) has been compiled to calibrate the model by using different government data sources in Bangladesh. A summary of the 2005 SAM is given below.

Accounts

The 2005 SAM identifies the economic relations through four types of accounts: (1) production activity and commodity accounts for 26 sectors; (2) nine factors of production with four different types of labour and five types of capital; (3) current account transactions between four main institutional agents; household members and unincorporated capital, corporation, government and the rest of the world; and (4) two consolidated capital accounts to capture the flows of savings and investment by private and public institutions.

Activity and commodity

The activity account is represented by 26 producing activities. A distinction is made between activity and commodity and the commodity account is denoted by 26 sectors.

Institutions accounts

Current account transactions are captured between four institutional agents: households and unincorporated capital, corporate enterprise, government and the rest of the world. Household account includes seven representative groups (e.g., five rural and four urban). Two consolidated capital accounts (domestic and rest of the world) distinguished by public and private sector origin are defined to capture the flows of savings and investment by institutions and the rest of the world respectively.

Household members

The 2005 SAM distinguishes seven household types, classified according to land holding size and occupation of the household's head in rural areas, and to level of education of the household's head in urban areas.

Factors of production

The SAM includes four factors of production: two types of capital, namely non-agricultural and agricultural capital, and two labour categories, skilled and unskilled.

The dynamic CGE model for the Bangladesh economy

The majority of the CGE models used in poverty and inequality analysis are static in nature. They are therefore unable to account for growth effects, which makes them inadequate for the long-run analysis of the poverty impacts of economic policies. These static models cannot capture accumulation effects, and fail to examine the transition path of the economy where short-run impacts of any policy reforms are likely to be different from the long-run impacts. To overcome this limitation, a sequential dynamic CGE model is suggested. In a sequential dynamic CGE model the economic agents do not have any intertemporal optimisation behaviour; rather, these agents are myopic. In this dynamic model a series of static CGE models are linked between periods, while exogenous and endogenous variables are updated with an updating procedure. Below a brief description of the static and dynamic aspects of the model is presented.

Static aspects of the model

In the case of production, each sector has a representative firm. The production system is characterised by a nested structure, where sectoral output is a Leontief function of value added and total intermediate consumption, and value added, in turn, is represented by a constant elasticity of substitution (CES) function of capital and composite labour.

Turning to consumption, a linear expenditure system (LES), which is derived from the maximisation of a Stone–Geary utility function, is applied to represent household demand function. The minimal consumption levels in the LES function are calibrated using guess-estimates of the income elasticity and the Frisch parameters. The model assumes household saving as a fixed proportion of the total disposal income.

Imperfect substitution between foreign and domestic goods is assumed, which is captured by the standard Armington assumption with a constant elasticity of substitution function (CES) between imports and domestic goods. On the supply side, constant elasticity of transformation (CET) between exports and domestic sales is assumed. The model also assumes a finite elasticity export demand function, which expresses the limited power of the local exporters in the world market.

The source of government income is the direct tax revenue from households and firms and indirect tax revenue on domestic and imported goods. Government allocates its expenditure between the consumption of goods and services (including public wages) and transfers. The loss in government revenue due to any tariff cut is compensated by indirect or direct tax mechanism, which is inbuilt in the model.

The model is solved for each period, and the general equilibrium in each period is achieved by the equality between supply and demand of goods and factors, and the equality between investment and savings. In each period the nominal exchange rate acts as the numéraire.

Dynamic aspects of the model

The model considers a capital accumulation equation, which updates capital stock in each period. The model assumes that the stocks are measured at the beginning of the period and flows are measured at the end of the period.

The model introduces an investment demand function which determines the pattern of re-allocation of new investment among sectors after any shock. Investment, in this function, is by sector of destination rather than by origin (product). The total investment by destination equals the total investment by origin in the SAM. The investment by destination matrix is used to calibrate the sectoral capital stock in the base run. The capital accumulation rate (ratio of investment to capital stock) increases with respect to the ratio of the rate of return to capital and its user cost.

Total labour supply increases at an exogenous rate, which is equal to the population growth rate and the labour force growth rate. Other nominal variables, such as transfers and the minimal level of consumption in the LES function, and government savings and current account balance also increase at the same rate.

An adjustment variable, which is introduced in the investment demand function, helps in bringing the equality between total savings and total investment in each period. The model allows all variables in the baseline to increase at the same rate in level, and the prices remain constant. This method is useful for the welfare and poverty analysis since all prices remain constant along the business-as-usual (BaU) path.

The results of policy simulations

In order to examine the link between trade liberalisation and poverty two simulations have been carried out with the model described above. They are:

- Full Liberalisation (FL) Scenario: Under this scenario, tariffs on all imports are reduced to zero. The base values of all other parameters are retained.
- Partial Liberalisation (PL) Scenario: Under this simulation, tariffs on all imports are reduced by 50 per cent. The base values of all other parameters are retained.

The main determinants of the simulation results are the values of trade elasticities, the share of imports and exports, the cost of inputs, and the general equilibrium effects of supply and demand. In all these cases, a decline in tariff rates leads to a decline in the production of the tariff-protected sectors. The resources will then move from this sector to other expanding sectors. The changes in export and import prices influence the domestic and composite good prices and the value-added price, and determine factors' reallocation.

Macroeconomic effects

The macroeconomic impacts are reported in Table 3.6. Under both the first and second simulation, the impacts on GDP and welfare illustrate the

Table 3.6 Macroeconomic effects (% change from the base year value)

Variable	Full tariff liberalisation		Partial tariff liberalisation	
	SR	*LR*	*SR*	*LR*
Real GDP	−0.18	1.32	−0.12	0.86
Welfare	−0.37	0.85	−0.24	0.55
Headcount ratio	0.74	−4.57	0.48	−2.97
Domestic terms of trade	10.73	8.98	6.97	5.84
Imports	11.45	25.28	7.44	16.43
Exports	18.22	41.13	11.84	26.73
Urban CPI	−9.13	−6.84	−5.93	−4.45
Rural CPI	−8.75	−6.61	−5.69	−4.30
Skilled wage rate	−10.51	−6.49	−6.83	−4.22
Unskilled wage rate	−8.86	−4.81	−5.76	−3.12
Agricultural capital rental rate	−8.63	−8.96	−5.61	−5.82
Non−agricultural capital rental rate	−9.65	−9.03	−6.27	−5.87
User cost of capital	−9.41	−7.32	−6.11	−4.76

Source: Author's calculations, based on simulation results.
Note: Short run (SR) refers to year 2008 and long run (LR) refers to year 2020.
Welfare is measured as the sum of individual household equivalent variations.
Domestic TOT is represented by the ratio of the domestic export and import price indexes.

importance of analysing trade liberalisation in a dynamic framework; both measures decline in the short run and then strongly increase in the long run compared to the BaU simulation. The short-run negative impact is explained by the fact that trade liberalisation contracts the import-competing and highly protected sectors, and capital cannot be quickly reallocated to the expanding export-oriented sectors. Impacts are also much larger than under the previous scenarios. Positive growth is observed in the domestic TOT (the ratio of export to import prices on domestic markets) in both the short run and the long run, given the decline in domestic import prices. Imports and exports register strong positive growth, particularly in the long run. Reduced domestic import prices lead to a fall in consumer prices both for rural and (slightly more) for urban households. Skilled and unskilled wage rates decline, although less so in the long run when capital is reallocated toward the expanding sectors. The reduction in unskilled wage rates is some-what smaller, given the expansion of unskilled labour-intensive textile and garment sectors. The user cost of capital also declines in both the short run and the long run.

The difference between the impacts of simulation 1 and those of simulation 2 is that, though the directions are the same, the magnitudes of the effects are smaller under the partial tariff liberalisation scenario.

Sectoral effects

Like the macro effects, the sectoral effects of two simulations are similar in pattern but the magnitudes are less prominent under simulation 2. Tariff elimination leads to an immediate reduction in the domestic price of imports that is proportional to the initial sectoral tariff rates (see Parts A and B of Table 3.7 for simulations 1 and 2 respectively). Domestic consumers respond by increasing import demand, once again in rough proportion to the fall in import prices, with the strongest increases in the grains, mill, food, textile and other industries (see Table 3.7 and Table 3.8 for simulations 1 and 2 respectively). The sectors that had low initial tariff rates (grains, livestock, other fish, woven and knitted ready-made garments) register negative import growth in the short run as consumers substitute towards goods for which prices drop more dramatically. In the long run, import volumes grow more (or contract less) in all sectors except leather.

The current account balance is fixed in the short run and subsequently increases at a fixed rate. Thus, the increase in imports leads to a real devaluation and an increase in exports. The export response is generally smaller in the long run, with the dramatic exception of woven and knitted ready-made garments and other textiles. In the long run, the woven and knitted ready-made garments sector flourishes, and their export volume increase by nearly 18 and 32 per cent respectively compared to the BaU scenario. With a negative sloping demand curve for exports, FOB export prices fall.

Table 3.7 Price effects trade liberalization under two scenarios

Part A: Percentage changes in prices from the BaU path (Full liberalization)

	PM		PD		PV		PX		PQ		PE_FOB	
	SR	LR	SR	LR	SR	LR	SR	LR	SR	LR	SR	LR
Paddy			-6.56	-5.12	-6.27	-4.89	-6.56	-5.12	-6.56	-5.12		
Grains			-6.28	-4.90	-6.53	-5.09	-6.28	-4.90	-1.86	-1.45		
Other crops	-10.85	-8.46	-6.04	-4.71	-6.07	-4.73	-5.99	-4.67	-4.33	-3.38	-1.13	-0.88
Livestock			-6.74	-5.26	-7.04	-5.49	-6.74	-5.26	-4.71	-3.67		
Poultry			-6.63	-5.17	-7.13	-5.56	-6.63	-5.17	-6.63	-5.17		
Shrimp			-10.86	-8.47	-6.06	-4.73	-7.52	-5.87	-10.86	-8.47	-1.61	-1.26
Other fish			-6.28	-4.90	-6.43	-5.02	-6.22	-4.85	-4.26	-3.32	-0.92	-0.72
Rice mill	-8.61	-6.72	-6.34	-4.95	-5.39	-4.20	-6.34	-4.95	-4.41	-3.44		
Grain mill	-21.87	-17.06	-3.39	-2.64	-5.39	-4.20	-3.39	-2.64	-1.65	-1.29		
Food	-28.67	-22.36	-7.65	-5.97	-5.33	-4.16	-6.72	-5.24	-10.84	-8.46	-0.73	-0.57
Mill cloth			-4.04	-3.15	-5.35	-4.17	-4.04	-3.15	-4.04	-3.15		
Woven RMG			-13.17	-10.27	5.31	4.14	-4.37	-3.41	-11.19	-8.73	-2.39	-1.86
Knit RMG			-16.13	-12.58	5.31	4.14	-3.43	-2.68	0.89	0.69	-3.35	-2.61
Other textile	-3.41	-2.66	-4.74	-3.70	5.37	4.19	-4.69	-3.66	-2.10	-1.64	-2.36	-1.84
Other industry	-17.25	-13.46	-7.77	-6.06	-5.32	-4.15	-7.30	-5.69	-10.34	-8.07	-0.62	-0.48
Urban construction			-7.07	-5.51	-5.30	-4.13	-7.07	-5.51	-7.07	-5.51		
Rural construction			-5.87	-4.58	-5.28	-4.12	-5.87	-4.58	-5.87	-4.58		
Public construction			-7.76	-6.05	-5.29	-4.13	-7.76	-6.05	-7.76	-6.05		
Utility			-5.86	-4.57	-5.33	-4.16	-5.86	-4.57	-5.86	-4.57		
Trade			-5.80	-4.52	-5.36	-4.18	-5.80	-4.52	-5.80	-4.52		
Transport			-6.18	-4.82	-5.33	-4.16	-6.18	-4.82	-6.18	-4.82		
Housing			-5.48	-4.27	-5.28	-4.12	-5.48	-4.27	-5.48	-4.27		
Edu & health			-5.92	-4.62	-5.40	-4.21	-5.92	-4.62	-5.92	-4.62		
Pub admin			-6.05	-4.72	-5.42	-4.23	-6.05	-4.72	-6.05	-4.72		
Pri service			-5.80	-4.52	-5.39	-4.20	-5.80	-4.52	-5.80	-4.52		

Table 3.7 (continued)

Part B: Percentage changes in prices from the BaU path (Partial liberalization)

	PM SR	PM LR	PD SR	PD LR	PV SR	PV LR	PX SR	PX LR	PQ SR	PQ LR	PE_FOB SR	PE_FOB LR
Paddy			-3.14	-2.45	-2.95	-2.30	-3.14	-2.45	-3.14	-2.45		
Grains			-3.02	-2.36	-3.08	-2.40	-3.02	-2.36	-0.93	-0.73		
Other crops	-5.43	-4.24	-2.88	-2.25	-2.86	-2.23	-2.86	-2.23	-2.11	-1.65	-0.54	-0.42
Livestock			-3.2	-2.50	-3.3	-2.57	-3.2	-2.50	-2.26	-1.76		
Poultry			-3.19	-2.49	-3.37	-2.63	-3.19	-2.49	-3.19	-2.49		
Shrimp	-4.31	-3.36	-5.17	-4.03	-2.88	-2.25	-3.62	-2.82	-5.17	-4.03	-0.76	-0.59
Other fish	-10.93	-8.53	-3	-2.34	-3.05	-2.38	-2.97	-2.32	-2.08	-1.62	-0.44	-0.34
Rice mill	-14.33	-11.18	-3.04	-2.37	-2.54	-1.98	-3.04	-2.37	-2.17	-1.69		
Grain mill			-1.65	-1.29	-2.54	-1.98	-1.65	-1.29	-0.87	-0.68		
Food			-3.68	-2.87	-2.56	-2.00	-3.25	-2.54	-5.14	-4.01	-0.36	-0.28
Mill cloth			-2.01	-1.57	-2.57	-2.00	-2.01	-1.57	-2.01	-1.57		
Woven RMG	-1.71	-1.33	-6.5	-5.07	2.55	-1.99	-2.16	-1.68	-5.55	-4.33	-1.13	-0.88
Knit RMG	-8.63	-6.73	-8.28	-6.46	2.55	-1.99	-1.72	-1.34	0.35	0.27	-1.68	-1.31
Other textile			-2.32	-1.81	2.57	-2.00	-2.3	-1.79	-1.12	-0.87	-1.16	-0.90
Other industry			-3.79	-2.96	-2.56	-2.00	-3.57	-2.78	-5.12	-3.99	-0.31	-0.24
Urban construction			-3.45	-2.69	-2.55	-1.99	-3.45	-2.69	-3.45	-2.69		
Rural construction			-2.85	-2.22	-2.54	-1.98	-2.85	-2.22	-2.85	-2.22		
Public construction			-3.79	-2.96	-2.54	-1.98	-3.79	-2.96	-3.79	-2.96		
Utility			-2.83	-2.21	-2.56	-2.00	-2.83	-2.21	-2.83	-2.21		
Trade			-2.79	-2.18	-2.57	-2.00	-2.79	-2.18	-2.79	-2.18		
Transport			-2.98	-2.32	-2.55	-1.99	-2.98	-2.32	-2.98	-2.32		
Housing			-2.64	-2.06	-2.54	-1.98	-2.64	-2.06	-2.64	-2.06		
Education & health			-2.85	-2.22	-2.59	-2.02	-2.85	-2.22	-2.85	-2.22		
Pub admin			-2.92	-2.28	-2.6	-2.03	-2.92	-2.28	-2.92	-2.28		
Private service			-2.79	-2.18	-2.58	-2.01	-2.79	-2.18	-2.79	-2.18		

Source: Author's calculations, based on simulation results.

Note: 1. PD = Domestic goods price, PV=Value-added price, PX=Aggregate output price, PQ=Price of composite goods, PE_FOB=FOB export price.

Table 3.8 Effects of trade liberalization on volumes under two policy scenarios

Part A: Percentage changes in volumes from the BaU Path (Full liberalization)

	M		X		E		Q		D	
	SR	LR	SR	LR	SR	LR	SR	LR	SR	LR
Paddy	-7.85	-10.06	-2.08	-2.67			-0.45	-0.58	-2.08	-2.67
Grains	9.65	12.37	0.85	1.09			-2.61	-3.34	0.85	1.09
Other crops	-9.96	-12.77	1.83	2.34	9.4	12.05	2.18	2.8	1.73	2.22
Livestock			-0.85	-1.09			-0.89	-1.14	-0.85	-1.09
Poultry			-0.72	-0.92			0.95	1.22	-0.72	-0.92
Shrimp			4.1	5.26	13.78	17.67	0.49	0.63	-1.16	-1.49
Other fish	-9.1	-11.67	-0.48	-0.62	7.57	9.71	-0.58	-0.74	-0.58	-0.74
Rice mill	2.53	3.24	-0.58	-0.74			-0.46	-0.59	-0.58	-0.74
Grain mill	27.89	35.76	-2.6	-3.33			-2.18	-2.8	-2.6	-3.33
Food	35.07	44.96	-2.24	-2.87	5.97	7.65	3.88	4.98	-3.2	-4.1
Mill cloth	-7.27	-9.32	-2.62	-3.36			-1	-1.28	-2.62	-3.36
Woven RMG	-5.43	-6.96	18.35	23.53	21	26.92	6.84	8.77	6.98	8.95
Knit RMG	16.51	21.17	31.57	40.48	31.69	40.63	-4.25	-5.45	13.22	16.95
Other textile	9.04	11.59	18.29	23.45	21.33	27.35	17.47	22.4	18.23	23.37
Other industry			-2.74	-3.51	5.01	6.42	2.14	2.74	-3.23	-4.14
Urban construction			1.11	1.42			2.81	3.6	1.11	1.42
Rural construction			0.2	0.26			1.89	2.42	0.2	0.26
Public construction			1.42	1.82			3.13	4.01	1.42	1.82
Utility			0.13	0.17			1.81	2.32	0.13	0.17
Trade			-0.76	-0.98			0.9	1.16	-0.76	-0.98
Transport			-0.42	-0.54			1.25	1.6	-0.42	-0.54
Housing			-1.19	-1.53			0.46	0.59	-1.19	-1.53
Education & health			0.11	0.14			1.79	2.29	0.11	0.14
Pub admin			1.17	1.5			2.88	3.69	1.17	1.5
Private service			-0.89	-1.14			0.77	0.99	-0.89	-1.14

Table 3.8 (continued)

Part B: Percentage changes in volumes from the BaU Path (Partial liberalization)

	M		X		E		Q		D	
	SR	LR	SR	LR	SR	LR	SR	LR	SR	LR
Paddy	-3.71	-4.75	-0.9	-1.15			-0.16	-0.2	-0.9	-1.15
Grains	4.7	6.02	0.51	0.65			-1.15	-1.47	0.51	0.65
Other crops	-4.73	-6.06	0.87	1.12	4.31	5.52	1.06	1.36	0.83	1.07
Livestock			-0.31	-0.4			-0.33	-0.42	-0.31	-0.4
Poultry			-0.27	-0.35			0.47	0.6	-0.27	-0.35
Shrimp	-4.39	-5.63	1.84	2.36	6.17	7.91	0.3	0.38	-0.44	-0.57
Other fish	1.42	1.82	-0.2	-0.25	3.5	4.49	-0.23	-0.3	-0.23	-0.3
Rice mill	12.07	15.48	-0.23	-0.29			-0.17	-0.22	-0.23	-0.29
Grain mill	14.45	18.52	-1.13	-1.45			-0.94	-1.21	-1.13	-1.45
Food			-0.93	-1.19	2.89	3.71	1.74	2.23	-1.37	-1.75
Mill cloth	-3.51	-4.5	-1.14	-1.46			-0.41	-0.52	-1.14	-1.46
Woven RMG	-2.58	-3.31	8.22	10.54	9.41	12.06	3.23	4.14	3.29	4.22
Knit RMG	7.57	9.7	14.31	18.35	14.37	18.42	-1.99	-2.55	6.39	8.19
Other textile	4.25	5.45	8.29	10.63	9.6	12.31	7.96	10.2	8.27	10.6
Other industry			-1.26	-1.61	2.43	3.11	1.07	1.37	-1.48	-1.9
Urban construction			0.59	0.76			1.35	1.73	0.59	0.76
Rural construction			0.18	0.23			0.93	1.19	0.18	0.23
Public construction			0.76	0.98			1.52	1.95	0.76	0.98
Utility			0.14	0.18			0.89	1.14	0.14	0.18
Trade			-0.26	-0.33			0.48	0.62	-0.26	-0.33
Transport			-0.12	-0.16			0.62	0.8	-0.12	-0.16
Housing			-0.5	-0.64			0.24	0.31	-0.5	-0.64
Education & health			0.02	0.03			0.76	0.98	0.02	0.03
Pub admin			0.48	0.61			1.22	1.57	0.48	0.61
Private service			-0.35	-0.45			0.39	0.5	-0.35	-0.45

Source: Author's calculations, based on simulation results.
Note: 1. M =Imports, X=Exports, E=Domestic Output, E=Exports, Q= composite goods, D=Domestic Sales.
2. Short run (SR) refers to year 2008 and long run (LR) refers to year 2020.

Output expands most in woven and knitted garments and other textile sectors. Export-intensive ready-made garments benefit from export expansion, and all these sectors register input cost savings, as evidenced by the positive evolution in value-added prices despite falling output prices. Greatly increased import competition for textiles is offset by increased input demand from the ready-made garments sector. In contrast, production contracts in the heavier manufacturing sectors for which export demand stagnates or declines. As a result, non-agricultural capital and labour migrate to the textile and garments sectors and away from the other manufacturing sectors, with relatively little movement in the agricultural sectors. In the long run, the non-agricultural capital stock response is much larger and tempers the reallocation of skilled and unskilled labour. There are also moderate capital stock increases in the agricultural and service sectors.

In the short run, nominal factor returns fall by roughly 10 per cent as a result of declining domestic prices (see Table 3.7). Overall investment falls in response to the average reduction in capital returns relative to the user cost of capital. This makes the long-term reduction in wage rates somewhat smaller, especially for unskilled wages. The average returns to capital fall slightly more in the non-agricultural sector, although these rates converge after long-term adjustment in sectoral investment rates (see Parts A and B of Table 3.8).

Welfare effects

Under both the scenarios, a fall in nominal income for all households is observed in both the short run and the long run (see Table 3.9). This reduction is smallest among the poorest households – urban households with illiterate or low-educated heads and rural landless or marginal households – given their reliance on unskilled wages. Medium- and high-educated urban households, as well as non-agricultural rural households, are the biggest losers as a result of their high endowments in non-agricultural capital and skilled labour. In the short run, real consumption decreases for all households as nominal income falls more than consumer prices. However, the opposite is true in the long run. The figures of EVs are very much in line with real consumption growth, with the poorest household categories emerging as the biggest winners.

Poverty effects

FGT poverty indexes are used to evaluate the impacts of the simulation on the poverty profiles of the nine representative households (Foster, Greer and Thorbecke 1984) (see Table 3.10).[1] The variations in consumption for each household group from the dynamic model are applied to generate new consumption vectors for individual households from the Bangladeshi household survey.[2] Two different poverty lines for rural and urban households are used, which are endogenously determined by the model taking into account the

Table 3.9 Income and welfare effects (percentage change from BaU path)

Scenario	Variable	Period	Rural					Urban			
			Landless	Marginal farmer	Small farmer	Large farmer	Non-Agricultural	Illiterate	Low education	Medium education	High education
Full liberalization	Income	SR	-8.25	-8.47	-8.59	-8.48	-8.72	-8.42	-8.59	-9.08	-8.93
		LR	-4.60	-5.08	-5.39	-5.91	-5.33	-4.91	-5.32	-5.92	-5.96
	CPI	SR	-8.06	-8.02	-8.03	-8.01	-8.18	-8.35	-8.43	-8.53	-8.69
		LR	-6.09	-6.05	-6.05	-6.04	-6.18	-6.27	-6.33	-6.37	-6.46
	Welfare (EV)	SR	-0.19	-0.46	-0.52	-0.28	-0.52	-0.06	-0.15	-0.47	-0.10
		LR	1.61	1.01	0.62	0.11	0.86	1.41	0.99	0.40	0.23
Partial liberalization	Income	SR	-5.37	-5.50	-5.58	-5.51	-5.67	-5.47	-5.58	-5.90	-5.81
		LR	-2.99	-3.30	-3.51	-3.84	-3.47	-3.19	-3.45	-3.85	-3.87
	CPI	SR	-5.24	-5.21	-5.22	-5.21	-5.32	-5.43	-5.48	-5.54	-5.65
		LR	-3.96	-3.93	-3.94	-3.92	-4.02	-4.08	-4.11	-4.14	-4.20
	Welfare (EV)	SR	-0.13	-0.30	-0.34	-0.18	-0.34	-0.04	-0.10	-0.30	-0.06
		LR	1.05	0.66	0.41	0.07	0.56	0.92	0.65	0.26	0.15

Source: Author's calculations, based on simulation results.
Note: Short run (SR) refers to year 2008 and long run (LR) refers to year 2020.

Table 3.10 Poverty effects (percentage point change from the BaU poverty levels)

Scenario	Poverty index	Period	Rural households					Total rural	Urban households				Total urban
			Landless	Marginal farmer	Small farmer	Large farmer	Non-agriculture		Illiterate	Low education	Medium education	High education	
Full liberalization	P0	SR	0.21	0.77	1.83	2.95	0.91	0.92	0.00	0.00	1.43	0.00	0.06
		LR	-6.30	-3.12	-3.88	0.00	-4.56	-4.83	-4.28	-6.75	0.00	0.00	-4.71
	P1	SR	0.43	1.25	2.17	1.74	2.31	1.47	-0.11	0.54	3.30	0.00	0.12
		LR	-7.02	-6.13	-4.45	-2.52	-4.30	-5.62	-6.06	-6.58	-1.51	0.00	-6.04
	P2	SR	0.57	1.67	2.59	2.46	2.90	1.80	-0.14	0.71	3.36	0.00	0.09
		LR	-3.34	-2.92	-2.12	-1.20	-2.05	-2.68	-2.89	-3.13	-0.72	0.00	-2.88
Partial liberalization	P0	SR	0.18	0.68	1.61	2.60	0.80	0.81	0.00	0.00	1.26	0.00	0.05
		LR	-5.54	-2.75	-3.41	0.00	-4.01	-4.25	-3.77	-5.94	0.00	0.00	-4.14
	P1	SR	0.38	1.10	1.91	1.53	2.03	1.29	-0.10	0.48	2.90	0.00	0.11
		LR	-6.18	-5.39	-3.92	-2.22	-3.78	-4.95	-5.33	-5.79	-1.33	0.00	-5.32
	P2	SR	0.50	1.47	2.28	2.16	2.55	1.58	-0.12	0.62	2.96	0.00	0.08
		LR	-2.94	-2.57	-1.86	-1.06	-1.80	-2.36	-2.54	-2.76	-0.63	0.00	-2.53

Source: Author's calculations, based on simulation results.
Note: Short run (SR) refers to year 2008 and long run (LR) refers to year 2020.
P0 = Headcount poverty, P1 = Poverty gap, P2 = Squared poverty gap.

rural and urban changes in poverty indexes (CPIs). Changes in poverty indexes are determined by changes in the poverty line and changes in nominal consumption (or income). The poverty line represents the cost of a basic-needs basket of goods. If the change in poverty line is greater (smaller) than the change in nominal consumption, then poverty is likely to decrease (increase). The poverty effects of two simulations are reported in Table 3.10

The poverty effects under two simulations are similar in pattern but different in magnitude. In the short run, headcount poverty increases for all households, except those headed by highly educated heads, for which there is no change, and those headed by illiterate heads, for which poverty falls. Also the depth of poverty (P1 – poverty gap) and the severity of poverty (P2 – poverty gap squared) increase in the short run. However, in the long run poverty indices fall for all households, especially among the poorer households. It suggests that accumulation effects captured by the model play a major role in alleviating poverty, because poverty falls dramatically in the long run.

Conclusion

Bangladesh has liberalised its economy considerably since the mid-1980s. The pace of liberalisation has been particularly rapid in the 1990s. The liberalisation reforms have reflected in a notable reduction in the anti-export bias in the incentive structure, but the incentives are still moderately biased in favour of import competing production at some moderate level. Although liberalisation should encompass many factors affecting trade and business practices, in Bangladesh overwhelming attention has been given to trade-related instruments. In fact, policy makers are so inclined to measures related to tariffs and QRs that most of the time reform measures are used interchangeably with trade liberalisation measures. Reform of institutions has largely been overlooked. Embarking on such trade reforms as tariff cuts and elimination of QRs is relatively easy. However, significant growth-enhancing effects perhaps require reforms in other difficult areas. In this regard, there are suggestions that institutional reforms should be considered the key to Bangladesh's growth-supporting strategy. Maybe it is high time that Bangladeshi authorities considered trade policy reform as an integral part of institutional reform. There is certainly a need for further trade liberalisation to remove anti-export bias. However, this will have to be supported by other more difficult reform measures. It is understood that, since the 1990s, Bangladesh has embarked on a fast-paced tariff reform programme; however, it may not be possible to continue further liberalisation on a comparable tempo. Nevertheless, it would be unwise to reverse the process of liberalisation and thus the progress achieved in the previous decade.

It is also important to recognise the difference between trade policy and policy of trade liberalisation. The distinction is very important for protecting some policy space that is required to promote development priorities. An overall pro-liberalisation policy does not exclude the possibility of policy support for certain specific sectors. In fact, across the board drastic tariff reduction may not be desirable not only because of the revenue concern of the government but also because of the need for providing some support to domestic industries with high growth and poverty alleviation potentials. By adopting a pro-active and analytical policy regime, effective support to the growth of small and informal sector activities with significant poverty alleviation effects can be provided, but many such opportunities seem to have been missed in the absence of a clear-cut trade policy philosophy and lack of manoeuvrability.

Finally, analysis using the dynamic computable general equilibrium model suggests that there are marked differences between the short-run impacts and the long-run impacts of tariff liberalisation. In the short run there are possibilities of reduced welfare and increased poverty; however, in the long run, if resources are reallocated towards the more efficient and expanding sectors, there could be positive outcomes of tariff liberalisation in terms of welfare gains and poverty reduction.

Notes

1 The FGT indexes allow comparison of three measures of poverty: headcount ratio, poverty gap index and squared poverty gap index. To estimate these three indexes, a poverty line is first defined. The poverty line is the minimum income that is required to maintain a subsistence level of consumption. The first indicator, the headcount ratio, is the proportion of the population with a per capita income below the poverty line. This is the simplest measure of poverty. The second indicator, the poverty gap, measures the depth of poverty as the average distance separating the income of poor households from the poverty line. The final indicator, the squared poverty gap index, measures the severity of poverty, taking account of the inequality of income distribution among the poor.
2 Poverty analysis is performed with DAD (Distributive Analysis–Analyse Distributive) software.

4 Bhutan

Chencho Dorji

Located in the eastern Himalayas, Bhutan is a small landlocked country surrounded by India on three sides and the Tibetan region of China in the north. It is an extremely mountainous country covering about 47,000 sq. km., with altitude changing from 200 to 7,500 metres above sea level. It was not colonised, and managed to maintain an undiluted culture based on Vajrayana Buddhism. The total population is about 700,000 and around 80 per cent of the total population live in rural areas. The fertility rate is high and the population growth rate is around 2.0 per cent in Bhutan. The adult literacy rate is low. The annual GDP growth rate was around 3.0 per cent for the past decade. Per capita national income has more than doubled in the first decade of this century (from $730 in 2000 to $1,900 in 2008). The country is still classified as a Least Developing Country by the United Nations. After long years of the monarchy system of the Kingdom of Bhutan, a new democratic system was introduced recently to form a National Council and a National Assembly. The first democratic elections were held in March 2008.

Bhutan started to integrate into the world economy in the 1960s, ending economic isolation. In addition to its gradual trade liberalisation process, Bhutan has entered into a number of preferential trade agreements in recent years. In terms of the theme trade–poverty nexus in South Asia, Bhutan can be used as a case study of a small and landlocked country, with a small and scattered population, rich cultural heritage, well-maintained natural biodiversity, empowerment of women at the forefront of the development policy and decades of sound political stability. The concept of Gross National Happiness has been its overall guiding principle. All these unique characteristics of Bhutan provide an interesting and a special case different from large countries in the region like India and Pakistan.

This chapter is organised as follows: section 2 provides the trade policy framework which includes trade policy, trade regime, regional free trade agreements and the foreign development policy framework; section 3 outlines the trends in economic growth and poverty; section 4 discusses the relationship between trade, growth and poverty; section 5 summarises the key findings of the report and some policy measures for poverty reduction.

Trade and investment policy reforms

Trade liberalisation

For Bhutan, like any other small landlocked developing country constrained by limited domestic resources and a small domestic market, gradual integration into the global trading system is of paramount importance. This has been recognised by its series of five-year plans. Its liberalisation and other economic reform programmes have been implemented under its five-year plans. Thus, the importance of opening up the economy has been highlighted in the Ninth Five Year Plan (NFYP, 2002–7) and in the recently finalised Tenth Five Year Plan (TFYP, 2008/9–2012/13) documents as a key objective of the government. It is important to note here that there are a number of features of Bhutanese integration into the world economy. First, the reform process in Bhutan is not 'crisis driven' compared with many developing countries' reforms based on the 'conditionality' of global institutions such as the IMF and the World Bank. Second, its gradual integration can be considered as one based on self-adjustment and participating in preferential trade agreements. Finally, its trade liberalisation process is related to the process of obtaining WTO membership.

The objectives for international trade for the NFYP are to stimulate growth of exports and enhance export earnings; to create an open, liberal and stable environment conducive for the growth of private sector and trade; to promote the integration of Bhutan into the international and regional trading system, and to promote more competitive and fair trade practices. Similar to the NFYP, the TFYP documents also accord high importance to trade as a tool for economic growth and poverty alleviation. This view has been clearly supported by the recent budget for 2009/10 presented by the Royal Government of Bhutan (RGOB). In view of the limited domestic market and narrow trade portfolio, the Royal Government's focus during the plan period will be to diversify exports, especially that of non-hydro export base and trading markets.

The most important trade policy instrument employed by the Royal Government of Bhutan is the bilateral free trade agreement (FTA) with India. Since India accounts for about 95 per cent of Bhutan's export trade and over 80 per cent of its import trade, this agreement ensures that Bhutan follows, by and large, an open economic policy.

Bhutan also has a preferential trade agreement (PTA) with Bangladesh, which is Bhutan's second largest export market. Bangladeshi products are granted duty-free access in the country while Bhutanese exports are imposed 50 per cent of the normal duty in Bangladesh. As the agreement period between the two countries is drawing to a close, the two governments will soon discuss the considerations of a new agreement. The Bhutanese will seek to negotiate for a deeper reduction in tariff and elimination of non-tariff barriers, and expansion of product coverage under the existing PTA. The concession was further enhanced on about 18 products in August 2003, whereby only 15 per cent of the duty is now applied. However, a large number of products covered by this concession are timber products which are no longer exported by Bhutan. Hence, the concession has not been very meaningful.

The customs tariff in Bhutan was introduced for the first time during the early 1970s, and the tariff nomenclature was revised to the Harmonised Commodity Description and Coding System (HS) in 1996 which is under the governance of the World Customs Organisation. Customs duty is levied only on imports from third countries on the CIF value of the goods as per the rates prescribed in the Customs Tariff Schedule. Trade with Countries Other Than India (COTI) used to be controlled by a rigid quota system until the early 1990s, and now the quota system has been replaced by the tariff system in a move to a more liberalised system. Presently, the tariff regime comprises of the Bhutan Sales Tax (BST) and the customs duty. BST is imposed on all imports and on sales in hotels, restaurants and on cement in the domestic economy. Thus, in principle BST is a trade-neutral tax since it is imposed on a commodity regardless of its origin and thus does not have a protective effect – it is primarily a revenue-raising instrument.[1] BST has seven slabs, ranging from zero to 50 per cent. The highest rate of 50 per cent is applied on alcoholic beverages and tobacco products (the import and sale of tobacco has been banned since December 2004).

The customs duty has eight slabs, ranging from zero to 100 per cent, and the highest rate corresponding to 100 per cent duty is applied to alcoholic beverages, tobacco and imports of antiques and other luxury items. The customs duty is the only tax that has a protective and trade-distorting effect but the actual impact of the customs duty is, however, very minimal for a number of reasons:

- It is not applicable to trade with India, which accounts for 70–80 per cent of all imports.
- Even where it is applicable, i.e. on hard currency imports from countries other than India, there are many exemptions and leakages that dilute its effect.[2]
- In addition, customs duty is also minimised because traders often under-invoice the value of their imports.

Because of all these factors, customs duty is rather a marginal phenomenon in Bhutan–neither its revenue effect nor its trade-distorting effect is large enough to make a difference to the course and structure of the Bhutanese economy.

As such, Bhutan has liberalised its trade policy by replacing quantitative restrictions with tariffs and by integrating into the various bilateral, multilateral and international trade agreements and, it has not tried to bring down the tariff rates, unlike the other liberalising countries. On the contrary, the present sales tax and customs duty were revised upwards by an average of 30 per cent in September 2004.[3] As a result, its average most-favoured-nation

Table 4.1 Trade penetration ratio, 1981–2006

Period	Export / GDP ratio (%)	Import / GDP ratio (%)	Trade / GDP ratio (%)	Trade gap / GDP ratio (%)
1981–4	11.2	44.3	55.6	−33.1
1985–9	21.3	41.7	62.9	−20.4
1990–4	27.7	40.6	68.3	−13.0
1995–9	32.6	41.0	73.7	−8.4
2000–3	21.9	37.6	59.4	−15.7
2004–6	34.8	49.6	84.4	−14.7

Source: Estimated from ADB (1999, 2000) and RMA (2000, 2004, 2007).

(MFN) average applied tariff rate increased from 15.3 per cent in 1995/99 to 21.9 per cent in 2007. On the other hand, the trade weighted applied tariff rate increased marginally from 14.6 to 14.8 per cent during the same period. There is a marked increase in tariff on agricultural imports compared with the modest increase on non-agricultural products.

From a virtually closed economy in the 1960s, Bhutan transformed itself completely in the subsequent decades into a classical case of a small open economy characterised by a high degree of dependence on trade (Table 4.1). By early 1980, the trade to GDP ratio had reached about 55 per cent – a far greater trade ratio than anything observed in the rest of South Asia. The trade ratio declined for the period 2000–3, but then increased and reached 84.4 per cent (2004–6), thereby reflecting the Royal Government's commitment to liberalise trade policy. The trade sector was also the highest contributor to national revenue and accounted for around one third of total national revenue in 2005/6, exceeding electricity revenue generation by a percentage point.

What is remarkable about this upward trend in the importance of trade relative to GDP ratio is that almost all the increases in the trade ratio resulted from faster growth of exports rather than of imports. The import–GDP ratio declined slightly from 44.3 per cent in early 1980s to 41 per cent in late 1990s, while the export–GDP ratio tripled during the same period, rising from 11 per cent to 33 per cent. Thereafter the ratios of both exports and imports to GDP declined from the giddy heights of the late 1990s, but, as noted above, with the commissioning of the Tala project these ratios returned to their upward trend.

Despite rapid growth of exports, trade deficits have remained large as a result of the very high level of imports, which stems from the continued inability of Bhutan's economy to expand its productive base (outside the power sector). For most of the plan periods, the country has consistently been import-dependent, with imports exceeding 60 per cent to 70 per cent of GDP. The current account deficit remains large and growing in absolute terms (Table 4.2). From Nu 1,279.7 million in 1995/6, the current account deficit

Table 4.2 Current account balance, 1995/6–2006/7 (Nu million)

Period	Balance without grants	Balance with grant	Total grant	Grant from India	India's share of grant
1995–6	(−)1,279.7	1,556.3	2,836.0	1,168.9	41.2
1996–7	(−)2,009.0	653.5	2,662.5	1,378.0	51.8
1997–8	(−)1,792.8	1,487.6	3,280.4	2,460.4	75.0
1998–9	(−)4,762.0	384.2	5,146.2	3,812.1	74.1
1999–2000	(−)5,134.4	1,049.6	6,184.0	5,098.0	82.4
2000–1	(−)4,908.6	343.3	5,252.0	4,092.3	77.9
2001–2	(−)5,990.4	−652.2	5,338.2	3,586.6	67.2
2002–3	(−)6,633.3	2,467.5	9,100.8	7,250.9	79.7
2003–4	(−)6,902.6	2,220.3	9,122.9	6,954.0	76.2
2004–5	(−)15,836.0	−10,487.4	5,348.6	2,628.0	49.1
2005–6	(−)8,877.2	−1,695.7	7,181.5	3,417.2	47.6
2006–7	(−)11,640.2	−5,057.8	6,582.4	3,791.2	57.6

Source: Estimated from RMA (2000, 2004, 2007).

(excluding grants from abroad) rose to Nu 11,640.2 million in 2006/7. The current account deficit (excluding grants from abroad) is large and continues to widen over time. Generous external grants, especially from India, have helped to sustain such a deficit.

Ever since planned economic development started in Bhutan in the 1960s, India has been the major trading partner, currently accounting for about 90 per cent of its exports and 80 per cent of its imports. India's predominance in Bhutan's external trade can be related to India's geographic proximity, Bhutan's landlocked nature, the bilateral FTA, free current account convertibility between the ngultrum and the Indian rupee and generous grants from India.

Among Bhutan's major exports to India, the sale of electricity comprises almost 40 per cent of all exports; others include minerals and chemical products, wood and wood products, fresh fruit and vegetables. Imports from India comprise minerals, chemicals, heavy machinery used in the industries and construction of hydro-power plants. Bhutan also imports most of its consumer products from India. The export portfolio, in terms of both products and markets, is very narrow, with the top ten commodities accounting for over 80 per cent of the total export values and with 94 per cent of these exports bound for India. To some extent, the predominance of bilateral trade with India signifies Bhutan's limited ability to diversify its export market (Table 4.3).

In terms of direction of trade, 77.2 per cent of Bhutan's exports in 2006 were to India, followed by Hong Kong with a 15.3 per cent share in total exports, Singapore (3.1 per cent) and Thailand (1.5 per cent). India is also the largest source of imports for Bhutan with a 68.7 per cent share of the total in 2006, followed by Indonesia (7 per cent), the Russian Federation (4.6 per cent) and Singapore (2.7 per cent).

Table 4.3 Bhutan's current account balances with India and others (Nu million)

Year	Trade with India		Trade with others	
	CA balance without grants	CA balance with grants	CA balance without grants	CA balance with grants
1995–6	−208.8	960.1	−1,070.9	596.2
1996–7	−463.5	914.5	−1,545.5	−261.0
1997–8	−982.8	1,477.6	−810.0	10.0
1998–9	−3,059.5	752.6	−1,702.5	−368.4
1999–2000	−3,560.5	1,537.5	−1,573.9	−487.9
2000–1	−3,643.7	448.6	−1,264.9	−105.2
2001–2	−3,741.1	−154.5	−2,249.3	−497.7
2002–3	−4,772.0	2,478.9	−1,861.3	−11.4
2003–4	−4,926.4	2,027.6	−1,976.2	192.7
2004–5	−7,119.7	−4,176.1	−7,647.8	−5,242.8
2005–6	−4,584.3	−1,956.3	−2,204.6	1,055.8

Source: Estimated from RMA (2000, 2004).

Regional free trade agreements

Bhutan has intensified its participation in the world community by becoming a member of many international organisations, both associated with and independent of the United Nations, including the United Nations Industrial Development Organisation, the Board of the United Nations Conference on Trade and Development, the UN Economic and Social Commission for Asia and the Pacific. Bhutan is also a member of the South Asian Association for Regional Co-operation and its various initiatives, the International Fund for Agriculture Development, the Asian Reinsurance Corporation, the International Monetary Fund, the Asian Development Bank, the International Centre for Integrated Mountain Development, the International Organisation of Supreme Audit Institutions, the International Telecommunications Union, the Asia-Pacific Telecomm Unity, the Association of Development Financing Institutions in Asia and the Pacific, the Asian Institute of Transport Development, the World Bank, the World Customs Organisation, the World Tourism Organisation and the World Intellectual Property Organisation, among others.

Bhutan was a member of the South Asian Preferential Trading Arrangement (SAPTA) and also fully participated in and supported the negotiations for the South Asian Free Trade Area (SAFTA), which was signed in January 2004. The SAFTA Agreement, which entered into force on 1 January 2006, laid down a tariff reduction programme spanning ten years, beginning 2006. While providing for shorter implementation periods for the non-LDC member countries, the agreement established a longer time frame for the LDC member countries. However, there are still some outstanding issues that are presently being negotiated.

Bhutan became a member of the sub-regional group the Bay of Bengal Initiative for Multi-Sectoral Technical and Economic Cooperation (BIM-STEC) in February 2004. Since then, Bhutan has been participating in the negotiations under BIMSTEC.

Bhutan signed bilateral trade agreements with two countries – India and Bangladesh. These agreements basically relate to trade in goods. The agreement with India provides for free trade and commerce between the two countries, while the agreement with Bangladesh is on an MFN basis, with preferential duty on a limited number of products.

The Agreement on Trade and Commerce between the government of the Kingdom of Bhutan and the government of the Republic of India provided for duty-free trade between the two countries. That was an essential condition in view of the long open border between the two countries. It also provided for transit of goods between Bhutan and third countries without the application of tariffs by India.

The Agreement on Trade between the Kingdom of Bhutan and the People's Republic of Bangladesh provided for concessions on duties on a range of negotiated product lines. Bhutanese exports to Bangladesh increased from US$ 5.01 million in 2002 to US$ 10 million in 2006. Bhutan intends to deepen the agreement with Bangladesh through further negotiations and to work consistently towards the improvement of trade between the two countries, in accordance with the Decision of 28 November 1979 on Differential and More Favourable Treatment, Reciprocity and Fuller Participation of Developing Countries (the Enabling Clause). Trade relations between Bhutan and Bangladesh began as early as 1980. The current trade agreement, signed in May 2003, expired in May 2009. The renewal of the same between the two countries is expected to be signed in November 2009, to extend for another five years. The new agreement is likely to include 17 new export items each from the two countries. During the Bhutan–Bangladesh trade meeting held in Thimphu during 12–17 August, Bangladesh approved an additional trade route (Tamabil port) between Bhutan and Bangladesh. During the trade meeting, Bhutan also proposed a free trade agreement with Bangladesh.

The success of bilateral trade agreements in improving market access for exporters in Bhutan is apparent. Therefore, in order to facilitate market access for Bhutanese exporters to new markets, the RGOB intends to initiate bilateral trade talks with other regional South Asian and Southeast Asian nations starting with Nepal and Thailand, with whom Bhutan has direct air links.

Foreign direct investment policy

The Royal Government approved the foreign direct investment (FDI) policy in 2002 and actively initiated measures to put in place the institutional and legal framework for creating an enabling environment for industrial development. The new policy replaced the *ad hoc* system of foreign investment approval of the past and put in place a transparent system for approval and regulation of all foreign investments, with the exception of portfolio investments, which were not allowed. Foreign investments in different forms had been permitted by the Ministry of Trade and Industry in the past.

In total, 15 sectors were identified in the positive lists where FDI would be encouraged, based on sectoral policies and procedures. The sectors open for investment were mineral processing; agriculture and agro-processing; forestry and wood-based industries; livestock-based industries; light industries including electronic industries; engineering and power-intensive industries; tourism including hotels; transport; roads and bridges; education; business infrastructure; information technology; private security services; financial services; and housing. Once the Royal Government was confident that the impact of FDI was positive to the economy, the sectors/activities open for FDI would be reviewed and the list of sectors might be extended.

The criterion for investment to be approved was the fulfilment of minimum investment size, namely a minimum of US$ 1 million project cost for manufacturing and US$ 500,000 for the services sector. In both cases, manufacturing and services, a foreign investor could only hold a majority shareholding of up to 70 per cent of the equity. The investment had to fall under the 15 listed open areas for FDI and had to be in line with the sectoral policies concerned, e.g. power-intensive industries. The views of the Ministry of Trade and Industry could be obtained on the suitability of the proposal, regarding proposed location as well as power availability.

While the adoption of an FDI policy is significant, the policy is still conservative, reflecting the cautious approach by the government to protect local entrepreneurs. Considering the small Bhutanese market and the few comparative advantages that Bhutan offers, it is unlikely that foreign investors will rush into Bhutan apart from limited sectors like tourism and power-intensive industries.

The country had virtually no foreign direct investments until the Eighth Plan period. In the Ninth Plan, FDI grew from Nu 101 million in 2001 to Nu 118 million and 157 million in 2002 and 2003. In the subsequent years, FDI declined to less than Nu 3.5 million. Even at its peak in 2003, FDI inflows constituted less than half a per cent of GDP and were entirely for the tourism industry.

Trends in economic growth and poverty

Growth trends

The Royal Government's development philosophy has always focused on improving the general well-being of people by promoting equitable and balanced socio-economic development. This people-oriented development philosophy has really helped in improving the quality of their lives. One of the highlights of the socio-economic development in Bhutan is reflected in its

GDP per capita, which rose to an all-time high of US$ 1,200 in 2006. Even in absolute terms, this represents a fairly high level of GDP per capita by both LDC and regional standards. The country's HDI value has similarly been rising steadily over the years, with the 2006 HDI value assessed at 0.600[4] as compared to 0.583 in 2003[5] and 0.550 in 1998.

Table 4.4 presents recent trends in economic structure, sectoral growth and overall economic growth. The economic growth over the ten years 1998–2008 averaged around 8.3 per cent, and the economy continues to transform into a more modern economy, with the tertiary and secondary sectors growing much more than the primary sector. Economic growth in 2008 was very impressive. The target economic growth rate for the TFYP period is around 8 per cent, with the major contributing sectors to this higher target growth rate being electricity and the construction of hydro-power projects. The faster growth in these sectors is changing the economic structure, with the share of renewable natural resource (RNR) consisting of agriculture, livestock and forestry declining from 37.7 per cent of GDP in 1988 to 18.7 per cent in 2008. Nevertheless, agriculture still remains the main contributor to the national economy and remains critically important as the majority of Bhutanese derive their livelihood from this sector.

The recent fast economic growth has depended upon the construction of major hydro-power. During the 1980s GDP stood at 25 per cent, thanks to the commissioning of the Chukha Hydro Power Corporation and establishment of power-intensive industries; in the early 1990s it dipped, due to political problems in the southern region, but from late 1999 onwards growth again surged as a result of the increase in the export power tariff from Nu 1 per unit to Nu 1.5 per unit, and also as a result of a boom in construction

Table 4.4 Recent trends in sectoral composition and growth in Bhutan

Panel A

% of GDP	1987	1997	2007	2008
Agriculture	37.7	32.5	20.9	18.7
Industry	25.7	33.2	42.9	46.1
Services	36.6	34.4	36.2	35.2

Panel B

	1988–98	1998–2008	2007	2008
Annual GDP growth	4.9	8.3	14.0	13.8
Annual GDP per capita growth	5.4	5.4	12.0	12.0
Annual growth in agriculture	1.8	2.4	1.2	1.1
Annual growth in industry	5.3	11.1	30.4	25.6
Annual growth in manufacturing	10.5	4.3	4.9	5.4
Annual growth in services	7.7	9.2	7.3	7.9
Annual growth in exports	n.a.	22.7	29.3	20.6

Source: World Bank, http://devedata.worldbank.org/AAG/btn_aag.pdf

and transportation-related activities with the Kurichu, Bashochu and Tala power projects. In 2008, real GDP growth stood at 13.8 per cent, primarily fuelled by the commission of the Tala power project. This rapid growth did not transform the Bhutanese economy into a modern industrial society, in the sense of creating a strong manufacturing base with evidence of some employment generation. The manufacturing sector in Bhutan has always been capital-intensive: in fact it has been one of the weakest links to the industrial sector, with low employment elasticity and limited spill-over effects to the other sectors. Apart from being the highest contributor to GDP, it is also the one of the highest contributors to the national exchequer.

Poverty trends

According to the 2008 *Economic and Social Survey of Asia and the Pacific* (UNESCAP 2008), chronic neglect of the agricultural sector in Asia and the Pacific is condemning 218 million people to continuing extreme poverty, and widening the gap between the region's rich and poor. The survey points out that a third of the region's poor, largely living in rural areas, could be lifted out of poverty by raising agricultural productivity. It also calls for a comprehensive liberalisation of global trade in agriculture, as this would take a further 48 million people out of poverty in the region.

'Agriculture appears to be neglected even though it still provides jobs for 60 per cent of the working population and generates about a quarter of the region's gross domestic product,' UNESCAP said in its survey. 'In South Asia, growth in agriculture dropped from 3.6 per cent in the 1980s to 3 per cent in 2002–3.'

Until recently, Bhutan did not attempt to measure poverty through the standard procedure of estimating a poverty line. With the Poverty Reduction Strategy Papers initiated by Bretton Woods and the need to monitor the Millennium Development Goals, the Royal Government conducted a household income and expenditure survey in 2000. Based on this, a more sophisticated survey called the Bhutan Living Standard Survey was conducted in 2003. Using the data generated by the survey and applying the standard procedure for estimating poverty, Bhutan for the first time came up with official estimates of poverty in 2004. Again in 2007, the National Statistics Bureau with the assistance from the United Nations System in Bhutan came up with new poverty estimates so as to give a detailed picture of poverty down to dzongkhag level (i.e. the level of one of Bhutan's 20 administrative regions) based on consumption–expenditure data and other poverty indicators sourced from the Bhutan Living Standard Survey 2007 (National Statistics Bureau of the Royal Government of Bhutan 2007).

The main features of the poor in Bhutan, as identified in the country paper Regional Poverty Profile, 2006–7 (SAARC 2007) are: limited or small land holdings or physical assets; lower human capital: ill health and less education; inability to own a decent house; vulnerability to food shortage or insecurity;

large household sizes (or number of dependants); geographical isolation or remoteness with limited or lack of rural communication facilities; transportation and marketing facilities and infrastructure (inaccessibility); dependence on subsistence agriculture; lack of sufficient resources to send children to school; shortage of labour within rural households; and vulnerability to natural disasters such as floods and hailstorms, destruction of crops by wild animals, and pest outbreak, etc.

As per the Poverty Analysis Report (PAR; National Statistics Bureau of the Royal Government of Bhutan 2007a), the poverty rate in Bhutan is 23.2 per cent; further, the report points out that poverty in Bhutan is a rural phenomenon, i.e. as many as 31 per cent of the rural population fall below the poverty line, compared to 2 per cent of population living in the urban areas. There is also a great deal of regional variation in poverty. The eastern and southern area is notably poorer than the rest of the region. According to the 2007 Bhutan Living Standard Survey (BLSS), carried out by the National Statistics Bureau (National Statistics Bureau of the Royal Government of Bhutan 2007b), 23.2 per cent of the Bhutanese population were found to be poor, mainly among the rural populace in Zhemgang, Samtse, Mongar, Lhuentse and Samdrup Jongkhar dzongkhags.

Poverty in Bhutan is largely a rural phenomenon, as is evident from the findings of the Household Income and Expenditure Survey 2000 (National Statistics Bureau of the Royal Government of Bhutan 2000) and PAR 2007 (see Table 4.5), and Bhutan today is still one of the least developed countries.

The current national poverty line in Bhutan is set at a minimum monthly earning of Nu 1,096 a person (basic food requirements: Nu 688; and non-food requirements: Nu 408). The Bhutan Living Standard Survey of 9,798 households put the number of people below the poverty line at 146,100 out of an extrapolated population figure of 630,000, based on the 2005 population survey. Bhutan has emerged from being the world's poorest country with a

Table 4.5 Trends in the incidence, depth and severity of poverty

Measure		*Years*				
		1980	*1990*	*2000*	*2004*	*2007*
Head count poverty ratio	National	—	—	36.3	31.7	23.2
(incidence of poverty)	Rural	—	—	41.0	38.3	30.9
	Urban	—	—	6.4	4.2	1.7
Poverty gap index	National	—	—	0.1105	0.0859	0.061
(depth of poverty)	Rural	—	—	0.1269	0.105	0.081
	Urban	—	—	0.014	0.007	0.004
Squared poverty gap index	National	—	—	0.0468	0.0308	0.023
(severity of poverty)	Rural	—	—	0.0539	0.0378	0.030
	Urban	—	—	0.0291	0.0016	0.001

Source: National Statistics Bureau of the Royal Government of Bhutan 2000, 2004, 2007

low level of human development index (HDI) to today's nation of sustained and successful economic growth, and is now categorised as among the medium human development countries.

The Gini index was estimated at 0.352 for the country as a whole, 0.317 in urban areas and 0.315 in rural areas in 2007. The Gini coefficient for urban and rural areas is very similar, signifying that inequality in both areas is very pronounced. To put it another way, the richest 20 per cent of Bhutan's population consumes 6.7 times more than someone from the poorest 20 per cent of the population and also, on average, household size and the dependency ratio are larger for the poor than for the rich.

The high inequality in rural areas is also indicated by the distribution of land. Less than 10 per cent of households own 10 acres or more of land, accounting for over 30 per cent of the total agricultural land available, while 14 per cent of total agrarian households own less than an acre, accounting for only 1.4 per cent of the available land. However, the problem of landlessness is not so acute as in many developing countries – only 2.6 per cent of households are estimated to be landless in Bhutan.

Analysis of the poverty profile shows that, apart from the region in which a person lives, there are other variables that are closely correlated with poverty. Two such important variables are physical infrastructure and educational level of the household. Greater proximity to roads is associated with a lower incidence of poverty, and lack of education is more pervasive among the poor. This is evident from the Poverty Assessment and Analysis Report (Royal Government of Bhutan 2000), which provides a strong correlation between poverty and road access – concentrations of the poor were found in the non-road-accessible areas of Mongar, Pemagatshel, Zemgang and Samdrupjongkhar districts. Many rural families in Bhutan are again caught in an inter-generational poverty trap, meaning that children born into poor families cannot always avail themselves of the educational opportunities open to them. As a result, lack of education condemns them to a life of poverty, both for themselves and for their own children in future.

Rural poverty is directly linked to low levels of agricultural productivity and inadequate access to markets, economic opportunities, resources, assets and social services. Poverty is thus to a great extent equated with and a resulting condition of the underdevelopment of rural areas. The situation is further exacerbated by the high degree of vulnerability of rural communities to inclement weather conditions, pests and wildlife predation, and natural disasters.

Nexus between trade–growth–poverty

In spite of vast improvement in human development and sustained economic growth over the past decade, roughly a quarter of Bhutan's population is still under the national poverty line and much of its rural areas still remain underdeveloped. In Bhutan, owing to the lack of time series data on poverty, it has been difficult to empirically link the nexus between trade, growth and poverty. The data presented in Table 4.5 provide the information for three periods, but these are not comparable to each other owing to different methodology, geographic coverage and type of questionnaire used. However, looking at Table 4.5 we can get some insight of how poverty in Bhutan is moving; comparing these three periods, the poverty ratio has been going down, from 36.3 per cent in 2000 to 31.7 per cent in 2004 and then to 23.2 per cent in 2007. The nexus between trade, growth and poverty could be linked to macroeconomic policy, as has been highlighted by the report *Macroeconomics of Poverty Reduction in Bhutan* (Osmani *et al.* 2007). Thus, the link between the two can be looked at from the following policy options:

- Fiscal policy and poverty reduction
- Trade policy and poverty reduction
- Poverty alleviation measures.

Fiscal policy and poverty reduction

The fiscal policy conducted in Bhutan is especially relevant to poverty reduction, particularly the overall fiscal stance and the sectoral allocation of budgetary expenditures.

The overall fiscal stance of Bhutan has been characterised by a cautious approach towards low budget deficits combined with the policy of pegging the ngultrum to the Indian rupee. This has helped the poor by creating demand for productive employment and by keeping inflation low.

The other aspect of fiscal policy that has a positive effect on the rural populace is the way in which the fiscal resource is allocated to different sectors of the economy and different regions of the country, as global experience shows that investments in health and education yield great benefits, empowering people to lift themselves out of the poverty trap. In Bhutan, the manner in which the budget is allocated has many implications for the poor. The Royal Government has always followed a pro-poor distributive allocation of its resources to the social sector. Since the inception of planned economic development in the 1960s, the Royal Government has spent well over a quarter of its budget on the social sector.

Improving the social conditions of people through enhancing access to social services, and the enhancing the efficiency and quality of such services, was a strategic thrust area of the Ninth Plan; during this, a quarter of its development plan outlay was allocated to the social sector. With this strong redistributive policy, Bhutan has exceeded its commitment to the Global 20:20 Compact agreement, which requires that developing countries should devote 20 per cent of their national budget to social programmes – Bhutan is among the few countries to have done so. As a result of these sustained social investments, Bhutan has achieved significant progress in advancing the general social conditions in the country, a development reflected in continued

Table 4.6 Comparison of major social indicators

Social and human development indicators	End of Seventh FYP (1997)	End of Eighth FYP (2002)	End of Ninth FYP (2007)
Education (%)			
GPER	72.0	81.0	102
NPER	—	62.0	79.4
Primary school completion rate	60.5	78.8	87*
Teacher–student ratio (primary)	1:41	1:31	1:34
Teacher–student ratio (secondary)	1:38	1:36	1:32
Gender parity in education			
Girl–boy ratio (primary)	81:100	88:100	93:100
Girl–boy ratio (secondary)	77:100	87:100	98:100
Girl–boy ratio (higher secondary)	41:100	61:100	85:100
Girl–boy ratio (tertiary)	29:100	39:100	54:100
National literacy (%)	—	—	60
Adult literary	54	—	53
Health and sanitation			
Life expectancy	66	—	—
Population growth rate	3.1	2.5	1.3
IMR (per 1,000)	70.7	61.1	40.1
U-5MR (per 1,000)	96.9	84	61.5
MMR (per 10,000)	380	255	150–200
Trained birth attendance (%)	10.9	23.6	51
Access to improved sanitation	80 (1996)	88 (2000)	89
Access to improved drinking water	—	78 (2000)	84
Nutrition (children)			
% underweight	17	—	—
% stunted	40	—	—
% wasted	2.6	—	—
Human development			
HDI	0.5505 (1990)	0.583 (2003)	>0.600 (2005)

Source: National Statistics Bureau of the Royal Government of Bhutan 2000, 2004, 2007.
Note: * Extrapolation for 2007 based on 10 years trend.

improvements in most of the social and human development indicators. A comparison of the major social indicators over the Seventh, Eighth and Ninth Plans is illustrated in Table 4.6.

Trade policy and poverty reduction

Over the decades, Bhutan has really benefited from the open trade policy regime. The living conditions of the rural people have greatly improved – most households have access to modern household equipment such as a gas stove,

TV set, refrigerator, telephone, etc., and the rural populace can also now find markets for their products in India, Bangladesh and Japan, especially cash crops like apples, oranges, cordyceps, matsutake and potatoes.

The open trade regime has created greater scope for specialisation in production and increased availability of a wide range of consumer goods. The consumption pattern of the people has changed over time; previously the staple food was not rice, but now, with the availability of varieties of rice, it has become the main staple for most Bhutanese. Large imports of rice and other essential foodstuffs has helped the Bhutanese poor, both directly and indirectly. Directly, it has helped by keeping the cost of living down. Indirectly, it has helped them by removing the wage–goods constraint, which has allowed faster growth and thereby faster expansion of opportunities for productive employment.

But in Bhutan, increasing specialisation promoted by the open trade regime has not been of much help to the poor because Bhutan's comparative advantage lies in natural resource–capital-intensive activities, which do not employ much labour. The other key issue is that Bhutan is a low-income country. Theory states that low-income countries are abundant in labour, implying that they will export labour-intensive commodities, which can have positive implications for poverty reduction through employment generation. But this theory is not supported in the case of Bhutan. Even though Bhutan is a low-income country, it faces the problem of underemployment and is dependent on cheap migrant workers from India.

Thus, this does not mean that the poor of Bhutan will gain from the opposite policy of trade restriction and inward orientation. The future of the poor clearly lies in an outward-oriented strategy, but one in which the unskilled poor people of today will be able to work as skilled workers, engaged in the production of low-volume, high-value products destined for the world market. For this to materialise, a range of policy measures will have to be adopted to create the necessary dynamic comparative advantage.

Poverty alleviation measures

One way to look at the factors leading to a reduction of poverty over the three time periods is to examine the way in which government and non-government organisations have initiated poverty alleviation measures over the years, measures that have had a positive and direct impact on the lives of the rural people. Most of these measures address the problems faced by the people in a very short time frame, by giving them economic power and the means to lift themselves out of the vicious cycle of poverty.

The main focus and thrust of poverty reduction in the country during the past five years have been through a three-pronged approach – improving accessibility of remote areas, providing access to markets, and providing electricity to rural households. The Ministry of Agriculture's target during the Ninth Plan (2002–7) was to construct more than 500 km of farm roads and open up the majority of remote isolated settlements through the triple-gem approach of production, access and market (PAM). At the time of writing, it had constructed about 600 km of farm roads, and about 200 km more was planned for the extended period of the Ninth Plan (2007–8). Various weekend market sheds have also been constructed in the 20 districts to provide opportunities for the people to bring their farm produce to market and earn some cash income.

Through the rural electrification programme, more than 65 per cent of rural households have been provided with electricity via a network of facilities such as transmission grid, micro- and mini-hydro projects, and other alternative sources of energy such as solar and wind power. As it is difficult and expensive to take transmission grids to remote isolated areas for the supply of electricity, such areas have been provided with either micro-hydro projects or solar panels. The rural electrification programme is said to have had a very positive impact on enhancing income-generation opportunities for people, as well as improving their health conditions through better lighting and cooking by avoiding use of kerosene oil for lighting and wood for cooking. The skilled women are now able to weave even at night and earn additional income for the family, something that was not possible in the past.

The RGOB has in the past addressed poverty reduction mainly through broad sector programmes. It has made massive social investments in expanding and improving primary education and primary health care. While such expenditures have greatly helped to improve all-round living conditions and ameliorate poverty, experience and lessons from the implementation of the Ninth Plan development activities indicate that poverty reduction could be better served, accelerated further and complemented with specific and improved targeting.

Targeted poverty reduction interventions will be initiated and implemented over the Tenth Plan period and will include relevant programmes for specific areas where the poor reside, based on poverty mapping from the survey of 2007 (National Statistical Bureau of Bhutan 2007). The following are some of the strategic measures the government will undertake in a move towards synergising integrated rural and urban measures for poverty reduction:

- encouraging specialisation based on local and regional comparative advantages in producing goods and services;
- promoting relevant skill development in the rural labour force;
- enhancing micro-credit to the rural populace;
- establishment of community forests and expansion of commercial harvesting of non-wood forest products (NWFP);
- establishment of integrated gewog centres (a gewog is a subdivision of a dzongkhag) to improve the delivery of development services at the local level;
- distribution of land to landless people, and a comprehensive programme of resettlement for the landless or land-poor families to areas where arable and productive land is available.

The overall rural development strategy through poverty reduction during the Royal Government's forthcoming Tenth Five-Year Plan will be to continue developing the agriculture sector as well as non-agriculture sectors in the rural economy. This is expected to enhance household food security and nutrition, stimulate productive capacities, generate employment and augment incomes. Foremost, though, is the need to ensure food security, as without this, households will have neither the time nor the inclination to engage in other activities that could potentially lead to longer-term livelihood improvements. The promotion of horticulture and cash crops – including the development of organic niche products in suitable areas – and efforts to raise livestock production are some of the strategic initiatives that will be undertaken to improve rural livelihoods. In addition to helping rural communities boost agriculture productivity and production, the Royal Government will support the development of small-scale and cottage industries, local handicrafts, textiles and arts, and various other off-farm activities and enterprises. The development and expansion of rural economic infrastructure such as local markets, farm and feeder roads, irrigation schemes and electricity will also be undertaken, as they are vital for stimulating and sustaining a thriving rural economy. The implementation of the Integrated Gewog Centres (IGC) concept and establishment of these centres in the various gewogs will greatly facilitate and improve the delivery of a variety of development services.

An effective rural development strategy will also focus equally on improving the non-income aspects of poverty and expose the nexus between growth, poverty and inequality. This will be addressed through implementing various activities to further develop social infrastructure and expand access to social institutions. As there is a clear linkage between poverty and the lack of educational attainment according to the Poverty Analysis Report (National Statistical Bureau of Bhutan 2007), further expansion and quality improvements in educational services in rural areas will constitute the major priority development activity in the Dzongkhag and Gewog Development Plans.

Apart from government, there are some agencies that look after the welfare needs of vulnerable people. The Tarayana Foundation, a non-profit organisation, wholeheartedly works to uplift and enhance the lives of people in rural communities in Bhutan. The Foundation complements and supplements the efforts of the Royal Government in poverty reduction by espousing the national goal, Bhutan 2020: A Vision for Peace, Prosperity and Happiness. Despite the pro-poor development strategy of the government, small communities in far-flung areas are still lagging behind. The Foundation was established to help these communities achieve self-sufficiency through small and targeted interventions. The Foundation strives to improve rural livelihoods by promoting participation in mainstream development initiatives and enhancing income-generating activities. (For more details of its activities please refer to the Foundation website: www.tarayanafoundation.org).

The SAARC Development Goals (SDGs) were conceptualised and formulated as a strategic regional response to the urgent imperatives of ridding South Asia of poverty and achieving the international Millennium Development Goals (MDGs) by 2015. Indeed, in certain aspects the SDGs seek to go much further than the MDG targets, and faster. The SDGs are also in a sense a road map for the implementation of the SAARC Social Charter. Endorsed at the Thirteenth SAARC Summit in Bangladesh in 2005; the SDG mandate covers several important development goals within the four broad areas of livelihood, health, education and environment. Taking into consideration both the South Asian context and specificities and the relevant linkages with international goals such as the MDGs, the SDGs include 22 priority goals for the period 2007–12, eight of which pertain to livelihood, four to health, four to education and six to the environment. Progress towards achieving these specific SDGs will also effectively determine the success the countries will have in combating poverty in the region. In recognition of its importance, the Thirteenth SAARC Summit declared 2006–15 as the SAARC Decade of Poverty Alleviation.

Conclusion

The following conclusion can be made from the above analysis. Bhutan, with a sound political system, sustained economic growth and the conscious effort made by the Royal Government to look after the people's basic needs, at present enjoys a relatively high degree of human development. Nevertheless, in 2007 about 23.2 per cent of the population fell below the poverty line and, of this, the rural populace (30.9 per cent) is most vulnerable. Poverty in Bhutan has become an inherited liability: children born into a poor family are trapped in the vicious cycle of poverty in the absence of necessary education facilities and lack of access to finance.

In order to break the inter-generational poverty trap, government policy on public investment needs to be supplemented by a vibrant private sector which can provide income and employment to the rural poor. Economic growth is mainly fuelled by public sector investment (hydro-power) and foreign aid. In order to have steady and stable growth, the economy needs to diversify its domestic resource base by developing a strong private sector which can help in boosting the export sector. Bhutan's economic growth is heavily dependent on one sector, the hydro-power and construction sector, which has very limited gains for the poorer section of society because of lower employment elasticity and weak forward and backward linkages in the economy, and thus it is important that any revenue earned from this sector needs to be equally distributed among all sections of the people. For this to happen an appropriate redistribution mechanism needs to be put in place.

Growth trends show that rural sector growth is stagnating through decline in the share of the primary sector to GDP and the concentration of economic activities in the urban areas. This urban–rural drift is forcing the rural populace to migrate to urban areas in search of better opportunities, thereby leading to increased pressure on the limited urban infrastructure and ultimately leading to increases in urban poverty and underemployment in rural areas. Thus, a pro-poor policy such as rural development, with transfer of resources and personnel to rural areas, needs to be put in place.

Notes

1 In accordance with the Free Trade Agreement with India, the Indian exporters can claim BST as a rebate against the Indian sales tax, hence nullifying the impact of BST on Indian imports and, moreover, the import of raw materials is exempt from BST.
2 Customs duty is exempt on imports of industrial plant, machinery, their spare parts and raw materials only if the final product has at least 40 per cent value addition and/or the convertible currency earned by the company during the year covers at least the cost of raw materials, and also if a large part of the imports from third countries is related to either government or donor-related procurement, which is exempt from customs duty.
3 The stated rationale behind the upward revision was to mainly 'conserve hard currency' by discouraging third-country imports, as most of the essential items are domestically available or could be brought from India. The sales tax and customs duty were also increased for plastic items, to discourage the use of plastic because of environmental concerns.
4 Rough estimate.
5 The HDI value is based on national data and, as such, varies from figures in the Global Human Development Reports that have lower figures computed for educational attainment and GDP per capita in US$ PPP terms.

5   India

Rashmi Banga and Shruti Sharma

The ongoing process of economic globalisation has led to an ever-growing debate on the relationship between trade, growth and poverty reduction. An important dimension which has often been ignored in this debate is the impact of openness to trade on growth and poverty at the sectoral level. Since the relationship between trade and poverty is multi-faceted, to estimate the overall impact of trade on poverty as a whole may not be appropriate. What is desirable is to estimate the impact of trade on producers and consumers in different sectors. This will enable the economy to be better prepared to face the challenges of trade. In this context, the main objective of this chapter is to empirically estimate the impact of exports and imports on indicators of poverty, i.e. wages and employment of unskilled labour in agriculture and manufacturing sectors in India.

One of the concerns that arise in undertaking such an exercise for India is the absence of continuous time series data on the number of people below the poverty line or of the poverty gap. The data on headcount ratio (HCR) or poverty gap are available from large sample surveys which have been carried out since 1972–3, every five years, by the National Sample Survey Organisation. However, these survey results are not comparable. In particular, the results for 1999–2000 are not comparable to those in 1993–4. This makes it difficult to empirically estimate the impact of any trade-related variables on direct indicators of poverty over time. The chapter therefore estimates the impact of trade on an indirect indicator of poverty, which is wages of unskilled workers in the manufacturing sector and the agriculture sector.

Another concern that arises in estimating the impact of trade on indicators of poverty in the manufacturing sector is the lack of data on trade at the industry level. The data at the industry level is available from the Annual Survey of Industries (ASI), while the data on trade is available at the product level. To undertake this exercise, a concordance matrix has been constructed to match eight-digit HS 2002 codes to three-digit National Industrial Classification (NIC), and trade data at the industry level is arrived at.

The analysis has been undertaken for the organised manufacturing sector at three-digit industry level for the period 1998–9 to 2005–6.[1] For the agriculture sector, the impact of trade on wages of unskilled agricultural labour is estimated at the state level for total agricultural products and separately for five agricultural products, i.e. cereals; fruits and nuts; vegetable, roots and tubers; and oilseeds. The period of analysis is 1990–1 to 1999–2000, for which the data on wages to unskilled agricultural workers is available.

The chapter is organised as follows: section 2 briefly reviews the empirical studies on the trade–poverty nexus in India; section 3 outlines the trends in trade, growth and poverty in India; section 4 discusses the methodology adopted to estimate the impact of trade on wages; section 5 presents the empirical results in the manufacturing and agriculture sectors; finally section 6 derives conclusions and policy implications.

Trade liberalisation in India: a brief review

After independence, India adopted a mixed economy strategy with self-reliance being the principal objective. Import substitution and export pessimism was an underlying strategy assumption. However, doubts about the effectiveness of this policy regime arose as early as the mid-1970s and since then a series of reforms have been undertaken towards opening of the economy, though effective reforms have taken place only since the early 1990s. These reforms have furthered the globalisation process with respect to cross-border movement of capital, goods and services.

Compared to many other developing countries, India has been a slow globaliser. Benchmarking the extent of liberalisation of India with respect to other developing countries, we find that the effective import duties[2] in India in 1990 were on an average 45 per cent while not exceeding 25 per cent in any of the Asian developing countries.[3] Consequently, the growth rate of merchandise imports remained low in India, i.e. 5 per cent in the 1980s and 9 per cent in the 1990s.

India began to adopt open trade and investment policies from 1991. Some of the liberalisation measures taken were reduction of import tariff rates (e.g. the simple average of all rates was brought down from 71 per cent in 1993/4 to 35 per cent in 1997/8 and to about 29 per cent in 2002/3[4]), simplification of FDI norms (reduction of FDI caps, permitting FDI in sectors previously not open), reforms in the infrastructure sector, deregulation and restructuring of the financial and telecom services sectors, relaxation of import and industrial licensing, etc. Consequently, in the 1990s, total imports of goods and services in India grew at a rate of 10 per cent as compared to 5 per cent in the 1980s. Exports of goods and services also witnessed a rise from 7 per cent in the 1980s to 11 per cent in the 1990s with exports of services rising from 5 per cent to 15 per cent in this period.

After more that fifteen years of liberalisation, India is the second fastest growing economy in the world. The growth rate of the economy in 2005–6 was 8.1 per cent. It ranks almost at the top in almost all the indices and surveys that rank economies around the world as future business destinations or market potential (e.g., AT Kearney, Goldman Sachs).[5] There has also been a spurt in the growth of trade and FDI (Government Economic Surveys, various issues).

However, the impact of globalisation has been felt in different degrees and extents in different sectors of the economy.

Agriculture

The Indian agriculture sector continues to remain the mainstay for a large majority of the population (about 600 million people in India depend directly or indirectly on this sector). Given the large livelihood implications, trade measures to open up for exports, imports and foreign investment and related restructuring measures have not been adopted for agriculture. Agricultural policy in India has been guided by domestic supply and self-sufficiency considerations. In addition, incentives and subsidies are partly constrained by the government policy of providing support prices to farmers and providing supplies to the general population at low cost through the public distribution system.[6] However, some measures of decontrol have been adopted in the last fifteen years. For example,

- the removal of state controls of the inter-state movement of certain grains and of administered prices;
- making the public distribution system more targeted, while continuing procurement by government agencies (which in fact had increased, in part due to a rise in minimum support prices);
- the freeing of trade in agricultural commodities from controls (under the Essential Commodities Act 1955);
- the removal of licensing and stocking requirements and movement restrictions, enabling free and unrestricted stocking and trading in wheat, rice, coarse grains, edible oils, oil seeds and sugar.

The sector still has a range of measures such as import and export controls, including tariffs, state trading, export and import restrictions and licensing, etc. Some of the controls are imposed or relaxed in times of shortages, over-production or price fluctuations, which are not very infrequent as indicated by the recent decision to import wheat and the reduction of tariffs on wheat to 0 per cent to encourage imports. Many of the policies related to agriculture are still adopted in an *ad hoc* manner.

India has protected its agriculture sector from import threats by keeping bound tariffs on agricultural products much higher than the average applied tariffs. Average bound agriculture tariff is 114 per cent: 100 per cent for primary products, 150 per cent for processed products and 300 per cent for edible oils. Certain items (comprising about 119 tariff lines) were historically bound at a lower level in the earlier rounds of negotiations. Out of these low bound tariff lines, bindings on 15 tariff lines (included skimmed milk powder, spelt wheat, corn, paddy, rice, maize, millet, sorghum, rape, colza and mustard oil, fresh grapes, etc.) were successfully negotiated to revise the binding levels upward to provide adequate protection to domestic producers (under GATT Article XXVIII) in December 1999.[7]

Another important liberalisation measure has been the removal of quantitative restrictions in 2000 and 2001, which India had maintained for balance of payments reasons (using GATT Art VIII (B)), on 1,429 items. Since by the late 1990s India's current account, capital inflows and foreign exchange reserves had been strengthened, the US brought a case in the WTO dispute settlement for the elimination of QRs, and won the case. Almost half of the agriculture tariff lines in HS 2002 codes at six-digit level were protected by QRs.

Agriculture has also benefited from price realignments resulting from the manufacturing sector reforms. However, the sector is largely untouched by reforms. The government came out with a New Agricultural Policy in 2000 with an aim of attaining 4 per cent growth. However, this growth target has mostly not been met. In fact, the sector is plagued with low productivity and volatile growth.

Manufacturing

Policies related to the Indian manufacturing sector have undergone considerable change since 1991 and thus the sector itself has experienced a rapid transformation. Various measures have been adopted to reduce trade and investment barriers, restructure, privatise and decontrol the sector. This sector has in fact witnessed maximum policy changes since 1991 compared to the other two sectors.

One of the significant liberalisation measures that have been undertaken to boost trade is the reduction of peak as well as average customs tariff rates for manufactures. The peak rate of customs tariffs was 150 per cent in 1991–2. Since then, the rate has been reduced in the successive union budgets with the aim of bringing India's tariff rates in line with the rates prevailing in the South East Asian countries (which is about 5 per cent). The simple average tariff rate was 81.8 per cent in 1990, which declined to 29 per cent in 2002. The peak rate for non-agricultural goods was brought down to 12.5 per cent in 2006–7. Comparing the applied rate in 2001–2 with bound rate at the WTO, out of 3,298 tariff lines bound by India at the WTO (mostly at 40 per cent or 25 per cent), 1,040 lines had applied rates equal to the bound rates (for five lines, applied rate exceeded the bound rate). In other cases, the applied rate was lower than the bound rate.[8]

Another significant measure that has been undertaken is the removal of FDI caps and permitting FDI in the closed sectors. Almost all the sectors are now eligible for the automatic approval route through the Reserve Bank of India except for some cases. Some of the important areas that have been opened up for 100 per cent FDI are the infrastructure sector (airports, power except atomic energy, manufacture of telecom equipment), mining, construction development projects, floriculture and horticulture, petroleum and natural gas except refining, SEZs and Free Trade Warehousing Zones, etc.

The impact of liberalisation measures on the Indian manufacturing sector has been positive in terms of growth, productivity and competitiveness. The sector responded to reforms positively, though there was some slowing down of growth in 1996/7 (mainly due to infrastructural bottlenecks), but there has been a major upturn in industrial activity since 2002/3. Between 2000/1 and 2002/3 the industrial growth rate was 5.2 per cent, which rose to 7.6 per cent[9] in 2005/6. The share of industry in GDP in 2005/6 was 25.8 per cent. Within the industrial sector, the share of registered manufacturing improved from an average of 58.8 per cent during 1970–82 to 65.7 per cent during 1992–2004. Further, there has been an improvement in the relative share of textile products, chemical and chemical products, rubber and petroleum products and electric machinery.[10] Many studies have shown that liberalisation, in terms of both trade and FDI, has had a positive effect on industrial productivity and growth (e.g. Goldar (2004); Virmani *et al.* (2004); Banga (2005a)). FDI has also been found to have led to technology transfer to domestic firms and to have had significant productivity and wage spillovers.

Services

The services sector in India has undergone many changes in its structure and has grown faster than the other two sectors since the early 1990s. The sector has had a high growth in the last fifteen years in both absolute and relative terms (with respect to the manufacturing and agriculture sectors), thereby increasing its share in India's GDP, FDI and trade.

The trend of growing importance of services in India is consistent with the similar trend in the rest of the world. However, it appears that India's services sector has grown faster than the global services sector. Between 1990 and 2003, the international trade in services has increased at the rate of 6 per cent per annum. In India between 1994 and 2004, the services sector grew at the average rate of 7.9 per cent per annum, whereas agriculture grew at the rate of 3 per cent per annum and manufacturing at the rate of 5.3 per cent per annum. Within services, business services grew the fastest in this period, followed by banking and insurance.[11] The contribution of services to India's GDP is also higher than that of the other two sectors. In the average contribution to GDP between 2000 and 2004, services contributed 50 per cent to India's GDP compared to 27 per cent contribution of manufacturing and 23 per cent of agriculture.[12] In recent years, the services sector has grown even faster and has increased its share in India's GDP. Recording a double-digit growth in 2005/6, it now constitutes more than 60 per cent of GDP.[13]

Notably, there has not been any integrated policy approach towards the services sector in India.[14] A variety of approaches have been adopted for different sectors such as banking, insurance and other financial services, and telecom.

India undertook commitments in the GATS in 1995 covering a number of sectors such as financial, telecom, professional, R&D, construction, health and tourism services. However, India's commitments were much less liberalising than its unilateral regime even in 1995. India did not even commit fully to the Telecom Reference Paper of the GATS. In subsequent years, India liberalised its services sector by a large measure. Thus, the gap between India's commitments under the GATS 1995 and its present regime has widened even more. In the revised services offer, which is a part of the new round of negotiations launched in 2001 under the GATS, India improved upon its commitments and offered commitment on a few previously untouched sectors (e.g. the accountancy, architectural, higher education, environmental, life and non-life insurance, transport and wholesale trade sectors) and improved upon its commitment on a few others (e.g. 100 per cent foreign equity permitted in computer and related services and R& D services; FDI in banking permitted at 49 per cent and number of licences increased from 12 to 20; increase in FDI in most telecom services from 25 per cent to 49 per cent).

Trends in trade, poverty and inequality

Trends in trade

India's trade, in terms of both exports and imports, has grown at an unprecedented rate since 2000 (Figure 5.1). Global merchandise exports increased from US$ 44 billion in 2000 to US$ 181 billion in 2008. The average annual growth rate in India's total merchandise exports to the world in the period 2004–6 was 20 per cent. Imports grew as fast as exports. From US$ 51 billion in 2000 they reached US$ 315 billion in 2008.

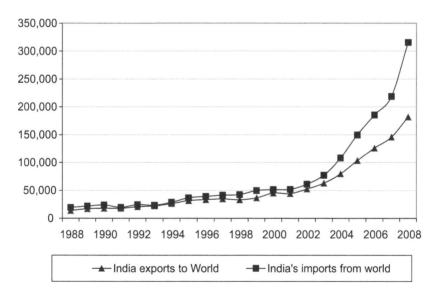

Figure 5.1 India's Global exports and imports: 1988–2008

Table 5.1 India's industrial tariffs

Tariff year	Simple average	Weighted average
1990	81.84	49.58
1992	56.34	27.86
1997	30.09	20.14
1999	32.95	28.52
2001	32.32	26.50
2004	29.12	22.84
2005	18.30	13.42

Source: Government of India (2008)

In the period post-liberalisation, the composition of India's exports has experienced some change. The share of agriculture and allied activities in India's exports has been fluctuating in the period 1994–5 to 2004–5. It was 16 per cent in 1994–5, increased to 19 per cent in 1995–6 and peaked in 1996–7 to 20.5 per cent. Subsequently, it fell to 18.8 per cent in 1997–8 and further declined to 17.3 per cent in 1998–9. The downward trend continued in 1999–2000 and the share reduced considerably to 15.2 per cent and further to 13.5 per cent in 2000–1 and 13.4 per cent in 2001–2. It dipped to a low of 11.9 per cent in 2002–3. From here on, the share of agriculture and allied activities picked up and was 16.4 per cent in 2003–4 and 16.8 per cent in 2004–5.

The manufactured goods sector has always been the largest contributor to India's exports. It was 78.4 per cent in 1994–5 and 75.4 in 1995–6. In 1996–7, its share further declined to 74.1 per cent but increased subsequently to 75.7 per cent in 1997–8. In 1998–9 this share was 77.8 per cent and it peaked to 80.1 per cent in 1999–2000. In 2000–1 it dropped a little to 78 per cent, and the downward trend continued in 2001–2, when it was 76.1 per cent. It increased marginally to 76.6 per cent in 2002–3 and further to 73.4 per cent in 2004–5, but declined in 2004–5 to 73.7 per cent.

India's tariff levels have experienced a significant decline ever since it embraced liberalisation in 1991 (Table 5.1). Considering Simple Average Tariffs, the tariff level dropped from 81.84 per cent in 1990 to 56.34 per cent in 1992. In 1997, the tariff level dropped even more sharply to 30.09 per cent, but then increased in 1999 to 32.95 per cent. There was a marginal decline in 2001 to 32.32 per cent, which further decreased to 29.12 per cent in 2004 and 18.30 per cent in 2005. As far as Weighted Average Tariffs go, the tariff level was down to 27.86 in 1992 per cent from 49.58 per cent in 1990. In 1997 this level was 20.14 per cent and it increased in 1999 to 32.95 per cent. In 2001 Weighted Average Tariffs declined to 26.50 per cent and continued the downward trend in 2004 (22.84 per cent) and 2005 (13.42 per cent).

Composition of India's export basket

There has been some diversification in the composition of India's export basket, especially since early 2000. As seen in Table 5.2, the share of

Table 5.2 Change in composition of India's export basket, 2004–8

Sl. No		2004	2006	2008
1	Engineering goods	15,724.1	27,478.6	41,722.3
2	Petroleum products	6,891.2	18,870.3	30,446.1
3	Chemicals and related products	10,951.7	17,242.1	22,906.0
4	Textiles	13,385.0	19,419.5	20,467.4
5	Gems and jewellery	14,242.1	16,048.5	18,835.5
6	Agricultural and allied products	6,091.5	8,549.9	14,999.0
7	Ores and minerals	4,327.1	6,024.6	8,474.8
8	Leather and leather goods	2,555.5	3,350.7	3,434.4
9	Marine products	1,365.5	1,759.7	1,466.5
10	Plantations	790.6	1,191.0	1,055.4
	Total	**79,834.1**	**126,125.5**	**167,768.5**

Source: Government of India (2008).

petroleum products in India's export basket has been increasing since 2004. India exported US$ 6.8 billion worth of petroleum products in 2004 which rose to US$23.6 billion in 2007 and further to 30.4 billion in 2008. Its share in India's ten major sectors of exports rose from 8.6 per cent to 18 per cent. Interestingly, the share of textiles, which was the predominant sector in the export basket in 2004 (16.8 per cent), has been declining and reached only 12 per cent in 2008. The engineering goods sector continues to have the highest share in India's export basket. Its share has further increased from 19.7 per cent in 2004 to 25 per cent in 2008. The share of chemical and chemical products has remained the same over time (13.7 per cent) while the share of gems and jewellery has declined from 18 per cent in 2004 to around 11 per cent in 2008.

Interestingly, exports of India's agricultural products have been rising steadily from US$ 6.0 billion in 2004 to US$ 14.9 billion, though their share in India's export basket still remains low (around 9 per cent). Although exports of ores and minerals have nearly doubled from US$ 4.3 billion to US$ 8.4 billion in 2008, the share of this sector in the export basket remains around 5 per cent. Marine and plantations have around 1 per cent share, which has not changed over time.

The above trends in the composition of India's export basket show that there has been some diversification in the past five years, with engineering goods, petroleum products and chemical products increasing their share, while traditional exports like textiles, gems and jewellery and leather and leather products have been losing their shares.

The direction of India's exports

In the 1990s, more than half of India's exports were directed towards EU markets and around 15 per cent to the US. Around 16 per cent went to Russia and a similar percentage to developing countries, with Asian markets being more dominant. However, over time there has been some diversification in terms of the direction of India's exports. The EU's share declined from 56 per cent in 1995–6 to 39 per cent in 2007–8, while the share of the US declined from 17.4 per cent in 1995–6 to 13 per cent in 2007–8. The share of the UAE increased from 4.5 per cent in 1995–6 to 9.7 per cent in 2007–8. There has been a considerable increase in the share of Asian developing countries in India's export basket, from 23 per cent in 1995–6 to 31.5 per cent in 2007–8. Africa's has also increased over time. However, the bulk of India's exports, i.e. 53 per cent, is still directed towards the EU and the US.

Trends in income, growth and employment

India moved to a high growth trajectory with GDP growth exceeding 8 per cent every year from 2003–4 to 2007. There has been a steady growth in GDP per capita in India since 1980 and this has improved considerably since the 1990s. Per capita GDP grew at an average annual growth rate of 2.9 per cent in the period 1980 to 1990, while it grew at 3.9 per cent in the period 1991 to 2000. From 2000 to 2005 the average annual growth of GDP per capita was 5.24 per cent. The most informative statistic available on unemployment is the daily status of unemployment provided by NSSO.[15] Employment almost doubled in the year 2004–5 as compared to 1983, but the growth rate of employment was much higher in the period 1999 to 2004–5 as compared with 1993 to 1999–2000, in which it actually fell below the level of 1983–4 to 1993–4 (Table 5.3).

The unemployment rate has increased despite an expansion in work opportunities, from about 20.27 million unemployed during 1999–2000 to about 34.74 million in 2004–5. This was because the labour force grew at a rate of 2.84 per cent, higher than the increase in the workforce. Unemployment rates are over two percentage points higher than ten years earlier (at 6.07 per cent in 1993 compared with 8.28 per cent in 2004) and the employment-to-population ratio is lower than it was ten years earlier. While part of the reason for decline

Table 5.3 Employment and unemployment rate in India

	1983–4	1993–4	1999–2000	2004–5	1983 to 1993–4	1993–4 to 1999–2000	1999–2000 to 2004–5
	Millions				*Growth p.a. (%)*		
Population	718.10	893.68	1,005.05	1,092.83	2.11	1.98	1.69
Labour force	263.82	334.20	364.88	419.65	2.28	1.47	2.84
Workforce	239.49	313.93	338.19	384.91	2.61	1.25	2.62
Unemployment rate (per cent)	9.22	6.06	7.31	8.28			
No. of unemployed	24.34	20.27	26.68	34.74			

Source: Government of India (2008).

in this ratio could be extended time spent in education, it can also be indicative of low employment opportunities.

As per the National Commission for Enterprises in the Unorganised Sector (NCEUS), organised sector employment increased from 54.12 million in 1999–2000 to 62.57 million in 2004–5. However, the increase has been accounted for by increase in unorganised workers in organised enterprises, from 20.46 million in 1999–2000 to 29.14 million in 2004–5. Thus, the increase in employment in the organised sector has been on account of informal employment for workers.

Trends in poverty and inequality

In India, the estimates of the incidence of poverty by the Planning Commission on the basis of the headcount ratios given by various rounds of the NSS show that poverty has been consistently declining for the country as a whole. The percentage of people below the poverty line declined from 54.88 in 1973–4 to 38.36 in 1987–8. In the period post-liberalisation, this fell further, to 35.97 in 1993–4 and then to 26.1 in 1999–2000. These figures, however, are not comparable as they have been calculated for different recall periods – the uniform recall period (URP) for 1993–4, and the mixed recall period (MRP) for 1999–2000. In 2004–5, the estimated poverty ratio by the URP method was 27.5 (making it comparable with the 1993–4 ratio) whereas by the MRP method it was 21.8 (making it comparable with the 1999–2000 ratio). The state-wise incidence of poverty (for which it is available) for the discrete years 1973–4, 1987–8, 1993–4 and 1999–2000 is given in Table 5.4.

Table 5.4 State-wise incidence of poverty in India, 1973–4 to 1999–2000

States	*People below poverty line (%)*					
	1973–4	*1977–8*	*1983–4*	*1987–8*	*1993–4*	*1999–2000*
Andhra Pradesh	48.86	39.31	28.91	25.86	22.19	15.77
Bihar	61.91	61.55	62.22	52.13	54.96	42.6
Gujarat	48.15	41.23	32.79	31.54	24.21	14.07
Haryana	35.36	29.55	21.37	16.54	25.05	8.74
Karnataka	54.57	48.78	38.24	37.53	33.16	20.04
Kerala	59.79	52.22	40.42	31.79	25.43	12.72
Madhya Pradesh	61.78	61.78	49.78	43.07	42.52	37.43
Maharasthra	53.24	55.88	43.44	40.41	36.86	25.02
Orissa	66.18	70.07	65.29	55.58	48.56	47.15
Punjab	28.15	19.27	16.18	13.20	11.77	6.16
Rajasthan	46.14	37.42	34.46	35.15	27.41	15.28
Tamil Nadu	54.94	54.79	51.66	43.39	35.03	21.12
Uttar Pradesh	57.07	49.05	47.07	41.45	40.85	31.15
West Bengal	63.43	60.52	54.85	44.72	35.66	27.02
India	**54.88**	**51.32**	**44.48**	**38.36**	**35.97**	**26.1**

Source: Government of India (2006).

The rural and urban Gini coefficients calculated for India give us an indication of the level of inequality in these areas. The rural Gini for India was 30.10 in 1983. It increased marginally in 1986–7 and 1987–8 and then dropped to a low of 27.71 in 1990–1. In the subsequent period it continued to increase and was back to the 1983 level in 1997 (marginally higher – 30.11). The urban Gini, on the other hand, was 33.40 in 1983, increased to 33.95 in 1990–1 and rose further to 36.12 in 1997. Inequality, therefore, has been on the rise in both the rural and urban sectors in India.

In a state-level study on poverty and inequality in India, Deaton and Dreze (2002) have calculated the Gini coefficient for 14 states as a whole in order to gauge inter-state inequality. The Gini coefficient according to his calculations increased from 0.152 in 1980–1 to 0.159 in 1985–6 and further to 0.171 in 1990–1. In the period post-liberalisation, it increased sharply to 0.230 in 1995–6 and rose slightly above this figure to 0.233 in 1998–9. This is indicative of the increase in inter-state inequality that has characterised India's growth, especially in the period post-reform.

Jha (2000) looked into these trends in the post-reform period and found that although poverty had declined marginally, inequality, both rural and urban, had been exacerbated. Deaton and Dreze (2002) also studied trends in poverty and inequality in the 1990s and arrived at the conclusion that poverty during the 1990s had indeed declined. Topalova (2005) studied the impact of liberalisation on poverty and inequality at the district level. She found that the poverty alleviation effect was less in those districts where industries that were more exposed to liberalisation (i.e. where tariff reduction were higher) were concentrated.

Impact of trade on employment and wages: methodology

An important channel through which trade can affect poverty is through its impact on wages and employment (Winters *et al.* 2004). To estimate this impact we derive the labour demand equation and wage rate equation.

Labour demand equation

To derive the labour demand equation, we assume two inputs constant elasticity of substitution (CES) production function, which allows for non-constant returns to scale provided the function remains homogenous of degree μ, i.e.

$$Q = \chi \, [s(k)^{-\rho} + (1\text{-}s) \, (Le^{\lambda t})^{-\rho}]^{-\mu/\rho} \ \dots \ (a)$$

Where $\chi > 0$ and $0 < s < 1$

Q is the output, k is the capital, s is the share parameter and ρ determines the degree of substitutability of the inputs. The elasticity of substitution can take any non-negative constant value (including unity, as in the Cobb–Douglas case) and technical progress is labour-augmenting at rate of λ. χ is the efficiency parameter as it changes output in the same proportion for any given set of input levels and the parameter can be interpreted as a distribution parameter since it determines the distribution of income through the factor payments.

$$Ln(L) = \ln(Q) - \tfrac{1}{(1+e)}\ln(\tfrac{w}{p}) - \tfrac{\rho}{(1+\rho)}\lambda_t + [\tfrac{1}{(1+e)}]\ln[1 - (\tfrac{s}{\beta})] - \tfrac{\rho}{(1+\rho)}\ln(\chi)$$

To examine the factors that affect the demand for labour and consequently the employment in an industry, we use marginal productivity theory and equate marginal product of labour (MP_L)

$$= \ln(Q) - \sigma\,\ln(\tfrac{w}{p}) - (1 - \sigma)\lambda_t + [\sigma\,\ln(1 - (\tfrac{s}{\beta}) - (1 - \sigma)\,\ln(\chi)] \;...(b)$$

to the real wage (W/P) (first order conditions, assuming mark-up is constant). Taking logs and rearranging (a) we get:

λ_t is taken as exogenous technical change which may occur through different channels, e.g. exports and imports may affect the technology and productivity which has an effect on demand for labour, i.e.

$$\lambda_t = f\,(\lambda_1\,\text{Time} + \lambda_2\,\text{FDI} + \lambda_3\,\text{Exports} + \lambda_4\,\text{Imports}) \;...\;(c)$$

Allowing for persistence in labour demand and adding fixed effects we have

$$\text{Ln (L)}_{it} = \alpha + \beta_0 \ln\,(L)_{it\text{-}1} + \beta_1 \ln\,(Q)_{it} + \beta_2 \ln\,(W/P)_{it} +$$

$$\beta_5 \text{ EXPORTS}_{it} + \beta_6 \text{ IMPORTS}_{it} + + \alpha_i + e_{it}$$

Thus, demand for labour in the manufacturing sector is a function of:

$$L_{it} = F\,[L_{it\text{-}1},\, Q_{it},\, (w/p)_{it},\, \text{EXPORTS}_{it},\, \text{IMPORTS}_{it},\, \text{Time, Fixed Effects}] \;...\;(1)$$

Wage-rate equation

In a competitive labour market, firms will hire workers until MC_L (which is wage rate) equals MR (which is Price $\times$ MP_L). However, in the developing economies wage rate is influenced by a number of additional factors, e.g. minimum wage rates set up by the government and the relative bargaining power of the labour unions. Following Greenway *et al.* (1999) we adopt a dynamic specification in order to allow for the possibility of sticky wage adjustment through time:

$Ln\ W_{it} = \beta_1 \ln W_{i,\ t-1} + \beta_0\ X_{it} + \lambda_i + u_{it}$

where W = wage rate, X = explanatory variables, λ_i = industry specific fixed effects

$X_{it} = f\ (SIZE_{it},\ K/L_{it},\ LP_{it},\ EXPORTS_{it},\ IMPORTS_{it})$

where SIZE = size of the industry (log of output); K/L is capital–labour ratio; LP is labour productivity; EXPORTS is exports of the industry; IMPORTS is the import intensity, i.e. imports of the finished goods produced by the industry divided by the total output of the industry; *i* represents the industry and *t* represents the time period.

The equation to be estimated *for the manufacturing secto*r therefore is:

$Ln(w/p)_{it} = F\ [Ln(w/p)_{it-1},\ LnSIZE_{it},\ LnK/L_{it},\ LnLP_{it},\ LnEXPORTS_{it},$ LnIMPORTS; Fixed Effects] ... (2)

For the agriculture sector, the wages of unskilled agricultural workers differ across states, though not across crops. We therefore undertake state-level analysis where wages of unskilled workers are influenced by the following factors:

$Ln\ W_{it} = \beta_1 \ln W_{i,\ t-1} + \beta_0\ X_{it} + \lambda_i + u_{it}$

where W = wage rate, X = explanatory variables, λ_i = state specific fixed effects,

$X_{it} = f\ (SDP_{it},\ RAINFALL_{it},\ SHAREAGRI_{it},\ IRRIGATEDAREA_{it},$ $NOTRACTORS_{it},\ FERT_{it},\ MINWAGES_{it},\ EXPORTS_{it},\ IMPORTS_{it},$ state-specific fixed effects)

where SDP = state domestic product, RAINFALL = average annual rainfall received, SHAREAGRI = share of agriculture in total SDP, IRRIGATEDAREA = extent of gross irrigated area in the state, NOTRACTORS = number of tractors used, FERT = amount of fertilisers used, MINWAGES = minimum wages of unskilled labour in the state, EXPORTS = share of state in total exports of the product, IMPORTS = imports of the product.

The equation to be estimated *for the agriculture sector* therefore is:

$Ln(w/p)_{it} = F\ [Ln(w/p)_{it-1},\ LnSDP_{it}, LnRAINFALL_{it};\ LnSHAREA$- $GRI_{it},\ Ln\ IRRIGATEDAREA_{it},\ Ln\ NOTRACTORS_{it}, Ln\ FERT_{it}, Ln$ $MINWAGES_{it}, Ln\ EXPORTS_{it},\ Ln\ IMPORTS_{it},\ Fixed\ Effects] ... (3)$

Empirical methodology

Keeping in mind the unique characteristics of Indian labour markets and the important role played by the government in wage-setting, we arrive at the wage equation. We assume that labour is available in perfectly elastic supply at any given wage rate. In this case, wages will be fixed exogenously depending on the minimum wages fixed by the government and the bargaining power of labour unions.

For the purpose of estimating the impact on employment and wage we need to take into account rigidities in the Indian labour market. We therefore construct Dynamic Panel Data (DPD) models, which are estimated using Generalised Method of Moments (GMM) following Arellano and Bond (1991). GMM has become an important tool in the empirical analyses of panels with a large number of individual units and relatively short time series. This model can be written as

$$y_{it} = \alpha y_{i,t-1} + \eta_i + v_{it}$$

where $i = 1, \dots, N; t = 2, \dots, T; T \geq 3$ and $\alpha < 1$

For such models the within-group estimator (for the fixed effects models) and the GLS estimator (for the random effects model) are not applicable. Therefore a GMM estimator is applied. Adopting standard assumptions concerning the error components and initial conditions (i.e. error terms are not autocorrelated) Arellano and Bond (1991) propose moment conditions.[16] The validity of moment conditions implied by DPD models is commonly tested using a conventional GMM test of over-identifying restrictions associated with Sargan (1958).

Database construction

For the manufacturing sector, no single source of data exists for the Indian economy that provides the data required by this study. The study therefore draws data from two different sources, i.e. the Annual Survey of Industries (ASI), which is published by the Central Statistical Organisation, Government of India, and the Directorate General of Commercial Intelligence and Statistics (DGCI&S), under the Ministry of Commerce, Government of India, for trade data. ASI provides a reasonably comprehensive and reliable disaggregated estimate for the manufacturing industries. It covers all the production units registered under the Factories Act, 1948,[17] 'large ones' on a census basis (with definition of 'large' changing over time) and the remainder on a sample basis. DGCI& S provides data at eight-digit level on HS 2002 codes. A concordance matrix is constructed to arrive at trade data at ASI three-digit industry level NIC codes.

The data used in the study is constructed for 54 industries at three-digit level of industrial classification (National Industrial Classification) for the period 1998–9 to 2005–6.[18]

There are considerable problems in obtaining good-quality time series data on wages by skill level. For our purpose, we use the available information on wages contained in the ASI database. This source provides the average number of full-time production-process 'workers' and 'employees' (which includes, in addition to 'workers', non-production workers like supervisors, clerks, etc.) employed per day after taking account of reported multiple shift working. Wages of production workers is taken as wages of unskilled workers.

For the agriculture sector, the data is collected from the AGRIHARVEST, which is a compiled database provided by the Centre for Monitoring Indian Economy (CMIE). The state-level wages of unskilled agricultural labour have been collected from the Department of Agriculture, Ministry of Agriculture. Exports and imports data at the state level is constructed by applying the ratio of share of state in total production of the agricultural product.

The analysis is carried out for five categories of agricultural products, i.e. fruits and nuts; vegetables, roots and tubers; cereals; oilseeds; and total agricultural products. The analysis is undertaken for the period 1990–91 to 1999–2000 (for which the data on wages of unskilled agricultural labour was available) for 14 states of India.

Empirical results

Impact of trade on wages and employment of unskilled labour in India

To estimate the impact of exports and imports on wages of unskilled labour (blue-collar workers), we undertake an inter-industry analysis for 54 industries for the period 1997–8 to 2005–6. Since wages and employment in Indian industries are characterised by downward rigidities (as discussed earlier), we use Generalised Method of Moments (GMM-IV) one-step estimators, following Arellano and Bond (1991).[19]

Table 5.5 presents the results of the Dynamic Panel Data (DPD) estimation of wage equation, i.e. equations (1) and estimation of labour demand equation (2). The dependent variables are Log of wages of unskilled workers and Log of number of unskilled workers. All estimates are based upon heteroscedastic robust standard errors. Consistency of the GMM estimates requires that there is no second-order correlation of the residuals of the first-differenced equation. Our results of the AR(2) test on the residuals as developed by Arellano and Bond (1991) do not allow us to reject the hypothesis of the validity of instruments used. We also use industry dummies at two-digit level to control for industry-specific effects.

The results with respect to the impact of trade on wages of unskilled workers show that, after controlling for inter-industry differences, export intensity of the industry has a positive and significant impact on wages; however, impact of imports of the products produced by the industry, i.e., import competition, does not have any significant effect on wages of unskilled workers. A plausible explanation for the result is the downward

Table 5.5 Impact of trade on wages and employment of unskilled workers in the Indian manufacturing sector, 1997–8 to 2005–6

Explanatory variables	Dependent variable: Log wages of unskilled labour (1)	Dependent variable: Log number of unskilled labour (2)
Log wages to unskilled workers lagged (l1)	−0.13*** (−7.19)	−0.02** (−14.99)
Log number of unskilled workers lagged (l1)	—	—
Log wage rate (predicted)	—	−0.01* (−0.74)
Log output	0.32*** (8.14)	0.04* (1.97)
Log labour productivity of unskilled labour	0.02* (1.77)	
Log TECH	0.01 (1.32)	
Log export intensity	**0.03*** (2.43)**	**0.01 (1.39)**
Log import intensity	−0.01 (−0.34)	−0.02 (−1.53)
Cons	7.31*** (17.06)	4.64*** (4.42)
Industry dummies	Yes	Yes
Wald chi² (6)	355.4*	821.3*
Auto correlation (z)	−1.20	0.91
N	302	302

Notes:
*** indicates significance at 1 per cent, ** indicates significance at 5 per cent, * indicates significance at 10 per cent.
The predicted value of wage rate arrived at from the wage equation is used as an instrument for wage rate in the employment equation.
Exports and imports variables have lagged values.
The estimations are carried out for 54 industries for the period 1997–8 to 2005–6.
The figures reported are the coefficients and the figures in bracket are the *t*−values.

rigidity in wages, given the minimum wage norms applicable in the organised manufacturing sector, while export orientation of the industry will create pressure on the industry to retain labour and improve their skills, which may raise their returns. The other variables have the expected direction. Output expansion and labour productivity will increase wages. While low-tech industries may pay higher wages to unskilled workers, the variable is not found to be statistically significant.

In terms of employment, the results are not very encouraging as we do not find any evidence that industries which are export-oriented lead to higher employment of unskilled labour. These results appear to be contrary to the results arrived at in other studies, such as those of Banga (2005b) and Goldar (2002), who find higher employment elasticity of demand in export-oriented industries in the post-reforms period. However, the dependent variable is employment of unskilled workers and not total employment. The results indicate that the export intensity of an industry does not lead to higher employment of unskilled labour after controlling for the output produced. One plausible reason for this could be higher outsourcing or higher employment of contract labour by export-oriented industries, which is not captured by the data used. Given the strict labour laws in India, this is a rising phenomenon. Import competition also does not have any significant impact on employment of unskilled labour. This is not very surprising given the lack of hiring and firing policy in India. Other variables are with the expected signs.

The rural and urban Gini coefficients calculated for India give us an indication of the level of inequality in these areas. The rural Gini for India was 30.10 in 1983. It increased marginally in 1986–7 and 1987–8 and then dropped to a low of 27.71 in 1990–1. In the subsequent period it continued to increase and was back to the 1983 level in 1997 (marginally higher – 30.11). The urban Gini, on the other hand, was 33.40 in 1983; it increased to 33.95 in 1990–1 and further to 36.12 in 1997. Inequality, therefore, has been on the rise in both the rural and urban sectors in India.

Impact of trade on wages of unskilled labour in the agriculture sector

The wages of unskilled labour in agriculture are taken as an indicator of poverty. Table 5.6 presents the results of the impact of exports and imports on the wages of unskilled labour in four different agricultural products – fruits and nuts; cereals; vegetables, roots and tubers; oilseed – and for all agricultural products. The estimation is undertaken for 14 states of India for which comparable data was available for the period 1991–2 to 2000–1.

The results show that after controlling for state specific variables that may impact the wages of unskilled labour in agriculture, for fruits and nuts exports increased the wages of unskilled labour but this is not statistically significant; however, higher imports of fruits and nuts led to a decline in the wages of unskilled labour in agriculture. In the case of cereals, the results indicate that exports of cereals led to a significant rise in the wages of unskilled workers and imports did not have any significant impact. For vegetables, we find that the results indicate imports of vegetables led to a fall in the wages of unskilled labour but the impact of exports is not significant. For oilseeds, we do not find any significant impact of exports or imports. With respect to agricultural products as a whole, we find that exports have not had any significant impact on the wages of unskilled labour. In other words, states with higher exports of agricultural products do not have correspondingly higher wages for unskilled workers, but higher imports of agricultural products have led to lower wages for unskilled workers in states where the production of the corresponding product is higher.

Other variables used indicate that wages of unskilled labour are positively affected if state domestic product is higher, rainfall is higher, agriculture has

Table 5.6 Impact of trade on wages of unskilled workers in agriculture

Explanatory variables	Fruits and nuts coefficient (t value) (1)	Cereals (2)	Vegetables, roots and tubers (3)	Oilseeds (4)	All agricultural products (5)
Lag	−0.26	0.51**	1.13***	0.65***	0.64
	(−00.4)	(2.07)	(4.91)	(5.05)	(3.00)
Log exports	0.30	0.05***	−0.004	−0.004	−0.03
	(1.53)	(2.43)	(−0.24)	(−0.10)	(−0.70)
Log imports	−0.25*	0.01	−0.009***	−0.0008	−0.11***
	(−1.83)	(1.58)	(−2.62)	(−0.02)	(−2.44)
Log state domestic product	0.80***	−0.07	0.25	0.27**	0.52***
	(2.91)	(−0.73)	(1.20)	(2.36)	(2.92)
Log rainfall	0.64***	0.13*	−0.04	0.03	0.001
	(2.46)	(1.85)	(−0.50)	(0.40)	(0.03)
Log share of agriculture	−0.97*	−0.20	−0.20	−0.06	−0.16
	(−1.57)	(−1.12)	(−1.10)	(−0.36)	(−0.69)
Log gross irrigated area	−0.4***	0.28*	0.28	−0.03	0.34*
	(−2.16)	(1.92)	(1.05)	(−0.24)	(1.76)
Log number of tractors	0.92	−0.05	0.08*	0.01	−0.01
	(1.64)	(−1.60)	(1.81)	(0.26)	(−0.32)
Log fertilisers	0.06	−0.13**	−0.29***	−0.13	−0.23***
	(1.30)	(−2.23)	(−2.49)	(−1.66)	(−2.42)
Log minimum wages	−0.06	−0.05	−0.04	−0.05	0.06***
	(−0.85)	(−0.93)	(−0.85)	(−1.20)	(3.06)
Constant	0.21	0.39	−1.56	—	−1.31*
Constant	(1.1.3)	(0.45)	(−0.82)	—	(−1.78)
No. of observations	83	92	88	84	89
Sargan test chi²	9.19	5.31	5.96	6.67	5.0
Auto correlation (z)	1.03	0.98	0.86	1.02	0.32

Dependent variables: Log real wages of unskilled labour in agriculture.
Notes:
*** indicates significance at 1 per cent, ** indicates significance at 5 per cent, * indicates significance at 10 per cent.
The figures reported are the coefficients and the figures in bracket are the *t*–values.
The estimations are carried out for 14 states for the period 1991–2 to 2000–1.

lower use of technology and minimum wages of unskilled labour are fixed at higher levels.

Conclusions and policy implications

The trade and poverty nexus is multi-faceted. A differential impact of trade may be transmitted through exports and imports in different sectors. Further, the impact on consumers and producers may differ. Level of development of the economies may further lead to differential impact of trade. To empirically estimate the overall impact of trade on poverty may therefore be ambiguous, as it may not be desirable to weigh gains over losses, or vice versa. However, it still remains important to empirically estimate the impact of trade on poverty in different sectors and through different channels, so as to formulate appropriate strategies and be better prepared for facing the challenges that trade may create in terms of social costs. In this context, this chapter has attempted to empirically estimate the impact of trade on labour markets, which may work through its impact on wages and employment, especially for the unskilled segment. The analysis was undertaken separately for the agriculture and manufacturing sectors.

The analysis with respect to the manufacturing sector has been undertaken by estimating the impact on wages and employment of unskilled labour in 54 industries of India for the period 1998–9 to 2005–6. The results indicate that exports have had a favourable impact on the wages of unskilled labour. Import competition does not seem to have displaced labour or adversely affected wages. Strict labour laws and downward rigidity of wages in India may be plausible reasons for this result.

Overall, the results of the agriculture sector indicate that for states which produce a higher proportion of the agricultural products that are exported, there is no evidence of corresponding rise in wages of unskilled labour, but states which produce a higher proportion of agricultural products that are imported do witness lower wages of unskilled labour.

The importance of existing regulations in protecting the wages and employment of unskilled labour in the manufacturing and agriculture sectors is highlighted by the results of the study. The existence of downward rigidity of wages because of minimum wage regulations and their enforcement, especially in low-tech industries, is required to mitigate the adverse impact that imports may have on wages. The study also indicates that minimum wages of unskilled labour at the states level has led to relatively higher wages of unskilled agriculture labour in states. This level of minimum wages should be revised and enforced in order to ensure appropriate returns to unskilled labour.

In agriculture, the study results support India's need to protect policy space, as losses in terms of lower wages due to displacement of labour appear to be significant. This is mainly due to the unlimited supply of unskilled labour that exists in the agriculture sector in India. On the other hand, results from the study suggest that gains from exports in terms of increased wages may not be sufficiently widespread to warrant negotiating a stance that seeks the opening of foreign markets in lieu of providing market access in agriculture. Thus, the results support the stand taken by India in WTO agricultural negotiations. Ultimately, trade's positive impact on wages and employment depends on the extent to which the poor are able to gainfully participate in the expanding sectors.

Notes

1 The choice of the period has been restricted as ASI changed the industrial classification in 1998–9.

2 Effective import duties = import duty revenue / value of imports (source: World Bank 2006a).
3 China 4 per cent, Malaysia 6 per cent, Viet Nam 14 per cent, Pakistan 25 per cent and Sri Lanka 14 per cent.
4 Trade Policy Reviews of 1998 and 2002 (WTO 1998, 2002).
5 According to a study by Goldman Sachs, the Indian economy is expected to continue growing at the rate of 5 per cent or more till 2050 and is slated to become the fourth largest economy by 2050. According to the ATKEARNEY 2004 Business Confidence Index India is the third most attractive destination, according to the ATKEARNEY 2004 Offshoring Index India is the best offshoring destination, and according to the UNCTAD and *Corporate Location* survey of April 2004 India is among the top three investment hotspots (DIPP 2003).
6 *India Trade Policy Review* 1998 (WTO 1998).
7 Ministry of Commerce and Industries, Government of India.
8 Goldar (2005).
9 Reserve Bank of India (2006).
10 Government of India (2006).
11 Banga (2005a).
12 Central Statistical Office; see www.mospi.gov.in/cso_test1.htm
13 Reserve Bank of India (2006).
14 Banga (2005a).
15 NSSO gives the average level of unemployment on a given day during the survey year, and thereby captures the unemployed days of the chronically unemployed, the unemployed days of the usually employed who become intermittently unemployed during the reference week, and the unemployed days of those classified as employed according to the criterion of current weekly status.
16 For details see Blundell and Bond (1998: 118).
17 The Factories Act, it may be noted, applies to those units employing ten or more workers and using power, or 20 or more workers not using power.
18 The period chosen has been constrained by the availability of comparable data from 1998 onwards (ASI changed its industrial classification from 1998–9).
19 The coefficients and standard errors reported are those of the one-step estimation since, as Arellano and Bond (1991) argue, inferences based on standard errors obtained from the two-step estimates can be unreliable. The Sargan test of over-identifying restrictions and the test for second-order autocorrelation are, however, based on two-step estimates (see Arellano and Bond 1991).

6 Maldives

*Jagath Dissanayake and
Suwendrani Jayaratne*

Located about 300 miles south west of India in the Indian Ocean, the Republic of Maldives is an archipelago of 1,192 small coral islands covering a small land area of 115 square miles (Athukorala 2004: 1402). Maldives initiated its trade liberalisation programme in 1989 initially by removing some of the import quotas and allowing private sector involvement in some of the export businesses (CIA 1996). Consequently, from the mid-1980s it has achieved an impressive economic growth, despite its sluggish economic performance since independence (in 1965). Maldives' per capita GDP in US$ has increased by about 16 times from 1985 till now (from US$ 250 in 1985 to US$ 4059 in 2008). The country's developments in the economic sphere have trickled down to other sectors, enabling Maldives to record impressive social indicators parallel to its growth in the economy: it has a Human Development Index (HDI) of 0.741 and ranks 100 out of 177 countries.[1] The poverty levels in Maldives have also been falling rapidly. However, considerable differences exist between the capital and its 26 atolls. For example, despite the rapid fall in overall poverty levels, there are significant differences between Malé and the atolls in terms of income distribution. Furthermore, Maldives' economy, which is based on a very narrow production base, remains highly vulnerable to external forces.

Maldives, therefore, provides a unique case study of the trade and poverty nexus in the South Asian region given its peculiarities as a Small Island Economy (SIE).[2] As Josling (1998) states, standard economic policy recipes may have different impacts on these countries given the special circumstances that arise by being 'small' and being surrounded by water. Against this background it is interesting to study the impact that trade has had on poverty in Maldives, relative to other countries in the region. As a SIE influenced by two decades of trade reforms, this chapter seeks to analyse the Maldivian experience on the trade–poverty nexus. The chapter is structured as follows. The second section of this chapter presents the trade policy framework of Maldives. The third section describes the post-reform trade performances, while the fourth section presents the trends in growth, poverty and inequality of Maldives in the post-liberalised era. The fifth section analyses the link between trade and poverty in Maldives. Summary and conclusions are presented in the last section.

Trade liberalisation in Maldives: a brief overview

As pointed out by Athukorala (2004: 1407), 'there is little room in the Maldives for using tariffs and other trade restrictions as means of promoting import substitution and infant industry' because of the small domestic market and limited resource base similar to that of Singapore. Despite the trade reforms undertaken at the unilateral, regional and multilateral levels since 1989, substantially high tariffs maintained for revenue reasons and direct import restrictions that favour state trading corporations have continued to remain important features of the economic landscape of the country. We briefly review the trade and investment policy regime in this section.

Liberalisation of trade and investment policies

The government of Maldives started its economic reform programme in 1989 by lifting import quotas and opening up some areas of exports to the private sector after which, further liberalisation of regulations took place in order to accommodate more foreign investments. Tariffs remain the main trade policy instrument and also the main source of tax revenue: they account for 70 per cent of tax receipts and 30 per cent of total government revenue (WTO 2009). This ratio has remained relatively unchanged from the 1990s. The tariff structure in Maldives remains complex with applied MFN tariff consisting of ten bands, duty free, 5 per cent, 10 per cent, 15 per cent, 20 per cent, 25 per cent, 35 per cent, 50 per cent, 100 per cent and 200 per cent, a specific duty for cigarettes (Rf 0.30 per stick), and many exemptions. The tariff structure has not undergone major changes in the recent past. While the number of tariff lines was 5,321 in 2002 (based on HS02 nomenclature), in 2008 it was 8,987 (based on HS07).

At the Uruguay Round Maldives bound about 97 per cent of its tariff lines at 30 per cent while the rest, mainly meat, alcoholic beverages, tobacco products, plastic bags, passenger motor vehicles, buses, motorcycles and their components, were bound at 300 per cent. Nevertheless, in 2008 96.3 per cent of tariff lines were bound, with 334 lines unbound. The latter were mainly in the fisheries and motor vehicle parts sector. The average bound MFN rate in 2008 was 37.1 per cent. However, it is notable that the number of applied tariff rates which exceeded the bound rates on 149 tariff lines in 2002 had increased to 218 in 2008 with justifications of these rates being made on religious and environmental grounds.[3] The average applied MFN rate was 21.4 per cent in 2008, and this is a slight change from the rates in 2002. This change is due to a change in nomenclature rather than a change in rates. A majority of the applied MFN tariffs range from 5 to 25 per cent. There is also a considerable difference of 15.7 percentage points between average bound and applied MFN rates, bringing in a degree of uncertainty. On the sectoral level the average tariffs for agricultural products were 17.2 per cent in 2008. This is a decline from 17.8 per cent in 2002. On the other hand, average tariffs of non-agricultural products have increased from 21.1 per cent in 2002 to 22 per cent in 2008.

In terms of non-tariff barriers, with the elimination of a majority of quotas from January 1998, there are only a few quantitative restrictions currently in place in Maldives. The staple foods, wheat flour, sugar and rice which enter the country duty-free are subject to quantitative restrictions in the form of import quotas. And a small number of items such as alcohol and spirits, pork and its by-products, and arms and ammunition are prohibited or restricted for reasons of safety, security, environmental or religious concerns. See Table 6.1.

The export regime in Maldives is relatively open. There are no duties levied on exports except a 50 per cent duty on the export of ambergris. However, since there are currently no ambergris exports from Maldives, the effect is nil.

Table 6.1 Tariff structure, 1995 and 2008

		MFN 1995–9[a]	MFN 2002[b]	MFN 2008[c]	Final bound[d]
1	Bound tariff lines (% of all tariff lines)	—	96.6	96.3	96.3
2	Simple average applied rate	—	20.8	21.4	37.1
	Agricultural products (HS01–24)	—	17.8	16.7	45.8
	Industrial products (HS25–97)	—	21.2	22.2	35.8
	WTO agricultural products	—	18.5	17.2	44.9
	WTO non-agricultural products	—	21.1	22.0	35.9
	Textiles and clothing	—	21.2	22.8	30.0
3	Tariff quotas (% of all tariff lines)	—	0.0	0.0	0.0
4	Domestic tariff 'peaks' (% of all tariff lines)[e]	—	1.4	1.5	2.6
5	International tariff 'peaks' (% of all tariff lines)[f]	—	59.9	64.0	100.0
6	Duty-free lines (% of all tariff lines)	—	0.1	0.2	0.0
7	Import duties (% of imports)	11.6	13.2		

Source: Compiled from WTO (2009) and World Bank (2010).
Notes:
a   Shows period averages. A dash indicates missing values.
b   The 2002 tariff schedule is based on HS02 nomenclature, consisting of 5,321 tariff lines;
c   The 2008 tariff schedule is based on HS07 nomenclature, consisting of 8,987 tariff lines.
d   Calculations for final bound rates are based on the 2008 tariff schedule.
e   Domestic tariff peaks are defined as those exceeding three times the overall simple average applied rate.
f   International tariff peaks are defined as those exceeding 15 per cent.

Foreign investors exporting garments had to pay a royalty when the Multi-Fibre Arrangement (MFA) was in place. Nevertheless, with the collapse of the garment industry in the country following the expiration of the MFA, this is no longer applicable. The export of timber and live fish is subject to export control. However, apart from these export restrictions, there have been no export taxes since 1996.

The investment regime in Maldives is quite liberal. Foreign investors may fully own and operate business enterprises. Registration and handling of foreign investment in all sectors is carried out by the Foreign Investment Services Bureau (FISB), with the exception of tourism, which is handled by the Ministry of Tourism. Most investment incentives apply equally to foreign and domestic investors. There are no exchange controls, and profits and capital proceeds can be repatriated. Foreign investments are, however, required to pay an annual royalty fee to the government. This amounts to 3 per cent of gross income or 15 per cent of profits, whichever is greater, for majority foreign-owned companies. For others, the greater of the two applies: either a royalty of 1.5 per cent of income or 7.5 per cent of profits.

Trade agreements and preferential access

Maldives has been a GATT contracting party since April 1983 and became an original member of the WTO in May 1995. It is a signatory to 17 multi-lateral agreements under the Uruguay Round and associated decisions and declarations, including the Doha Ministerial Declaration (Wijayasiri 2007). While Maldives provides MFN treatment to all WTO members it is also entitled to special and differential treatment under WTO agreements. Furthermore, Maldives has been actively participating in WTO-related activities.[4]

In addition to multilateral and unilateral trade liberalisation measures, Maldives has also engaged in bilateral and plurilateral trade liberalisation. It has already become a member of a number of Free Trade Agreements (FTAs). In terms of membership in regional associations, Maldives' membership is limited to one: the South Asian Association for Regional Development (SAARC). It was a founding member of the South Asian Preferential Trade Agreement (SAPTA), which came into effect in 1995. SAPTA was superseded by the South Asian Free Trade Agreement (SAFTA) which was signed in January 2004 and came into effect in July 2006. Maldives, which is considered a Least Developed Country (LDC) within SAARC, enjoys special and differential treatment. Under the agreement Maldives will fully implement SAFTA by 2017. However, 74.5 per cent of imports (in terms of value) to Maldives from other SAARC countries are subject to its negative lists while 57.6 per cent of its exports to SAARC are subject to the negative list of other countries (Weerakoon and Thennakoon 2006). In this context, the current trade benefits acquired by Maldives through SAFTA appear to be limited.

Maldives' only bilateral trade agreement is with India which came into effect on 31 March 1981. The agreement states that the two countries will not provide to each other any less favourable treatment than that they offer to another trading country. This, however, excludes trade facilitation measures offered to other countries. It has little impact on trade between the two countries, and functions as an MFN agreement (WTO 2003).

Maldives receives preferential trade treatment under the Generalised System of Preferences (GSP) with most industrialised countries except the United States. It is also eligible for the preferences extended under the EU's 'Everything but Arms' initiative. Maldives' utilisation rate of EU preferences is as high as 98.8 per cent (World Bank 2008).

Post-reform trade performance

The export sector in Maldives recorded an impressive growth during the first fifteen years of post-liberalisation. Total exports doubled during the first decade of post-liberalisation from US$ 32 million in 1989 to US$ 64 million in 1999. The sector grew more rapidly for another half a decade until 2004, recording nearly 20 per cent annual growth on average. Nevertheless, the share of exports to GDP remained constant, at around 14 per cent, since the inception of liberalisation.

Despite its rapid growth, the export sector of the country was confined to a few industries, with the fisheries sector being the only significant export industry of the country until the garment sector emerged in the 1990s. The garment industry grew rapidly, largely as a result of foreign investments, and contributed significantly to the export sector over a decade and a half. Liberalisation of investment regulations accompanied by export preferences enjoyed by the country under the MFA made the industry attractive for Foreign Direct Investments (FDI). Most investors in the sector were 'quota-hopping' investors from other countries in the region. Nevertheless, the sector collapsed in 2004 as a result of the MFA phase-out; by the time of its expiration the garment sector accounted for more than 30 per cent of total exports. Despite its significant role in the export sector, the garment industry had little value-addition and few leakages to the domestic economy such as employment generation for Maldivians. The bulk of the garment sector employees were expatriates and therefore the collapse of the industry had a limited impact on the rest of the economy.

The country experienced a substantial 15 per cent decline in its total exports in 2005 in the immediate aftermath of the MFA phase-out; however, it recorded a rapid rise during the following years. Maldives was able to sustain a 20 per cent growth in the export sector on average during 2006 and 2007. Though the fisheries sector was a significant export sector in the country, the growth of the sector during 2006 and 2007 can be solely attributed to re-exports, which mainly consisted of jet fuel. Re-exports from the country increased from less than US$ 40 million in 2003 to US$ 120 million in 2007 recording an average annual growth of 34 per cent. It accounted for more than half of the total exports by 2007, being the single largest component of the merchandise export sector. Total exports from the country in 2007 were US$ 228 million while re-exports and marine exports contributed 53 per cent and 46 per cent, respectively.

Recent developments in the re-export sector can be considered a significant milestone in the export economy of the country. Since Maldives is a SIE with limited physical and human resources, re-exports would possibly provide an option for the nation to earn more foreign exchange in its first stages of development, as was successfully done by Singapore. However, unlike Singapore, Maldives has not fully harnessed its potential, given the limited diversification within the re-exports sector.

Even after two decades of liberalisation, Maldives has been unable to exploit international trade as a tool for diversifying its export economy and continues to rely on very few export commodities. Diversification of the Maldivian economy has been difficult because of the country's geographic isolation and its small and dispersed population, which also renders public services, and transport links difficult to provide (IMF 2009). However, a commendable diversification is evident within the fisheries sector. Traditional dry fish exports have been diversified into fresh, chilled, frozen, dried and canned fish exports. Dried fish accounted for almost all the fisheries exports in the 1980s, but its importance as an export commodity had declined to less than 10 per cent of the total fish exports by the end of 2007. Canned fish, which requires skilled labour, new technology and much value-addition accounted for more than 10 per cent of total fisheries exports in 2007, while other forms, such as fresh, chilled and frozen, accounted for the rest of the 80 per cent.

Services exports, which narrowly concentrates on tourism, has been the main foreign exchange earner of the archipelago even in the days before the trade reforms took place. The tourism industry, which was limited to only two resorts with a bed capacity of 280 in 1972, developed to 60 resorts and more than 6,000-bed capacity by 1990, and further to 91 resorts with total bed capacity exceeding 18,000 after three and half decades (MMA 2007). Annual tourist arrivals were 675, 900 in 2007, a seven fold increase compared to that reported in the mid 1980s. Tourism currently generates 87 per cent of the country's total foreign exchange earnings (MMA 2007).

FDI has always played a crucial role in both merchandise and services export growth in Maldives. Average annual FDI inflows increased from US$ 3 million during 1985–9 to US$ 13 million during 2004–7, while the total stock of FDI stood at US$ 209 million at the end of 2007 (UNCTAD 2008). The main sectors which attracted FDI into the country include tourism, garments and fisheries. Tourism and fisheries industries have attracted steady FDI inflows into the economy. The recent destinations of FDI into the country are mostly visible in transport and telecom, water production and distribution, and financial sectors.

Though FDI inflows have increased over time, Maldives has not been able to fully exploit its potential of attracting FDI into the country because of a less conducive policy environment. Many successful examples, like Singapore, which relied on trade and foreign investment in its take-off, first made the country more investor-friendly in order to attract FDI. With recognition of the issue, the Maldivian government revised its FDI policy in 2007 to increase transparency and predictability, and to speed up approvals for incoming investment projects, which are essential ingredients of FDI policies of many of the countries successful in attracting FDI.

The country's imports have also increased throughout the last two decades at a rapid pace. Total imports were nearly US$ 100 million at the time of liberalisation and currently stand at more than US$ 1 billion. Being a net food-importing country, Maldives spends a large share of the import expenditure on food items. In 2007, 16 per cent of imports were food items, out of which nearly 14 per cent were staple foods such as rice, wheat and sugar. The rest of the imports mainly comprised intermediate capital goods (48 per cent) such as construction-related products, transport equipment and parts, and machinery and mechanical appliances and petroleum products (18 per cent).

Post-reform growth, poverty and inequality trends

Growth performance in the post-liberalisation era

The impact of trade liberalisation on the Maldivian economy is mostly visible through the growth of GDP. Maldives witnessed a rapid acceleration of its GDP growth in the immediate post-liberalisation era. The economy, which was already growing at a rate of 10 per cent on average during the 1980s, reported a 13 per cent annual growth rate during the first decade of post-liberalisation. It experienced 8 per cent growth on average during 1999–2007, exceeding the GDP US$ 1 billion mark in 2007. GDP per capita more than doubled during the first decade of post-liberalisation, from US$ 1,000 in 1989 to US$ 2,300 in 1999. In 2007, it was US$ 3,460, which is comparable with countries like China, Jordan and Ecuador. Maldivian per capita income is much higher compared to many other archipelagic states with a population of more than 100,000: in 2007, Samoa's was US$ 2,517, Vanuatu's US$ 2,218 and the Solomon Islands' US$ 763. The rich performance in growth during the last two decades was largely driven by developments in the tourism and fisheries sectors fuelled by FDI, favourable external conditions, and large inflows of foreign aid/grants and their proper utilisation. See Table 6.2.

Sectoral composition of GDP shows the narrow economic base of the country confined to a few sectors (Table 6.3). The economy is mainly concentrated on the services sector, which accounts for a substantial 80 per cent of GDP, making it the driving force of the economy. The tourism sector dominates the tertiary sector as well as the whole economy, being the single largest contributor to GDP in both the pre-liberalisation and the post-liberalisation eras. The share of tourism in GDP has slightly declined in the post-liberalisation era (28 per cent in 2007 compared to 33 per cent in 1989) while the transport

Table 6.2 Maldives' economic performance

	1990–5	1996–2000	2001–5	2006	2007	2008
GDP per capita at current market price (US$ million)	1,323	2,088	2,452	2,654	3,454	3,460
Real GDP growth (%)	8.3	7.7	4.5	18.0	7.2	5.8
Inflation (CPI) (%)	7.3	2.8	1.7	3.5	7.4	12.3
Broad money (M2) growth (%)	6.5	15.9	17.4	20.6	23.7	23.6
Current account balance (% of GDP)	−1.1	−7.5	−15.3	−33.0	−41.5	−51.7
Exchange rate, rufiyaa per US$ (monthly average)	10.8	11.7	12.6	12.8	12.8	12.8

Source: Compiled from Athukorala (2004); WTO (2009); Maldives Monetary Authority, *Annual Reports* (various years).

Table 6.3 Sectoral composition of GDP

Sector	1984	1989	1994	1999	2004	2007
Primary sector	19	7	13	10	9	7
Agriculture	7	5	4	3	2	2
Fisheries	12	11	8	6	6	4
Coral and sand mining	1	1	1	1	1	1
Secondary sector	13	12	13	15	16	17
Manufacturing	10	9	10	8	8	7
Electricity and water supply*	—	—	—	3	4	4
Construction	3	3	3	4	4	6
Territory sector	68	71	74	75	79	80
Tourism	29	33	34	33	32	28
Transport and communication	4	9	11	14	15	20
Government administration services	9	9	9	11	13	16
GDP per capita (US$)	771	1,074	1,407	1,934	2,682	3,460

Source: Calculated from Statistical Yearbooks (various years); MPND cited in UNDP (2005a), and calculated from Maldives Monetary Authority (2007).
Note: * From 1984 to 1999, electricity was included in manufacturing.

and telecommunications sector has emerged with a 20 per cent share of GDP in 2007 compared to less than 10 per cent in 1989.

The significance of fishing in the Maldivian GDP has declined substantially, from 12 per cent of GDP in the mid-1980s to 4 per cent in 2007. However, the fisheries remain a significant industry, being a key employment generator, particularly, for inhabitants in atolls. In fact, the atolls contribute to 93 per cent of total employment in the fisheries sector (Ministry of Planning and National Development 2006). More importantly, almost all the domestic exports of Maldives comprise of fisheries export: in 2007 fisheries accounted for 98 per cent of total domestic exports. Furthermore, the fisheries sector has also established significant links with the manufacturing sector through fish--processing activities such as fish-canning, which is added in the manufacturing activities.

The share of manufacturing in GDP increased from about 6 per cent in 1990 to 9 per cent in 2001–2, due predominantly to the expansion of the export-oriented garment industry (Athukorala 2004). However, after the collapse of the garment industry, the contribution of the manufacturing sector has again reduced to 6 per cent. The significance of the construction sector has been increasing in recent years due largely to the tsunami reconstruction activities, development works demanded by the booming tourism industry, state-oriented capital investment works, and residential and property development by the private sector (MMA 2007).

The contribution of the agriculture sector to GDP is decreasing and becoming negligible, something that has become more obvious in the post-liberalisation era. Lack of cultivable land, technical knowledge and skilled labour in the sector, distance between islands and small market size are some of the constraints for the development of the sector. However, agriculture remains vital for the Maldivian economy since it is an important source of income and employment generation, particularly for women; women living in outer islands account to 63 per cent of total agricultural sector employment (MMA 2007).

Poverty and inequality in the post-liberalisation era

The record in poverty reduction in Maldives during the past three and a half decades has been exceptional. In the 1970s, Maldives was the poorest country in South Asia. Three and a half decades later, its per capita GDP and social indicators rank it at the top of the region – per capita GDP is US $ 3,460; the adult literacy rate is 98 per cent; average life expectancy is 73 years; infant mortality is 21 per 1,000 live births; and maternal mortality is 141 per 100,000 (ADB 2007). However, improvements in poverty reduction are not very impressive at disaggregated levels due to widening inequality between the capital and the atolls during the past two decades. See Table 6.4.

Assessing the changes of poverty over time has been rather difficult in the case of Maldives because of the limited availability of statistics over a long period of time.[5] There is no nationally accepted poverty line in Maldives. A 'low' poverty line of Rf 10 (US$ 0.78) per person per day, and a 'high' poverty line of Rf 15 (US$ 1.17) per person per day are commonly used to categorise the poor (ADB 2007). Statistics suggest that poverty in the country has been declining considerably, particularly during the last decade, with the proportion of those living below Rf 7.5 coming down from 21 per cent to 6 per cent in the period 1997–2005. According to the internationally accepted poverty line of PPP US$ 1, the poverty incidence in Maldives was 4 per cent in 2005, a significantly lower value compared to many of the archipelagic

Table 6.4 Headcount ratios according to various poverty lines in Malé and the atolls, 1997–2005

Poverty line*	Maldives (%)			Malé (%)			Atolls (%)		
	1997	2004	2005	1997	2004	2005	1997	2004	2005
Rf 7.5	21	12	6	10	10	*	25	13	8
Rf 10	26	17	8	12	11	*	31	20	11
Rf 15	40	28	16	18	15	7	48	34	20

Source: UNDP (2005a).
Notes:
* indicates too few statistical observations to be statistically reliable.
In 1997, Rf 7.5 = US$ 0.63, Rf 10 = $0.84, Rf 15 = $1.27; in 2004, Rf 7.5 = US$ 0.58, Rf 10 = $0.78, Rf 15 = $1.17.

states, such as Vanuatu: 50 per cent (2002); Fiji Islands: 40 per cent (2002); Palau: 23 per cent (2000); and Samoa: 20.3 per cent (2002).[6] However, in the case of the atolls, the incidence of poverty is higher than the national level despite a declining trend over the years.

Incidence of poverty in the central, central south and south regions is much lower compared to that of other regions such as north and north central, possibly because of geographical proximity to the capital city and thereby accessibility to infrastructure and new markets. The severity of poverty declines as one moves from north to south. While the poverty levels of the south were not too different from those of the northern regions during the mid-1990s, the southern regions seem to have combated poverty more successfully by 2005.

Although poverty levels have been decreasing rapidly, the population remains very vulnerable with a high degree of transient income poverty. A large number of people have been moving in and out of poverty instead of moving out of poverty permanently. It is also a matter of concern that in the period 1997–2005, half the population in Maldives moved between poverty classes at least once (ADB 2007).

Rising income inequality has become yet another key concern of the country as it confines the accessibility of the poor to reap the benefits of liberalisation. The Gini coefficient of Maldives, which was 0.41 in 2004, is relatively higher compared to its South Asian neighbours: Bangladesh: 0.32, India and Pakistan: 0.33 and Sri Lanka: 0.34. However, the coefficient is similar to those in a number of other SIEs, such as Trinidad and Tobago: 0.40; Saint Lucia: 0.43; Fiji Islands: 0.49; Samoa: 0.44 and Tonga 0.42 (Sharma 2006; ADB 2007). As reflected by in-country regional Gini coefficients, although inequality has declined within Malé and within the atolls, this is not the case between Malé and the atolls (Table 6.5).

Moreover, regional differences in poverty can also be seen through the differences in average expenditure per person by deciles of the population. Though the average expenditure per person per day has risen over the past

Table 6.5 Gini coefficients by region, 1997 and 2004

	1997	2004
Maldives	0.42	0.41
Malé	0.39	0.33
Atolls	0.40	0.36
Between Malé and the atolls	0.12	0.18
North	0.39	0.36
Central north	0.41	0.38
Central	0.38	0.33
Central south	0.44	0.31
South	0.34	0.34

Source: MPND/UNDP (2004).

decade at both aggregate and regional levels, there is evidence to suggest a widening disparity between Malé and the atolls, with a slower improvement recorded in the atolls compared to Malé. Rising inequality further suggests that Maldives would have reaped the benefits of liberalisation and enjoyed greater improvement in poverty reduction if the inequality between Malé and the atolls had not increased.

The link between trade and poverty

The linkages between trade and poverty are unique to Maldives as an archipelagic state compared to those of its South Asian neighbours. However, the present analysis has been limited to a more qualitative approach largely because of the limited availability of data.

As suggested in the sections above, Maldives has achieved spectacular growth in the post-liberalisation era while at the same time recording a commendable growth in international trade. Moreover, the country has experienced a decline in national poverty over the same period. This clearly establishes a possible link between economic growth and poverty reduction. The linkage between trade and poverty reduction could be established through the linkages between growth and poverty, where GDP growth in Maldives has possibly been triggered by trade in the post-liberalisation era. However, the linkages between trade and poverty need to be examined with caution, given that the causality between trade and growth in Maldives has not yet been empirically established by a rigorous study. Thus, the present study goes on to analyse the key channels in which trade has affected poverty in Maldives, via employment, through the creation and disappearance of markets, transmission of border prices, and vulnerability.

Employment

A direct link through which trade liberalisation could affect poverty is through employment and wages. Employment and wages are key sources of keeping poverty at bay, while the loss of employment is a cause of plunging people into poverty. In Maldives, trade has opened new employment opportunities in the economy through new industries. This required bringing professionals in from abroad. While getting professionals into the country has enabled Maldivians to gain skills that are necessary to match those required by, especially, the new industries, it has also had negative impacts such as lowering market wages owing to the competitiveness of the expatriate workforce and a reduction of wages for manual labour in some industries. More importantly, however, the analysis of the dynamics of the Maldivian economy reveals an interesting finding: poverty in the country has reduced over time even though unemployment has increased. A possible reason for this paradoxical relationship may be that income of one employed household member has been increased to an extent that he/she can afford to support the rest of the family members who are unemployed.

However, total employment in the country has increased significantly over the last two decades, from 51,478 in 1985 to 110,231 in 2006 (ADB 2003; MMA 2007). More particularly, the spectacular growth in the tourism industry has opened up a large number of direct employment opportunities in the industry, particularly in Malé and nearby islands. Direct employment in the tourism industry was recorded as more than 17,000 in 2004 compared to about 10,000 in 1996 (Ministry of Tourism 2001; MPND 2005). Furthermore, such rapid growth in the industry has triggered construction of resorts and hotels, and thereby created a massive demand for workers in the construction industry. Wide-ranging other economic activities such as manufacturing and retail were also spurred on in the country after liberalisation and created ample job opportunities for the economy. Many Maldivians have migrated from their rural atolls to Malé to participate in these high-income earning activities, and this has enabled their families to emerge from poverty. Income levels in Malé have increased significantly during the last two decades, possibly up to a level where people who work in Malé can support their unemployed family members who live in the outer islands. In fact, there is a lower probability for households to be categorised as poor if they receive remittances from family members working in resorts or in Malé (ADB 2007).

Despite the large number of employment opportunities that emerged after liberalisation, Maldivians have not been able to fully benefit from such opportunities largely because of a skills mismatch in the labour market. Many of the jobs created in the post-liberalisation era, such as jobs in the service and construction sectors, have not attracted Maldivians, either because these posts needed special skills or because they involved unskilled menial work that the Maldivians did not want to engage in (Ghosh and Siddique 2000). Lack of skilled labour was considered a major challenge even for Singapore in the early stages of its development. Nevertheless, Singapore was able to attract industries into the country in the 1960s and early 1970s that demanded mostly unskilled labour, and eventually the population acquired the skills required to engage at the top end of the labour market.

In the case of Maldives, the local workforce has become less attractive or not attractive at all for skilled employment, owing mainly to the lack of educational attainment, which is not sufficient to acquire the required skills. Most Maldivians have completed only primary education, and this is a direct result of the under-developed education sector in Maldives that has long been suffering from rigid human and physical capital constraints. Human capital issues, which mostly prevail in schools located in atolls, have been reduced over time because of the liberal policies of the economy concerning the expatriate workforce. In fact, almost 79 per cent of teachers for secondary education in the atolls are expatriates (ADB 2001). This has increased accessibility to education for thousands of Maldivians, particularly those living in the atolls, and thereby might have helped them to become involved in income-earning activities created by trade liberalisation. However, physical capital constraints still remain a critical issue in the education sector.

Besides, the main reason for Maldivians not to engage in many unskilled job opportunities is the prevailing low wages in the market. This is mainly due to the suppression of wage rates and the acceptance of low wages by the expatriate workforce which flowed into the country during the post-liberalisation era. The wage rates that expatriate workers from Bangladesh and Sri Lanka receive are as low as US$ 80 per month, which is lower than the minimum wage rate expected by Maldivians (ADB 2001). In addition, the pressure to increase productivity levels to compete with the expatriate workforce regardless of the low wage rate offered has further made employment opportunities unattractive for Maldivians (ADB 2001). On top of that, the rise in prosperity of households due to economic developments over the years after liberalisation has reduced pressure from their families on young members to take any available job. This has resulted in voluntary unemployment in the country and has caused the unemployment levels to increase from 0.8 per cent in 1990 to 14 per cent in 2006.[7]

Changes in the structure of the economy resulting from trade liberalisation have also resulted in job losses in certain sectors. There has been a major occupational shift in Maldives during the post-liberalisation era, which has adversely affected female employment in the country. The female employment participation rate in 1978 was 60 per cent, one of the highest in the region at that time. The value dropped drastically to 21 per cent in 1995, one of the lowest levels in the world (ADB 2001). The major reason for this decline is the loss of employment opportunities for the female workforce in the fishing industry. In the 1970s, many women employed in the industry were engaged in drying fish, which was the main type of fish export from Maldives in the pre-liberalised era. However, with the diversification of the industry in the post-liberalisation era, the relative importance of dried fish declined, and therefore, the demand for women's services was significantly reduced. As a result, most of the women in the atolls who were previously employed became unemployed. No other suitable employment opportunities were created in the atolls in the post-liberalisation era. Furthermore, local handicraft production mainly carried out by women declined, because of the lack of competitiveness relative to cheap imports, particularly from China. New employment opportunities that opened up were confined to Malé and were not attractive for many women due to lack of skills, remoteness and cultural barriers. In fact, currently the Maldivians are far more likely to be poor if the households are headed by a female (ADB 2007).

Transmission of border prices

As has been noted in previous studies, the poor can benefit from trade liberalisation through price reductions. This is true in the case of the capital, Malé, where the prices of many consumer goods and durables, particularly imported goods, are lower than the prices in the atolls (MPND 2008). However, reduction in prices of both goods and services has not effectively taken place in the atolls. Disparities in prices between the capital and the outer islands largely reflect the disparities in infrastructure development. Even though many development projects, particularly in terms of infrastructure development, have been continuously carried out by both the government and multinational donor agencies, most of them have been confined to Malé. For instance, Malé has been largely advantaged by the presence of the international airport and the sea port. Unlike other developing nations in the region, such as India and Sri Lanka, which have more homogenous lands, equal distribution of infrastructure development throughout Maldives has proven more difficult through geographical disparities. The geography of Maldives is challenging, even by the standards of small archipelagic states (ADB 2007). The total population of Maldives is small and dispersed over 200 islands, which are distant and remote from each other, making connectivity complex and expensive. The fragmented geographical and population distribution has caused diseconomies of scale and has made transport of services and commodities highly expensive. For instance, the average construction cost of a primary school on an atoll is five times higher than the cost of a comparable school in Sri Lanka; and the cost of immunising a child is five times higher than the average of all developing countries, largely because of the transport costs of construction materials and of vaccines respectively (ADB 2001). Therefore, direct benefits of trade liberalisation, such as price reductions and access to better quality commodities, have been limited or have not taken place in the atolls.

Disadvantaged access to basic infrastructure and social services (education, health care services, and water and sanitation) and the limited employment opportunities in the rural atolls are clear evidence of poverty and vulnerability in these areas and have fuelled migration to Malé, where conditions are much better (ADB 2001). This suggests that the benefits of trade liberalisation are effectively enjoyed by the inhabitants of Malé but not by the people in outer islands. Indeed, the reduction in poverty in Malé in recent years has largely contributed to improvements in poverty reduction at the aggregate level while causing widening income inequalities.

Vulnerability

Maldives has one of the most open economies in the region, with a trade–GDP ratio (2005–7) of 192.0. This is higher than many of the archipelagic states such as Fiji (112.9), Samoa (92.8), the Solomon Islands (147.5) and Vanuatu (99.0).[8] High dependence on trade in goods and services has exposed the Maldivian economy to external shocks through changes in production and consumption, fluctuation in prices and thereby impacts on macroeconomic stability. Therefore, though Maldives has enjoyed a reduction in poverty over time, it continues to be highly vulnerable. Given that the poor are less cushioned than the rich in terms of savings and assets to absorb the shocks, vulnerability has more severe and faster impacts on the poor than on the rich.

Maldives is highly dependent on imports for its consumption needs, with a significant share being spent on food imports. Like many of the archipelagic states, such as Samoa, Vanuatu, Tonga and the Solomon Islands, Maldives is totally import-dependent on staples such as wheat flour and rice (Sharma 2006). Lack of arable lands in the country can be considered the main reason for Maldives to be in such a disadvantaged position. These land constraints suggest that the country has very little opportunities to increase its food supply other than relying on imports. Given its high import dependence on staple foods, domestic financial constraints or any destruction in international food supply would mean an enormous pressure on the economy, making the poor more vulnerable than the rich.

Another factor which makes the country highly vulnerable to external shocks is its heavy reliance on the narrow export base for exchange earnings. Thus, the country is left with only a few options for survival, particularly in a recession. The economy is highly susceptible to any changes in the tourism industry, the main source of foreign exchange accounting for nearly 60 per cent of the total. For instance, the entire industry and the economy at large was adversely affected by the European recession and the Gulf War in the early 1990s, and again by the 9/11 attack in 2001. In both situations tourist arrivals declined sharply, reducing government revenue and putting strong pressure on balance of payment positions. The fisheries sector, which was the second largest foreign exchange earner at that time, was also badly affected by the recession in Europe because of the reduction in world tuna prices. The production supply of the fisheries sector also suffers large fluctuations with adverse weather conditions, and this has occasionally led to short supply for the export sector, which results in reductions in foreign exchange earnings. The most recent evidence for such vulnerability is the reduction in fish catch volume by 38 per cent in 2007 compared to the previous year, due to bad weather conditions that prevailed throughout the year (MMA 2007). This ultimately caused a 20 per cent reduction in foreign exchange earnings from marine exports in 2007 compared to 2006.

The export base of the country has slightly strengthened and vulnerability has marginally reduced in recent years due to the emergence of the re-export sector, which mainly consisted of jet fuel. This is a commendable development in the economy in recent years. However, demand for jet fuel depends totally on the international transport industry, and therefore over-reliance on the industry may further increase the vulnerability of the country. The price and supply of oil has also been volatile throughout the past few decades. One of the best success stories of island economies largely benefiting from re-exports of jet fuel is Singapore. However, Singapore's steady development was triggered by a diversified export base. Therefore, Maldives would possibly benefit from this trade if it diversifies the economy further.

High reliance on the expatriate workforce is another factor that makes the economy of Maldives vulnerable to external fluctuations. In 2005, expatriates accounted for 46 per cent of the total employment compared to less than 2 per cent in 1985.[9] They are employed at both the top and bottom ends of the labour market, and a large number of key professions in the economy have been occupied by expatriates. Many of them have migrated from neighbouring countries in the region mainly through lack of better employment opportunities in their home countries. The vulnerability arises from the fact that expatriates are highly sensitive to labour market fluctuations in both their home countries and the other countries in the region. There is a high tendency for them to return to their home countries or to a third country when the relative economic conditions in such countries improve over time. Such improvements in other countries may eventually leave Maldives with an inexperienced workforce, making the economy more vulnerable in the long run. More importantly, outflow of the expatriate work force would be aggravated in a situation of a domestic instability such as an economic recession or political turmoil.

Summary and conclusion

The Republic of Maldives initiated its trade liberalisation programme in 1989 initially by removing some of the import quotas and allowing private sector involvement in some of the export businesses. Investment regulations in Maldives were also relaxed in subsequent years with the intention of attracting FDI into the country. As a result of the continuous reforms, Maldives currently has one of the most open economies in the region, with a high trade–GDP ratio. After the opening up of the economy, Maldives experienced an accelerated growth in exports, imports and GDP, and a significant reduction in poverty. In the 1970s, Maldives was the poorest country in South Asia. Three and a half decades later, its per capita GDP and social indicators rank it at the top of the region. Although poverty levels have decreased rapidly, inequality in the country has increased over time.

Analysis of the trade–poverty nexus in Maldives reveals that trade has had a direct positive impact on poverty through employment. Trade has created a large number of employment opportunities in Maldives, particularly in Malé. Most of the poor have migrated from rural atolls to the capital city to take part in such employment opportunities. These migrants have been able to increase overall household income. Nevertheless, many of the jobs which were mainly available for women in the pre-liberalised era have disappeared after liberalisation. As a result, currently the Maldivians are far more likely to be poor if the households are headed by a female. Besides, the present analysis suggests that the geographical disparity in the country has made connectivity between Malé and the atolls complex and highly expensive. As a result, the poor in Maldives have not significantly benefited from trade through reductions in border prices. Prices of many of the consumer goods in the atolls are generally higher than in Malé, mainly because of the high transport cost between Malé and the atolls. Furthermore, this analysis has found evidence to suggest that despite rapid growth in trade and GDP after liberalisation, the country remains vulnerable to external shocks, largely because of its narrow export base and high import dependence on staple food, and its expatriate workforce for domestic economic activities.

Notes

1 Values as at 2005.
2 A small island is defined as one with a total population below 1.5 million (Commonwealth Secretariat 1997).
3 Based on WTO Trade Policy Reviews of 2003 and 2009 (WTO 2003, 2009).
4 It expressed concern prior to the implementation of the Uruguay Round Agreements, predicting that this would heighten the level of inequality between the developed and LDCs, and has called for substantial reduction of tariffs, expressing concern that multilateral negotiations should move towards new areas like investment, competition, environment and labour standards, supported initiatives to stop LDC marginalisation, etc.
5 The first national socio-economic assessment, Vulnerability and Poverty Assessment (VPA-1), was carried out in 1997.
6 ADB, country profiles, various years.
7 The 1990 figure is from Ghosh and Siddique (2000); the 2006 figure is from MMA (2007).
8 WTO country profile: www.wto.org (accessed 3 February 2011).
9 Calculated from MMA (2007) and '25 Years of Statistics: Maldives', available at: www.planning.gov.mv/publications/25yearsstats/default.htm (accessed 3 February 2011).

7 Nepal

Yuba Raj Khatiwada

As a landlocked country, Nepal has initiated economic liberalisation, openness and outward orientation since the mid-1980s through the elimination of import licences and quotas, tariff reduction and rationalisation, the introduction of full convertibility of the rupee for current account transactions, and moving towards capital account convertibility. Nepal has also entered into a liberal global trading regime through membership of the WTO, SAFTA and BIMSTEC. This has significantly opened up the Nepalese economy and deepened integration with the global economy, but it has also raised vulnerability and risks to sustained growth, livelihood and poverty reduction.

This chapter provides an overview and empirical analysis of the linkages between trade liberalisation and poverty reduction in Nepal with the use of simple statistical tools and analysis of quantitative information.[1] Section 2 of the chapter gives an overview of the current trade policy framework of the country and key developments/changes in the trade policy over the past few decades. Section 3 analyses the trends in economic growth, poverty and inequality over the past few decades. Section 4 analyses the link between trade liberalisation and poverty based on the indirect two-stage relationship between trade and growth and growth and poverty, or direct impacts on the welfare of the poor. Section 5 summarises the key findings of the study and draws policy implications for poverty reduction through trade policy reforms.

Trade liberalisation in Nepal: an overview

The history of Nepal's trade regimes has three distinctive episodes. There was a free trade regime in 1923–56 in Nepal and it moved towards a protectionist trade regime from 1956, similar to other South Asian countries. The period of 1956–85 was a protectionist trade regime, and it started its liberalisation process in 1985. It implemented a series of trade and market-oriented reforms in the 1990s, partly related to the process of Nepal's World Trade Organisation (WTO) membership. It has removed most of the QRs and licensing requirements during the trade liberalisation process over the last fifteen years or so. Nepal's current simple average of tariff is around 12.6 per cent and the import-weighted tariff average is around 14.4 per cent. Because of Nepal's landlocked nature and its special relationship with India, Nepal's reform process was constrained and it has adopted a gradual liberalisation process. Nepal became a member of the WTO in 2004, as the first Least Developed Country (LDC) to join the WTO since its inception on 1 January 1995. This has opened up trade opportunities for Nepal as a member of the multilateral trading system.

Nepal's meaningful international trade began in the 1960s, but it accelerated with the trade liberalisation process only from the 1980s, when exports and imports grew on average by 19 per cent and 18 per cent respectively. In the 1990s, the external sector remained robust in general – exports grew on average by 28 per cent per annum whereas imports also grew by 20 per cent. After 2000, imports witnessed compression mainly because of low economic growth, depreciation of the rupee, and decline in demand for third-country goods for re-export purposes.

In addition to the unilateral trade liberalisation process, Nepal has also become a member of a number of bilateral and multilateral trading agreements. It shares a very open, porous, and long (1800 km) border with India, and has almost free flow of goods and services across the border. This is facilitated by free and unlimited convertibility of the Nepalese rupee against Indian currency. The trade treaty with India allows duty-free market access to primary goods and selected manufacturing goods to the Indian market. Imports from India are also subject to low tariff. Border trade with Tibet (China) is also liberal – people of both Nepal and Tibet living within 30 kilometres of the border can do free barter trade as per the Trade Treaty of 1968.

Nepal is a founder member of the South Asian Association for Regional Cooperation (SAARC). Under this, South Asia Free Trade Area (SAFTA) was launched from January 2006. Nepal, as an LDC, will get three years' grace period for its implementation.

Nepal has joined another regional group – BIMSTEC (Bay of Bengal Initiative for Multi-sectoral Technical and Economic Cooperation). The BIMSTEC FTA was established with the objective of strengthening and enhancing economic, trade and investment cooperation, and progressively liberalising and promoting trade in goods and services, among others. With the signing of the framework agreement, Nepal has agreed to enter into negotiations for eliminating the tariffs and non-tariff barriers in substantially all goods with a provision of maintaining a negative list and dual tracks ('fast' and 'normal') for liberalisation.

Nepal faces problems in its trade with India and the rest of the world, such as: (1) very stringent rules of origin (RoO); value-added requirements; and trade through specified trading corporations imposed by India after the 2002 Trade Treaty; (2) quarantine procedures for all agro products which are time-consuming, expensive and very bureaucratic (in particular, leaf tea, ginger, cardamom, broom-grass, green vegetables, etc., exported to India face such problems); (3) export barriers in terms of entry points, trade routes and mode of transport; (4) standards often far higher than those required by the standard-setting institutions, like the Codex Alimentarious Commission and the

European Union (EU); and (5) the difficulty of fulfilling such criteria given its existing technical, human and financial capabilities and resources. Nepal is currently facing many such problems and not benefiting from the Special and Differential Treatment provisioned in the global trade rules under the WTO.

At present, Nepal has a relatively open economy with almost free trade with India and a very liberal trade regime with the rest of the world. There are no quantitative restrictions or licensing requirements for trade and no foreign exchange restrictions on current account payment, as the country has entered Article VIII of the IMF Charter. Tariff rates have been substantially reduced over the last decade or so; and although the unweighted average import tariff rate is about 15 per cent, the applied tariff for most goods is around 10 per cent.[2]

Expansion of both exports and imports increased the trade–GDP ratio from a little over 20 per cent in the mid-1980s to more than 40 per cent in the year 2000. But the share declined to 35 per cent in 2007. The recent drop in the trade–GDP ratio is attributed to stagnating exports. Including services, the trade–GDP ratio which stood at about 50 per cent throughout the 1990s compared with less than 30 per cent in the 1970s, slipped down to about 45 per cent by 2007 thanks to a decline in service exports along with stagnating merchandise exports.

There has been a notable change in the structure of trade over the last two and a half decades. Share of primary goods exports declined from nearly 70 per cent in 1980 to 16 per cent in 2000; however, it rose to 22 per cent in 2007. Share of manufacturing goods exports, which increased from 30 per cent in 1980 to 85 per cent in 1995, came down to 76 per cent in 2007.

Woollen carpets and ready-made garments have dominated Nepal's exports for many years. From less than 6 per cent in 1980, their share in total exports rose to more than 70 per cent in most of the 1990s. In recent years, their shares have come down significantly. The share of woollen carpets in total exports declined from 45.0 per cent in 1990 to less than 10.0 per cent by 2007.[3] The share of ready-made garments, which was 27 per cent in 1990, declined to less than 9 per cent by 2007.

The structure of imports, however, hardly changed during these decades. Imports of primary goods hovered around 16–20 per cent of total imports, whereas the share of capital goods stood at around 29–32 per cent. The share of manufactured goods ranged between 38 and 47 per cent throughout the 1980s and 1990s, but declined to about 31 per cent in recent years.[4] The share of capital goods in total imports did not improve much over the period of 25 years – it has hovered around 30 per cent throughout the last three decades. If manufacturing growth had been rapid, a marked increase in imports of capital goods would have been evident.

Destination-wise, Nepal's trade is re-concentrating towards India. In the past decade, the share of India in Nepal's trade has more than doubled; it reached about 68 per cent of the trade in 2007 as against 28 per cent in 1995. Nepal's trade vulnerability has increased with lack of export diversification and trade re-concentration with India.

Economic growth, poverty and inequality

Growth and poverty: trends and their distribution

Nepal is historically a moderate growth performance country, with GDP growing, on average, by about 5 per cent per annum throughout the 1980s and 1990s and by about 4 per cent thereafter. The growth during these decades was higher than that in the 1970s (2.1 per cent on average) but the faster pace of trade and industrial liberalisation since the mid-1980s and particularly from the early 1990s did not have a major shift in the growth trend. The growth rate decelerated significantly after the 1990s due to the intensifying conflict in the country and adverse shocks faced on the external front.[5]

Nepal is one of the few countries where poverty fell significantly even with low economic growth. During the last decade, as GDP growth was on average only 4.2 per cent against a population growth of 2.2 per cent, per capita income growth remained at only 2 per cent. Despite such a low per capita income growth, there was significant progress in the reduction of absolute poverty. The proportion of the population below the poverty line came down to 31 per cent in 2004 from 42 per cent in 1996, implying a decline of 11 percentage points in eight years. This implies growth (per capita income) elasticity of poverty at (-)0.7. The country's per capita income level (about US$ 380 in 2007) is now the lowest in South Asia.

The reduction in poverty during 1996–2004[6] was not even across regions, sex and social groups. The decline was slower (from 43 to 34 per cent) in rural areas and faster (from 22 per cent to 10 per cent) in the urban areas. Some social and religious groups and geographic regions remained at a high intensity of poverty – 45 per cent of the Dalits, 44 per cent of the hill Janajatis, and 41 per cent of the Muslim people were still absolutely poor. Geographically also, poverty increased in some regions (rural eastern hills) even though there has been a significant reduction in poverty on average.

Poverty also has gender, spatial and occupational dimensions along with ethnic ones. While women are poorer than men, most households located in the areas not connected by roads, telecommunications and electricity, along with low service delivery in education, health services and drinking water, are absolutely poor. Among the poor, 95 per cent live in rural areas, 67 per cent are self-employed in agriculture, 71 per cent are illiterate, 54 per cent have a family size of seven or more, and 51 per cent hold less than one hectare of land. Most of such households are hard-to-reach poor; and thus additional efforts are needed to make trade help their poverty reduction.

Income inequality

From a poverty reduction perspective, a decline in inequality is important in many ways: (1) it will reduce poverty faster for a given level of income; (2) it will accelerate the poverty-reducing impact of economic growth; and (3) it may contribute to a larger rate of economic growth in the long term. Recent Asian trends show widening income inequality, and Nepal is now among the countries with the highest income inequality. The Gini coefficient of income distribution increased to 41.4 in 2004 from 34.2 in 1996. The share of the poorest consumption quintile in total consumption declined to 6.2 per cent in 2004 from 7.6 per cent in 1996 (CBS 2004). Similarly, while the share of the poorest income quintile in total income remained at 5.3 per cent in 2004, as in 1996, the income share of the richest income quintile increased from 50.3 per cent in 1996 to 53.4 per cent in 2004.

Decomposition of poverty reduction into: (1) economic growth and (2) income distribution components during 1996–2004 shows that growth alone contributed to a 24.1 per cent decline in poverty, whereas redistribution of income exacerbated poverty by 13.2 per cent, resulting in a net decline in poverty of about 11 percentage points from the level of 1996. Had income distribution remained neutral, the decline in poverty would have been more than 24 percentage points (CBS 2005).

There are a number of other indicators which speak of the widening of income inequality in the recent decade. The percentage of total farm holdings that operate less than 0.5 hectares of land has increased from 40.1 per cent in 1996 to 44.8 per cent in 2004 (Table 7.1). Moreover, an increasing proportion of agricultural households are becoming landless, as only rented-in land holdings increased from 4.8 per cent in 1996 to 7.3 per cent in 2004. Besides this, the external (trade and tourism) and domestic (conflict) shocks appear to have squeezed trading activities, with households engaged in trading enterprises reduced from 52 per cent of the households in 1996 to less than 32 per cent in 2004.

Table 7.1 Livelihood and inequality indicators (comparison of two living standard surveys)

Activities	1995/6	2003/4
Agricultural household (HH) with land (% of total HHs)	83.1	77.5
Average size of land (ha.)	1.1	0.8
HH operating <0.5 ha. (% of total olding)	40.1	44.8
Only rented in land (% of total HHs)	4.8	7.3
Consumption: share of poorest 20%	7.6	6.2
Consumption: share of richest 20%	44.9	53.3
Sample HHs with enterprises (% of total HHs)	24.2	28.3
HHs with trading enterprises (% of total HHs)	52.1	31.7
HHs with service enterprises (% of total HHs)	14.3	29.2
HHs receiving remittances (% of total HHs)	23.4	31.9
Share of remittance in HH income (%)	26.6	35.4

Source: CBS (1997, 2004).

The role of remittance in poverty reduction

Workers' remittance has been a critical factor not only for poverty reduction but also in maintaining external sector balance and building foreign currency reserves despite the weak merchandise exports performance of Nepal. After agriculture, foreign labour has been the second largest area for absorbing the country's labour force – migrant workers now constitute nearly 2 million, about 20 per cent of the labour force. Nepal now gets its largest amount of foreign currency from migrant workers than from any other source – nearly US$ 2 billion (Rs 123 billion) in 2007. In the recent decade (1996–2007) remittances have grown by more than 12 per cent per annum[7] and accounted for about 16–17 per cent of GDP in the recent years (Table 7.2).[8]

The proportion of households getting remittances increased from 23 per cent in 1996 to 32 per cent in 2004, and the amount of remittance quadrupled during 1995–2007. In 2004, remittances accounted for on average 35 per cent of the income of the households receiving any remittance. Income from external work and open trade regimes together has helped consumption poverty to improve and has brought many people above the poverty line. This explains how poverty could be reduced in Nepal amid conflict and a low growth rate.

Overall, the 11 percentage point decline in absolute poverty during 1996–2004 amid a per capita GDP growth rate of 2 per cent and growing income inequality is partly explained by remittances. But this alone cannot explain all the achievements made in poverty reduction. Underlying growth in the informal sectors of the economy, which are not properly covered by the national accounting system, and the role of micro-finance institutions, local bodies and non-government organisations are to be perceived as being equally important in this regard.

Table 7.2 Remittance inflows from migrant workers

Remittance amount (Rs million)						*Growth rates (%)*	
Items/year	1990	1995	2000	2005	2007	1996–04	2006–07**
Workers' service income	2,552	26,430	9,919	8,614	9,617.2	−8.3	5.7
Workers' remittance	1,748	5,064	36,818	65,416	100,145	30.6	23.7
Gurkha army pension			5,941	12,496	12,937	18.4*	1.7
Total remittance inflow	4,300	31,494	52,678	86,526	122,699	10.3	19.1
As % of GDP		4.8	14.4	13.9	16.4	17.1	
Poverty		42.0		30.8		−11.0	
Δ % poverty / Δ % remittance						−0.133	

Source: *Quarterly Economic Bulletin* (various issues), Nepal Rastra Bank.
Note: * Average of 2001–5 only; ** compound growth rate.

Trade–poverty links: qualitative assessment

Economies with trade openness have been able to enhance growth and reduce poverty faster than others. Evidence shows that acceleration of economic growth has taken place in countries with sound macroeconomic policies and trade openness; and poverty has been better addressed in high growth conditions (UNDP 2004a, 2004b). It is substantiated by high and sustained economic growth in South East Asian countries, China and, of late, in Vietnam, India and Bangladesh, resulting in marked reductions in poverty.

The link between trade liberalisation and poverty in the country can be analysed through: (a) the indirect two-stage relationship between trade and growth and growth and poverty, and (b) direct impacts on the welfare of the poor through: (1) price effects on consumer and producer goods; (2) effects on profits, wages and employment; (3) government revenue and expenditure; and (4) shocks, risks and vulnerability.

Effects of trade liberalisation on poverty through economic growth

Trade would promote growth through the generation of additional demand for goods and services, and poverty would be reduced if more employment were created in the process of output growth. As such, economic growth would help rural poverty reduction only if there were promotion of local resource-intensive or labour-intensive industries which use simple and cheap technology (UNESCAP 2001).

Despite all the initiatives towards trade liberalisation, Nepal's exports comprise less than 10 per cent of GDP, and thus the indirect impact of exports on poverty through the growth process appears to be low. However, as there has been a marked reduction in poverty during the last decade, the welfare gain from cheaper imports of consumer goods from both India and China cannot be ruled out.

Nepal's expansion of trade is somehow related to faster economic growth. During 1986–95, when both exports and imports accelerated, the average GDP growth also reached 5 per cent (Table 7.3). The trade elasticity of growth stood at about 0.2 during this period. But this was the period when poverty did not buzz to come down. There was no reduction in poverty during 1986–95, as reflected in the growth elasticity of poverty at only 0.1.

There are a few points worth noting in this trade–growth–poverty relationship. First, there is a large informal component in trade, particularly with India; it is not accounted for by the official trade statistics and thus the full impact of trade on growth cannot be observed. Second, the large inflow of remittances is not reflected in GDP; thus, growth measured by GDP underestimates the demand side of the national accounts, and this, followed by the underestimation of imports (and also domestic production to some extent) in the supply side, prevents a full reflection of trade, growth and poverty relationship.

Table 7.3 Relationship between trade, GDP growth and poverty reduction

Annual average growth rates (%)	1976–85	1986–95	1996–2005
Exports	15.4	23.0	3.7
Imports	16.0	23.7	4.4
GDP	3.7	4.9	4.2
Agriculture	2.0	2.8	3.5
Non-agriculture	6.2	6.8	4.7
Change in poverty	0.79	−0.05	−1.40
Rural	0.80	−0.06	−1.13
Urban	0.28	0.28	−1.50
Export elasticity of growth	0.24	0.21	1.14
Import elasticity of growth	0.23	0.21	0.96
Growth elasticity of poverty	0.21	−0.01	−0.33

Sources: *Economic Survey*, MOF (various issues); *Quarterly Economic Bulletin*, Nepal Rastra Bank (various issues); CBS (2005).

Direct implications of trade liberalisation on poverty

Based on the theoretical underpinning of the impact of trade liberalisation on poverty (Winters *et al.* 2004), the following issues, among others, have to be critically examined in order to assess the impact of trade reform on poverty: (1) price effects of trade liberalisation; (2) changes in the production pattern as well as prices of goods consumed and produced by the poor; (3) relationships between trade and employment; (4) relationships between trade and inequality; (5) the macroeconomic impact of trade liberalisation, including fiscal and balance of payments constraints on poverty reduction; and (6) the structural shift in production technology and social exclusion of poorer producers from livelihoods. The subsequent sections look at the effects of price and production, employment and fiscal and macroeconomic management and their poverty implications.

Price effects

Trade liberalisation in Nepal is associated with low inflation, but it is not necessarily a causal relationship. The prices of non-trade goods have little to do with trade liberalisation, except through the income effect. But prices of tradable goods have a direct bearing on trade liberalisation. Nepal observed single-digit inflation during the 1990s and at present, mainly because of tighter macro policies and better supply conditions, including imports of very cheap manufactured goods from China and imports of rice from India at a consistently low price for several years. The inflation rate, which hovered around 10 per cent during the 1980s and 1990s, would have fallen much lower had the rupee not depreciated by about 5 per cent per year during the period of trade liberalisation. The inflationary situation has further improved (to less than 5 per cent) in recent years as the rupee appreciated from 2004 onwards and food prices remained low until 2006.

Nepal imports inflation, mainly from India, in terms of import prices. Besides this, flows of daily consumption goods across the border act to equalise cross-border prices. As tradable goods account for more than 50 per cent of the consumption basket used to calculate the consumer price index, prices prevailing across the border have a significant bearing on Nepalese prices.

Price level is one channel through which trade and openness affect poverty. Global experience shows that countries that have opted for a more open and liberal trading regime have attained lower inflation than others. In Nepal also, the rate of inflation came down along with opening the trade regime. An empirical analysis of inflation with trade openness shows a significant negative relationship – a one percentage point rise in trade openness (measured by trade–GDP ratio) reduces price by 0.32 per cent.[9] Thus, overall, there have been some positive implications of trade liberalisation on the prices front, whereas little impact is observed in the real sectors of the economy.[10]

The expansion of trade with Tibet (China) and the import of cheap Chinese products have helped to keep the prices of non-food items low. As such, prices of clothing, footwear and recreational items remained low (and consumption high) during the last decade because of such cheap imports from China.

Household income and employment effects

Given the high incidence of rural poverty in Nepal, any analysis of the effects of trade liberalisation on poverty must focus on income generation and employment creation for the rural people, particularly in agricultural and small and medium enterprises. During 1996–2004, as the living standard surveys show, nominal per capita household income increased by an average of 9 per cent per annum, whereas nominal per capita consumption went up by 11 per cent (Table 7.4). There was not much improvement in wage and non-wage employment in agriculture and non-agriculture. There was an 8 per cent per annum rise in nominal wage during 1996–2004 which was not sufficient to increase the share of the low income group in total income. That the share of the lowest income (consumption) quintile in total income (consumption) deteriorated during 1996–2004 while that of the highest income (consumption) quintile increased significantly implies that the income so generated was more unequally distributed.

Most of the changes in income and employment mentioned here accrue to all the economic policies and programmes, including those related to trade. For trade-specific impacts, there is a need to analyse this impact through major export items such as woollen carpets, ready-made garments, pashminas, vegetable ghee, thread and yarn, textiles, etc. The declining share of most

Table 7.4 Household income, consumption and employment

Indicators		1995/96	2003/04	Average growth
Per capita income (Rs)	Poorest 20%	2,020	4,003	8.9
Richest 20%		19,325	40,486	9.7
Share in total income	Poorest 20%	5.3	5.3	0.0
	Richest 20%	50.3	53.4	0.8
Per capita consumption (Rs)	Poorest 20%	2,571	4,913	8.4
	Richest 20%	15,243	42,236	13.6
Share in total consumption	Poorest 20%	7.6	6.2	−2.5
	Richest 20%	44.9	53.3	2.2
Sources of income (%)	Farm income	61.0	48.0	−3.0
	Non-farm income	22.0	28.0	3.1
	Others	16.0	24.0	5.2
	o/w: Remittance	6.0	11.0	7.9
Wage employment (in %)		21.7	17.0	−3.0
	Agriculture	12.2	6.8	−7.0
	Non-agriculture	9.5	10.2	0.9
Non-wage (self-)employment (in %)		78.4	73.6	−0.8
	Agriculture	70.7	64.3	−1.2
	Non-agriculture	7.7	9.3	2.4
Unemployment (%)		4.9	3.8	−3.1
Underemployment (working <40hrs/week) (%)		47.1	47.8	0.2

Source: NLSS I (CBS 1996) and NLSS II (CBS 2004).

labour-intensive exports like carpets, garments and pashminas in recent years implies a squeeze in the job opportunities in these sectors. Immediate transition of labour force from this to any another industry has been difficult. Thus the poverty implications of the shrinking garment industry have been very high and damaging to the labour market.[11] The dismal performance of these items in recent years speaks of the short-lived effect of trade liberalisation on exports. Of the nearly 300,000 workers employed in carpets, garments and pashminas, two-thirds have lost their jobs with the decline in exports.[12]

In recent years there has been a growth of exports of some manufacturing products to India which have low value-added and low labour intensity. This has a very limited contribution to poverty reduction for a number of reasons, such as weak backward linkage of these products to the rural economy, little job creation and use of migrant workers, and little value-added. Value-added in key exports like vegetable ghee, plastic products and iron and steel is just 25 per cent, 38 per cent and 15 per cent respectively (CBS 2003).[13] The country has made progress in the export of some agro produce, such as tea, coffee, vegetable seeds, off-season vegetables, herbs, non-timber products and dairy products. But so far these do not figure significantly in major trade items and employment figures.

Wage implications

In Nepal, underemployment is a major problem with only 52 per cent of workers working for more than 40 hours a week (CBS 2004). More than 90 per cent of the labour market is informal, and the process of informalisation is growing owing to issues related to trade unionism and rigidity of the labour laws. Despite the high underemployment situation, there has been some improvement in wage rates in recent years. Most of this rise has come about because of the out-migration of the young population for work. Also, the strong growth performance of the Indian economy and subsequent rise in wage rates in India has discouraged Indian workers to come to Nepal for informal-sector jobs, and the trend has now reversed with Nepalese labour going to India as agricultural workers.

In nominal terms, the wages of all types of workers have gone up during the last two decades. The rise was higher during the 1990s. The differential wage rates for male and female workers continued during this period but the trend was towards convergence in the formal sector, a good sign of improving wage discrimination. However, the reverse was true for the informal sector. The average nominal wage growth rate for agricultural workers stood at 10.2 per cent in the 1990s and 5.1 per cent during 2001–5. Wages in other sectors moved up a bit faster during this period. Compared to nominal wages, there has been a marginal rise in real wage rates during the last decade or so. The real wage of carpenters, masons and agricultural workers went up during 1981–2005 by less than 2 per cent. The only sector where real wages went up by more than 2 per cent was the industrial sector (Table 7.5).

Nevertheless, the process of trade and investment liberalisation has had the following effects in the Nepalese labour market. First, the entry of multinational companies has had little employment effect as employment intensity of foreign capital is observed as very low.[14] Second, the so-called technological shift has also made the unskilled labour force redundant and encouraged the use of foreign labour. Third, in the process of privatisation as a means to enhance foreign investment, many workers were laid off and a number of instances of labour unrest have surfaced. Fourth, the multinational

Table 7.5 Trend of real wage rates by types of employment (average growth in %)

	1981–90	*1991–00*	*2001–5*	*1981–05*
Carpenter: Skilled	2.3	1.9	0.39	1.78
Semi-skilled	1.9	1.0	0.25	1.21
Mason: Skilled	2.3	1.7	0.28	1.63
Semi-skilled	2.1	0.6	0.46	1.17
Ind. labour: Skilled	−1.9	7.7	1.05	2.51
Unskilled	−0.9	4.6	3.46	2.17
Agri. labour: Male	2.9	0.5	1.44	1.65
Female	4.7	−2.5	4.84	1.81

Source: Nepal Rastra Bank.

companies are hiring labour on the basis of contracts, sub-contracts, daily wages or on a temporary basis at low wages, employing foreign labour, and undertaking production itself on a contract basis. It all adds to the informalisation of formal sector employment and loss of labour bargaining power.

Trade liberalisation and agriculture

Trade liberalisation is supposed to promote and commercialise agriculture by expanding domestic agriculture and creating an export market for the produce, smoothing the supply of inputs and bringing excess labour from the agricultural to the non-agricultural sector. Nepal, however, has not yet experienced much of this effect, as agriculture even in the post-reform period (1990–2007) continues to grow slowly, with little change in its structure. It grew by less than 4 per cent per annum, on average, during 1991–2007 compared with 5 per cent during 1981–90.

Trade liberalisation has not transferred technology to agriculture, as evidenced by the limited use of modern agricultural inputs and mechanisation technology. The agricultural system in Nepal still depends on indigenous technology. Most farmers use conventional agricultural tools, and the mechanisation of agriculture is at a very early stage. Only 0.6 per cent of the farmers in Nepal own tractors or power tillers, 0.9 per cent use threshers and 2.7 per cent own pumping equipment (CBS 2004).

Most of the agricultural produce in Nepal is non-marketed. Only half of Nepali agricultural households sell any agricultural produce in the market, compared to nearly all households in Bangladesh selling some of their produce (Sharma 2006). Such low levels of commercialisation and productivity of agriculture stand in sharp contrast with the country's significant potential, arising from its inherently favourable agro-climatic conditions and regional diversity.

Trade liberalisation affects the protection of agriculture through tariff reduction in agricultural produce in the process of creating a freer global or regional trading regime. In principle, Nepal's entry into the WTO, SAFTA and BIMSTEC calls for tariff reduction to a certain level. In practice, however, the requirement is minimum, as applied tariff rates are much lower than the binding rates. The unweighted average of the final bound level of tariff in agriculture products under the WTO is 42 per cent against the unweighted average applied tariff rate of 13.0 per cent.

Nepal withdrew price subsidy on chemical fertilisers, capital subsidy from shallow tube-wells, and interest subsidy to bank credit as an attempt to enhance input supplies by relieving traders from a subsidy-constrained supply system, rationalise public spending, and promote the private sector to participate in the agricultural inputs market. Overall, because of resource constraints, Nepal is not providing any trade and production distorting supports to the farmers. However, if the level of protection to agriculture following entry into the WTO is unlikely to change, the implication of IPR-related norms is likely to affect it.

Trade liberalisation is expected to put the agricultural product prices 'right' – normally higher than the suppressed level. High agricultural prices are, however, a double-edged sword which can cut both sides of the agricultural households. In a country where food sufficiency is reported by less than 40 per cent of the lowest consumption quintile of households and 60 per cent of the second lowest consumption quintile of households, and where food surplus is reported only by a little over 2 per cent, prices might adversely affect the food security situation of the households who have to buy food. As poverty is concentrated around landless and marginal farmers, the impact of trade on poverty reduction must be reflected in a better output and employment condition in agriculture.

Trade liberalisation and the manufacturing sector

Trade liberalisation can support the manufacturing sector by, among others, (1) reducing the tariff applied on raw materials and machinery; (2) encouraging foreign investment in manufacturing; (3) facilitating technology transfer; and (4) creating a competitive environment by the elimination of distorting measures like subsidies, transfers and differential tax rates. An expanded external market through trade liberalisation helps domestic and foreign investment in export-oriented industries. At the same time, trade liberalisation could reduce the degree of protection enjoyed by domestic industries, and therefore cause non-competitive domestic firms to close down.

Empirical analysis shows some positive effect of trade liberalisation on the manufacturing sector in Nepal. Regressing value-added in the manufacturing sector against value-added in the trade sector and openness, it is observed that each 1 per cent growth in value-added in the trade sector is associated with a 1.02 per cent rise in value-added in the manufacturing sector; and each one percentage point increase in trade openness results in the growth of manufacturing by 0.02 per cent.[15]

The poverty implications of manufacturing sector performance would partly depend on the growth of employment and wages in this sector. The census (CBS 1998, 2003) of organised manufacturing establishments shows a decline in the number of manufacturing establishments by 25 per cent during 1992–2002. The number of people engaged in manufacturing also declined by 14 per cent, and waged employees by 15 per cent. Output increased nearly threefold, but the wage bill less than doubled. During the same period, output per unit of input declined by 10 per cent and wages and salaries as a percentage of output declined by one third. Also, employment elasticity of manufacturing output declined from 3.1 in the 1980s to 1.5 in the 1990s. All this does not indicate an encouraging picture of the manufacturing sector when trade liberalisation develops momentum.

Foreign trade, industrial and foreign investment policies are interlinked. With liberal economic policy changes put in place, foreign direct investment went gone up – particularly in the fields of banking, hydro-power development and tourism. As a result, within the span of 15 years, the number of industries approved for joint venture investments increased almost tenfold. These industries under FDI are estimated to generate employment opportunities to about 94,000 people, nearly nine times the level of employment opportunities available to less than 11,000 people 15 years ago.

One of the major reasons behind FDI flows to Nepal is the unorganised labour market, which has an excess supply of labour willing to work at a wage which is not enough even to meet the poverty threshold level of consumption. Without plugging the loopholes for exploitative labour relation, the creation of job opportunities alone is not going to promote labour welfare. In a nutshell, no automatic positive linkage seems to have evolved between FDI and poverty in Nepal.

Fiscal implications of trade liberalisation and poverty

There are at least three channels of trade–poverty links through the fiscal sector: government revenue (through international trade tax and overall tax composition), public expenditure (through reallocation of resources); and public enterprise reforms (through price adjustments, privatisation, closure, etc.). Trade reform can affect government revenue, but the effects observed are less adverse than imagined. Even if tariff reduction leads to reduced revenue collection, there is no straightforward conclusion that the poor will suffer.[16] Public spending can protect the people adversely affected by trade liberalisation through resource reallocation, mainly as safety nets. Restructuring and privatisation of public enterprises in relation to trade reforms lead to closure, privatisation or liquidation of enterprises, resulting in loss of jobs or increased prices for services; but safety nets can be established to minimise the adverse effect on the poor.

Government revenue in Nepal, which had increased by about 17 per cent during the 1980s and 1990s, decelerated to less than 12 per cent during 2001–7. The slowdown in revenue growth in the later part of the 1990s and during 2001–7 was due to a lower contribution of tax revenue. In fact, tax revenue went up by an average of only 11.1 per cent during 1996–2000, lower than the growth rate of nominal GDP (11.8 per cent), reflecting a deterioration in the buoyancy of the tax system. During 2001–7, despite low revenue growth, the tax system became more buoyant – the growth of tax revenue (11.7 per cent) was higher than that of gross domestic product (7.0 per cent).

Despite several measures to widen the domestic tax base, international trade still accounts for nearly 45 per cent of total revenue and more than 55 per cent of tax revenue.[17] Any tariff reduction measures to be introduced in connection to bilateral, regional or multilateral trade agreements would have serious revenue implications: that is, revenue compensation measures have to come within the free trade negotiation agenda.

So far, the negative impact of tariff reduction in the process of trade liberalisation has been more than offset by the higher revenue base created by more imports, a wider income tax base, the introduction of VAT and its upward revision, and administrative measures to enhance tax compliance. But when it comes to the elimination of trade-related duties and charges, the reduction in some tariff lines as a commitment to the WTO and SAFTA and the saturation of the income tax base expansion, the revenue implications would be serious, and global and regional trade negotiations call for serious attention to revenue-compensating provisions.[18]

Trade liberalisation and macroeconomic indicators

Despite a widening trade deficit, Nepal's current account balance has remained positive because of service and transfer incomes, particularly from workers' remittances. The balance of payments position has remained comfortable throughout the last decade except for one year. This has led to a growing foreign exchange reserves position in the banking system with a capacity to cover more than ten months of imports of merchandise goods.

The strong external sector balance despite the huge trade deficit (to the extent of 18 per cent of GDP) has given the government a fiscal space to scale up public spending on pro-poor programmes and accommodate monetary policy to fiscal stimulus. The comfortable reserves have also provided a cushion for the import of essential consumption and capital goods needed for anti-poverty programmes. However, the huge trade deficit, unless offset by remittance inflow, will pose a huge challenge in the macroeconomic management and poverty reduction strategy of the country.

The strong reserves position has also helped to stabilise the exchange rate and thus avert any adverse consequences of exchange rate depreciation on prices and public spending.

Concluding remarks

Nepal has almost free trade with India and a very liberal trade regime with the rest of the world. Despite this, the country's export market is hindered by several structural and non-tariff trade barriers. Nepal is not benefiting from the Special and Differential Treatment provisions in the global trade rules under the WTO.

Empirical analysis shows some positive effects of trade liberalisation on the manufacturing sector in Nepal. However, agriculture continues to grow slowly, with little change in its structure. Trade liberalisation has not transferred technology to agriculture, as evidenced by the limited use of modern agricultural inputs and mechanisation technology.

Nepal is one of the few countries where poverty has fallen significantly even with low economic growth and low trade intensity. Workers' remittance has been the critical factor in poverty reduction. The growing income inequality amid a reduction in poverty in Nepal indicates that trade policies have to be made pro-poor.

Trade promotes the income and consumption of the poor if it is linked to their resources. But Nepal's export trade is not strongly linked to the domestic and particularly the rural resource base; thus, a restructuring of the trade sector is needed to make it work for meaningful poverty reduction. Trade has to be linked with sector strategies, particularly with agriculture and industry.

As the country moves to further duty reduction along with the elimination of other duties and charges and export service charges as per WTO commitments, revenue may fall if compensatory domestic tax measures are not introduced or if the measures so introduced do not cover the loss incurred in tariff reduction. Thus, extra efforts concerning domestic taxation are required. It is necessary to diversify export products and export markets and also to increase the competitiveness of existing exports. A host of measures, such as targeting potential export sectors, and preferential credit and tax incentives, need to be devised. 'Aid for trade' needs to be mobilised.

Openness alone has limited effectiveness in promoting broad-based economic growth in a country like Nepal. In particular, the existence of a large non-commercialised subsistence agricultural sector means that the supply response to trade policy reforms is likely to be limited. Thus strategic public interventions in the rural economy are needed to make trade work for the poor.

For preferential market access provided to LDCs to be commercially meaningful, rules of origin should not constrain their capacity. Nepal should be lobbying among LDCs for relaxing them. Moreover, the harmonisation of GSP rules of origin, which currently differ from one GSP scheme to another, would be an important step towards making market access commercially meaningful. An equally important issue towards trade promotion for Nepal would be non-tariff barriers including SPS and TBT.

Special and Differential Treatment to LDCs is mentioned in the WTO agreement, with technical assistance not necessarily binding. Integrated Framework is a welcome step but lacks sufficient resources to enhance hardware-related capacity building. Technology-intensive testing and certification systems are often needed to assure final products meet high standards, especially in areas of health and safety. There is a need for financial and technical support to be mobilised to enhance capacity in this area.

Preference erosion due to reduced industrial tariffs under various GSP schemes enjoyed by LDCs needs to be compensated by other means, including technical issues. Harmonisation of GSP rules of origin, which currently differ from one GSP scheme to another, would be an important step towards making market access commercially meaningful.

Materialisation of regional cooperation frameworks like SAFTA or BIMSTEC FTA requires effective differential treatment to LDCs like Nepal, supporting development of in-country trade infrastructure, and creating an inter-country physical trade link along with other policy measures.

Notes

1 This analysis of this paper mainly draws from the study done by the author for SAWTEE (2005).

2 The average tariff rate is high because of 80 per cent basic duty on automobile imports, which have a significant share in imports.
3 See Appendix 2 for the detailed data on the composition of trade.
4 This is mainly because of a significant decline in gold and other imports, most of which are being consumed across the border.
5 The shocks in exports of major commodities (mainly carpets, garments and pashminas) and services (tourism) were instrumental in slowing down GDP growth performance after 2001. The robust growth of exports during the 1990s was also restrained by new barriers imposed on duty-free exports of major manufactured items to India from 2002.
6 The only living standard surveys which are comparable for poverty measurement are those done in 1995/6 and 2003/4.
7 However, the estimated remittance in the balance of payments statistics of the Nepal Rastra Bank does not cover all the inflow, as a large chunk of the inflow is from informal sources.
8 In the 1990s, import of gold from personal finance was assumed to be financed by workers' remittance. So a gold import equivalent amount was recorded under service income as short-term workers' remittance. In recent years, gold imports have declined and remittance has been better recorded under transfer heads, resulting to a decline in service income accounts.
9 The estimation period was 1985–2005. The coefficient was statistically significant at the 5 per cent level and R2 was 0.26.
10 Regression of real GDP against trade openness showed an insignificant relationship for the period 1975–2005.
11 A recent survey (SAWTEE 2007) shows a direct relation between unemployment in the RMG sector and the removal of the quota system. Of the 133 past employees surveyed, 66 per cent cited closure of a garment factory as the reason for unemployment. The sample data indicates that about 60 per cent of workers left their jobs within the last two years.
12 As discussed before, the major factors behind the decline are the abolition of quotas on garment export in the USA since January 2005, saturation of the Nepalese carpet market and a quality problem with pashmina shawls.
13 Figures derived from manufacturing census tables. Comparison of the census input and output figures for 1991 and 2001 shows a decline in value-added in these products over time.
14 It is one employment per Rs 500,000 as compared with one per Rs 90,000 in organised domestic industries.
15 The estimated period is 1976–2005, the coefficients are statistically significant at the 5 per cent level and the explanatory power of the estimated equation was 0.99.
16 The government can either introduce new domestic taxes to compensate for the shortfall in revenue emanating from lowered tariff rates, or it can restructure allocation of public expenditure to protect the poor from such a revenue shortfall, if any. Nepal introduced Value Added Tax (VAT) in later 1990s as a compensatory measure to reduced tariff rates whereas public expenditure reforms leading to formulation of Medium Term Expenditure Framework was devised to protect the poor from any revenue shortfall arising from any shocks, including trade reforms.
17 Details of the revenue composition are given in Appendix 2.
18 However, a study shows that the estimated revenue loss due to tariff cuts on imports for the fulfilment of WTO obligations would be up to Rs 469 million for 2007 (UNDP 2007). The revenue loss due to the abolition of other duties and charges (ODC) would be Rs 433 million in 2007, with further increments in subsequent years. This accounts for only about 1 per cent of total revenue.

8 Pakistan

Rehana Siddiqui

In Pakistan, the focus of trade policies has changed over the years, from import substitution to export expansion and trade liberalisation in recent years. A number of studies have examined the relationship between economic growth and openness but the trade–poverty nexus is examined in only a few studies. The empirical studies support the view that growth rate of GDP has been responsive to exports expansion and rise in trade–GDP ratio (see, for example, Siddiqui 2004). However, a casual analysis of indicators of trade–economic growth–poverty, over time, does not reveal that trade liberalisation, despite its positive impact on growth rate of GDP, has resulted in poverty reduction.

Thus, it is important to study whether, in Pakistan, trade liberalisation alone has or has not resulted in poverty reduction. This chapter focuses on the nexus of trade–growth–poverty in Pakistan. The chapter is structured as follows: after the introduction, an overview of trade liberalisation in Pakistan is given in section 2. Trends in economic growth and poverty are elaborated in section 3. Empirical results on trade–growth–poverty are analysed in section 4. The paper is concluded with some policy suggestions in section 5.

Liberalisation in Pakistan: an overview

Pakistan adopted the Stabilisation and Structural Adjustment Programme in the late 1980s and 1990s. The aim was to improve the efficiency and competitiveness of the economy by reducing market intervention and fiscal and trade deficit and other distortion. In this study we focus on the trade-related policy measure. Various indicators can be used to assess the performance of the trade sector. An important indicator of success of trade liberalisation is openness, defined as total trade–GDP ratio, which remained stagnant around 30 per cent in the 1990s and afterwards, indicating no significant rise in the openness of the economy despite liberalisation of trade and reduction in quantitative and qualitative trade barriers. However, the terms of trade improved from 100 in 1990/1 to 123.5 in 1997/8 and deteriorated continuously afterwards to 62.59 in 2006/7, as a result of which export earnings were adversely affected (see Government of Pakistan 2009). Other indicators of trade policy outcomes are reported in Appendix 3 for recent years. The indicators show an improvement in trade and current account deficit until 2002–3 and deterioration afterwards. The growth rate of gross domestic product was around 5 per cent and declined to 2 per cent in 2000/1, then increasing to 7 per cent in 2006/7. A simple comparison shows a weak linkage between current account deficit and economic growth at the aggregate level; however, the decomposition of trade into its components, like imports and exports, is important to understand the linkage between trade expansion and economic growth and link it to the trade liberalisation policies adopted in Pakistan.

The focus of trade policies in Pakistan, as in any other developing country, has changed over time. The trade policy regimes can be divided into three distinct periods. In the initial phase, from 1947 to 1958, focus was on import substitution to expand the meagre domestic industrial base; in the second phase (from 1958 to the 1980s), an incentive structure was formulated for import substitution and export expansion. In the third phase (the 1990s and 2000s), export expansion was the major focus, followed by adoption of SAP and reduction in market interventions in the external sector.

Phase I: 1947 to 1958

In the initial phase after independence in 1947, the focus of the policies was to provide incentives to expand the limited domestic industrial base and set up essential consumer goods industries. The trade policy focused on adoption of import licensing policies, control of foreign exchange, and policies for export promotion. The tariff policy was adopted with the objectives of increasing government revenue and promoting import substitution. It also reinforced the impact of exchange control and import licensing policies. In this era, the major trading partners were the UK and India and other sterling areas. But the crisis followed by England's decision to devalue its currency in 1948 forced Pakistan to diversify its trading partners and devalue the currency in 1949.

In 1950, as a result of the Korean War, exports and foreign exchange earnings increased and foreign exchange policy was liberalised. With the end of the Korean War in 1951, earnings from exports of primary products declined, putting pressure on the balance of trade. Liberal imports under Open General Licence (OGL) continued until 1952. But rapidly deteriorating terms of trade and decline in foreign exchange reserves forced the government to tighten its import policy. The major focus of the import policy was on industrial raw materials, and licences were granted to 'established importers' and only to certain 'category holders'. In order to boost exports, various incentives were given but they were not effective. As a result, the currency was devalued again in July 1955 to raise export earnings and ease the pressure on the balance of trade (see Ahmed and Amjad 1984).

Phase II: 1958–1980s

In the second phase of 1958 to the 1980s, the focus was on industrialisation through protection of domestic industries. The tariff and non-tariff barriers were used to restrict imports and fiscal incentives were used to boost exports and imports. The regime imposed tariff and non-tariff barriers, like licensing, bans and quota restrictions, on imports. Import licensing, foreign exchange controls and bilateral trade agreements were used to regulate imports. An Export Bonus Scheme, giving different bonus vouchers for different categories of exports, was initiated. The impact of these policies was similar to the impact of currency devaluation (see Lewis 1971; Ahmed and Amjad 1984; Uddin and Swati 2006). However, the multiplicity of exchange rates and trade and fiscal incentives for industrialisation led to distortions in resource allocations and encouraged rent-seeking activities and an industrial structure that was heavily dependent on the protection provided by the government of Pakistan. As a result, the industrial base remained weak, inefficient and concentrated (see Lewis 1971). In addition, the incentives structure designed for export expansion led to contradictory outcomes and no net increase in trade. The accumulation of a heavy debt burden with an inefficient and concentrated industrial base increased the vulnerability of the economy to internal and external shocks. Moreover, the concentration and inefficiencies in the industrial set-up lowered the competitiveness of exports.

The concentration of industrial wealth and the resulting income and asset inequalities were one important factor in the separation of East Pakistan in the early 1970s. The concentration of industrial wealth and other distortions were also important reasons behind massive nationalisation of industries during the Bhutto regime in 1974. The nationalisation programme discouraged private industrial activities. During 1972–6, the government continued to adjust export and import taxes to maintain real exchange rate parity. The Export Bonus Scheme was abolished, and commodity-specific tariff rates were introduced to treat imports uniformly. Another important change in policy was devaluation in 1972. Although several measures were adopted to differentiate these reforms from those undertaken in the 1960s, the net impact of the reforms on trade in the two periods was similar, as both lacked long-term planning, and continuous intervention resulted in increasing uncertainty (see Guisinger and Scully 1991).

The trade policies were also sensitive to political changes (see Butt and Bandara 2009). In the 1980s, Zia's regime revived various policies of the 1960s. The process of denationalisation was started to reduce the burden on government and to deal with inefficiencies in public sector enterprises. The objective of the export policy in 1983–4 was to generate exportable surplus by increasing domestic production in the agriculture and industrial sectors, with a focus on export-oriented industries, and on the diversification of exports of goods and of trading partners. For the export expansion, the measures included compensatory rebates on various items; standardisation of tariff rates; excise and sales tax rebates; duty-free imports of machinery for balancing, modernisation and replacement (BMR) for export units; an export financing scheme; setting up EPZ in Karachi and Lahore; and delinking of the rupee with the US$ in 1982. However, the trade imbalance persisted, despite a substantial inflow of remittances, as imports exceeded exports and Pakistan accumulated huge debt over the years.

Phase III: the 1990s and 2000s

In the third phase, from the 1990s onwards, a set of reforms was initiated under the Structural Adjustment Programme (SAP) to reduce market interventions in order to improve efficiency of resource use and the competitiveness of the economy. Despite difficulties, Pakistan tried to honour its WTO commitments. The emphasis was on trade liberalisation and on opening the domestic market by reducing quantitative restrictions and rationalisation of the tariff structure. The tariff rate was reduced on a number of products from a maximum of 225 per cent in 1986/7 to 70 per cent in the 1990s, and to 25 per cent in recent years. In addition, the dispersion in tariff rates has been reduced to four slabs only, i.e. 5 per cent, 10 per cent, 20 per cent and 25 per cent, resulting in risk reduction. Simplification and rationalisation of tariff rates, the elimination of controls and other quantitative restrictions and abolishing the negative list are important steps in the direction of trade liberalisation. In the mid-1980s and by the end of the 1990s, only 2.7 of imports faced quantitative restrictions (QRs).

In the trade policy of 2007/8, the focus is on encouraging businessmen and entrepreneurs to install new machinery and add capacity, on measures to improve competitiveness and on availability of consumer goods at reasonable prices. To facilitate imports, the policy focuses on improving the registration and standardisation of imports, facilitating trade fairs in Pakistan, improving provisions for import of used machinery, facilitating overseas Pakistanis, and on importing pharmaceutical and chemical products for domestic industry.

Despite various efforts, the gains in terms of the import–GDP ratio remain modest. The ratio declined from 18.6 per cent in 1989–90 to 13.7 per cent in 2002–3, and increased to 22.43 per cent in 2006/7. However, the composition has changed significantly over time. The share of consumer goods in total imports declined from 19 per cent in 1989–90 to 10 per cent in 2005/6, and the share of capital goods varied between 33 and 37 per cent during 1989–2007. The rise is the result of BMR in the production sector of the economy, indicating an improvement in private industrial investment and in the economic conditions. The composition of exports also changed, as the share of manufactured in total exports increased from 56 per cent in 1989/90 to 77 per cent in 2006/7; however, due to deterioration in the terms of trade foreign exchange did not increase substantially. In addition, according to the World Bank (2004b: 22),

The removal of the QRs up to this point proceeded behind declining but still very high tariff barriers, however, and in 1998 some of the industries protected by the remaining QRs and also by Government or by government-controlled import monopolies were very large, including, for example, most of agriculture and the fertilizer industry.

Comparison with neighbouring countries shows that over time the quantitative restrictions were reduced in all South Asian countries. The comparison of Pakistan's tariff rates with the tariff rates in other South Asian countries shows that liberalisation of all trade, including trade in agricultural products, was much higher in Pakistan than in other South Asian countries. The comparison across South Asian economies also shows that restrictions on trade with India continued, except for the positive list of 677 items. The local-content/deletion programme for the auto industry continued, with the intention of gradual phasing out to meet WTO conditions. Under the local-content programme (deletion programme), local firms were entitled to tariff reduction or exemption on imported intermediate inputs and components in return for a commitment to buy or produce other materials and components domestically. However, the reduction in tariffs on imports made this provision less attractive for the local industry. The illegal trade between Pakistan and Afghanistan also affected the linkage between trade and economic growth. According to the World Bank (2004b: 5, 'One factor influencing trade policy liberalization in Pakistan is the recognition of the large volume of illegal imports via Afghanistan and from India that high protection has encouraged.'

An important source of non-tariff protection is the implementation of technical and health- and safety-based regulations. There are restrictions on imports of second-hand products, e.g. consumer durables like refrigerators, air conditioners and vehicles, to protect domestic industry. The regulatory duties are also imposed on domestic industries. Currently, only the regulatory duties are on steel products and new duties are not imposed. The National Tariff Commission has been established to manage enquiries from industries requesting regulatory duties and to advise the government.

In the 1990s and after, the focus on export expansion and export diversification continued. For example, the trade policy of 2007/8 focused on: development of an efficient, competitive and diversified export sector; provision of various incentives like income tax and sales tax; surcharges through the duty drawback facility; provision of credit for the export-oriented industries on easy terms; and support for ISO certifications, e.g. ISO 9000 and ISO 14000. In addition, the Trade Development Authority of Pakistan was created to develop an effective export marketing strategy and compliance with international standards and trade laws. Other measures included the revamping of Rules and Laws of Trade-Related Bodies, development of the new Trade Organisations Ordinance of 1961, a reform strategy for the improvement of the insurance sector, tariff rationalisation for inputs and output, strengthening of domestic commerce, the establishment of the Competitiveness Institute of Pakistan to develop effective research and information system to improve competitiveness, redefining the role of the National Tariff Commission as an effective trade defence organisation of Pakistan, and preferential trading arrangements with China and other countries in East and South Asia.

Despite the focus of trade policy on export expansion, the exports–GDP ratio remained stagnant and success in export diversification was limited. So far, the country is not able to increase its market share in world exports and diversify exports. Lower competitiveness and lack of access to other countries are the major reasons for the slow progress in export expansion. However, the composition of exports changed significantly as the share of manufactured goods in total exports increased to 77 per cent in 2006/7 from 56 per cent in 1989/90. The product-wise comparison of exports shows a high concentration around a few products like rice in the primary goods category and textile products in the manufactured goods category. This indicates a need for export diversification and expansion of the export base for improving the trade balance of the country.

Exchange rate policy

Until 1980, Pakistan followed a fixed exchange rate regime. The use of the exchange rate policy for trade (exports) expansion and industrialisation led to multiple exchange rates in the economy. In 1955 and 1972, the currency was devalued, resulting in an improvement in the current account balance for a short period of time. In 1982 the fixed exchange rate regime was abandoned and 'managed float' was introduced to determine currency prices. The domestic currency price was linked to a basket of foreign currencies, not the US$ alone. In 1996, the State Bank of Pakistan allowed interbank determination of currency prices.

The existing evidence shows that the devaluation increased exports only in the short run. However, before 1982 misalignment of the exchange rate was also a critical issue. After the adoption of a managed floating exchange rate regime in 1982, misalignment in currency prices reduced substantially. Fluctuations in exchange rates pass through domestic prices, resulting in a higher cost of production and cost of living with implications for poverty and the welfare of the population. In addition, the use of fiscal and monetary instruments maintained the stability of the real effective exchange rate (REER), making nominal devaluation ineffective in increasing exports (see Siddiqui and Akhtar 2000; Ahmed and Amjad 1984).

Resource inflow

The resource inflow in the form of foreign aid, remittances and foreign direct investment (FDI) affects the economic growth of a country mainly by easing the resource constraint. In Pakistan, foreign aid, without its efficient use, resulted in a heavy debt burden in the 1990s. However, in the 1990s the huge inflow of resources and debt rescheduling eased the repayment pressure and forwarded the burden of debt. Foreign direct investment increased from a meagre US$ 10.7 million in 1975 to US$ 1,295.9 million in 1996 and to US$ 5,124.9 million in 2006/7. However, this inflow was concentrated to a few areas, like energy.

The resource inflow in the form of workers' remittances increased from US $ 1,848.29 million in 2001 to US$ 5,493.6 million in 2006/7. Initially, Pakistan was not able to attract FDI like other Asian economies. The main reasons were cumbersome processes, long waiting periods and complex administrative procedures. In addition, in current years, despite simplification in procedures and ease in investment and profit repatriation, the inflow of FDI is limited because of the adverse law and order situation. A CGE-based analysis by Rizwana Siddiqui and Kemal (2006), shows that the inflow of resources in the form of remittances has a direct and larger impact on poverty reduction compared to resource inflow in the form of foreign direct investment.

Trends in growth and poverty in Pakistan

As in any other developing country, the definition of poverty and its estimates are controversial in Pakistan. The definition of poverty ranges from income/ expenditure poverty to food insecurity or lack of access to employment opportunities and to social services. Ignoring the methodological issues sur-rounding the controversy, we focus on the reported income/expenditure esti-mates of poverty in Pakistan. The incidence of poverty was high in the 1960s, declined in the 1970s and 1980s, started rising in the 1990s and slowed down in recent years (see Table 8.1). Table 8.1 also shows that, as expected, the incidence of poverty was higher in rural areas than in urban areas. The gap in rural and urban poverty was small during the earlier period, when the incidence of poverty was declining. However, in the later period, when the incidence of poverty is rising, the gap between rural and urban areas is widening. The poverty gap (P1) and severity (P2) increased despite lowering incidence of poverty in the 1980s. P1 and P2 are lower in the later period when the incidence of poverty was rising. The reason may be the presence of transient poor, who are poor because of some temporary shocks resulting in loss of income and pushing the household below the poverty line temporarily. Thus, there is a need for regional focus of poverty alleviation efforts.

Increased frequency of crises of finance, fuel, food, political instability and security has increased the vulnerability of the households closest to the poverty line. Del Ninno *et al.* (2006) discuss the issue of vulnerability of the poor to various risks. According to the study, some risks affect the whole population equally while other risks affect only a few groups, particularly the poor. In order to reduce vulnerability, sound economic and social policies areneeded. The study estimates that the incidence of vulnerability ranges between 47 and 67 per cent, with major sources of vulnerability being a low

Table 8.1 Poverty incidence in Pakistan, 1963–2006 (%)

Years	Total	Rural	Urban	P1	P2
1963–4	40.24	38.94	44.53	—	—
1966–7	44.50	45.62	40.96	—	—
1969–70	46.53	49.11	38.76	—	—
1979	30.68	32.51	25.94	—	—
1984–5	24.47	25.87	21.17	11.10	3.80
1986–7	26.90	29.40	24.50	—	—
1987–8	17.32	18.32	14.99	11.27	2.30
1990–1	22.11	23.59	18.64	13.10	2.20
1992–3	22.40	23.35	15.50	—	—
1993–4 (a)	20.80	24.40	15.20		
1993–4 (b)	23.60	26.30	19.40	5.31	1.55
1996–7	31.00	32.00	27.00	5.80	1.70
1998–9	32.60	34.80	25.90	7.58	2.20
2001	32.10	38.99	22.67	7.03	2.13
2003	31.80	38.65	22.39	—	—
2005	23.94	28.13	14.94	4.76	1.40
2006	22.60	27.00	13.10	4.00	1.10

Sources: World Bank, Poverty Indicators 1984–85 to 1996–97; Amjad and Kemal (1997); Bhatti *et al.* (1999); Jafri (1999); Arif *et al.* (2000); Qureshi and Arif (2001); World Bank (2001, 2002b); CRPRID/Planning Commission (2003); Government of Pakistan (2003); *Pakistan Economic Survey* (various issues).

level of resource availability (for 33 per cent of the population) and low and volatile consumption (24–34 per cent). In Pakistan, the issue of vulnerability is examined in terms of poverty bands. The population with 50 per cent of per capita income at the poverty line declined marginally from 1.1 per cent in 2001 to 1 per cent in 2005, and halved in 2006. The population in the range of 50–75 per cent of poverty-line income declined significantly from 10.8 per cent in 2001 to 6.5 per cent in 2005, and to 5.60 per cent in 2006. Similarly, in the categories of vulnerability (100–125 per cent income of poverty line), there is a decline in vulnerable population. However, the gains to the ultra-poor are not very high. If we include the vulnerable population in the target group for poverty alleviation efforts, the size of the group increases from 23.9 per cent to 44.4 per cent in 2004/5 and to 42.80 per cent in 2005/6.

The period-wise analysis shows that in the 1960s aggregate poverty increased, urban poverty declined and rural poverty estimates reported in different studies show a mixed trend. In this era, the focus of macroeconomic policies was on the protection of industries through tariff and non-tariff barriers on imports. Fiscal incentives in the form of accelerated depreciation rates, subsidies and tax holidays were provided to increase the role of private sectors in the growth process. They resulted in inefficient use of resources, industrial concentration and no incentive to become efficient. The green revolution in the 1960s increased agricultural productivity but the impact on poverty was not very significant. The reason could be low employment intensity in the agriculture sector and the large-scale manufacturing sectors. In addition, the real wages of the workers declined and the terms of trade were against the agriculture sector, which is still the largest employer of the workforce. The resource inflow in the form of foreign aid and grants at subsidised rates encouraged over-investment in the large-scale manufacturing sector. Overall growth rate was higher, around 6.8 per cent per annum, despite low employment generation, but it was not sustainable. According to Lewis (1971) the protection structure in Pakistan protected inefficient producers. There was little incentive for the inefficient to become efficient. Thus, the protection structure in the 1960s led to misallocation of resources and higher cost of domestic production, making the high growth of 1960s unsustainable.

After the political turmoil which started in the late 1960s and led to the creation of Bangladesh, the period of 1970–7 was a time of change in political and economic philosophy. In order to control monopolies and reduce wealth concentration, the government adopted the policy of nationalisation. This policy led to the nationalisation of major industrial units, and financial and educational institutions were also nationalised. The state-controlled institutions were set up for export promotion. The inflation rate increased. Worker migration to the Middle East led to an increase in foreign exchange reserves, resulting in the welfare improvements of households. This supports the argument in Siddiqui and Kemal (2006) that resource inflow in the form of remittances has a welfare improving effect at household level and, as a result, poverty declined during this period despite a modest growth rate of GDP, i.e. 4.5 per cent.

In the 1980s, the emphasis of government policy shifted again towards a market economy. The process of nationalisation was reversed, resulting in significant loss of employment. The incentive structure of the 1960s was partially revived. Fiscal incentives in the form of tax holidays, imposition of high tariffs on imports to protect domestic industry, and heavy foreign resource inflow to finance the Afghan War affected the sustainability of the economy. However, the growth rate of GDP was 6.7 per cent per annum, resulting in a lower incidence of poverty.

In the period of 1988–93, the reform programme was initiated with the help of multilateral institutions. The basic economic philosophy was to minimise government intervention and promote a market-based economic structure. It resulted in the removal of all qualitative restrictions on imports and exports and rationalisation of the tariff structure. The tariff slabs were gradually reduced, and the maximum tariff was also reduced to about 35 per cent. However, growth slowed down and poverty estimates show a rising trend.

In the 2000s, poverty started showing a downward trend. In this period, trade restrictions were reduced substantially and the growth rate of GDP increased to 9.0 per cent. The discussion raises the following critical questions: is there a linkage between poverty reduction and growth, and is there a linkage between poverty reduction and trade liberalisation? Osmani (2002: 15) argues that 'the pursuit of an open trade regime that does not discriminate against tradables in general and exports in particular, and perhaps actively promotes them, is essential for achieving pro-poor growth in developing countries'. Therefore, it is not just trade but also the pattern of trade that is important in determining its impact on poverty. The evidence reported in Table 8.3 shows that the growth rate of GDP and poverty are moving in the same direction. Openness and output growth are also moving in the same direction. Employment generation, key to poverty reduction, shows significant fluctuations over time. The evidence suggests that, in general, the growth process was employment-intensive. However, there seems to be a lagged effect of employment generation on the incidence of poverty.

Like other developing countries, Pakistan has taken various initiatives to reduce poverty. For example, the Poverty Reduction Strategy Paper (2001) focused on accelerating growth, with governance reforms creating income-generating opportunities, improving human development to reduce poverty and reducing vulnerability to shocks. Similarly, the focus of the Medium Term Development Framework is on the generation of employment opportunities and 'decent' work. For this purpose, various programmes have been initiated, such as the public works programme 'Tameer-e-Pakistan', the revival of Khushal Pakistan, social mobilisation, skills training for self-employment, overseas employment of engineers, nurses, welders, masons, carpenters, electricians, cooks, technicians, drivers, information technology workers and others.

The employment activation policies focus on technical/vocational training for the unemployed (Rs 5.3 billion), progressive education policy (secondary, tertiary and others), the establishment of a 'Labour Market Information System', and provision of employment safety-net policies – a minimum wage, social security (with a 7 per cent employee contribution), EOBI (an 8 per cent deduction), workers' welfare funds, a worker's children's education ordinance (Rs 100, paid by the employer), the *zakat* fund, *Baitul mal* (a subsidy scheme).

As part of the UN MDGs, Pakistan needs to reduce poverty by a half by 2015, to 13 per cent from 23 per cent in 1990. This means a target of reducing the incidence of poverty to 11–12 per cent by 2015. However, if we examine the pattern of incidence of poverty we see a rise in incidence of poverty to 32 per cent in 2001 and then a decline to 22.3 per cent in 2006/7. This raises a critical issue: will Pakistan be able to achieve the target set by the MDG? The current trend is mixed. There is a need to study how poverty incidence responds to various socio-economic indicators, including trade, and which of these indicators can help to achieve the MDG for poverty reduction.

Empirical investigation of the trade–poverty nexus

Model

Utilising the data for 1973–2005 for Pakistan, a simple regression model is estimated. However, only 15 observations are available for incidence of poverty. In a simple methodological framework, incidence of poverty is a dependent variable and growth rate of GDP is the main explanatory variable.

Other factors, representing trade and socio-economic characteristics, are divided into two groups. The first group includes indicators of openness (O). The second set is identified as structural indicators (S). The indicators of openness include: trade–GDP ratio, import–GDP ratio, export–GDP ratio, average rate on import duty, remittances–GDP ratio and foreign direct investment–GDP ratio. The structural variables include: unemployment rate and inflation rate (measured as changes in the consumer price index). In addition, a dummy variable, taking the value of 1 for the reform period, i.e. 1990/1 onwards, and 0 otherwise, is included to capture the effects of changes under the Structural Adjustment Programme.

Because of the limited number of observations, it is difficult to include all the variables in one regression and apply time series techniques. Six regression equations are estimated selecting one indicator of trade liberalisation. The structural variables are included in all the equations as control variables. Trend is included to capture the spurious correlation in the model due to time series data and a dummy variable is included to capture the change in poverty in the post-reform period.

The growth–poverty linkage is well established in the literature. The benefits of economic growth are expected to reach all segments of the population, unless the income distribution worsens with economic growth. The trade–GDP ratio is defined as the sum of imports and exports as a percentage of GDP. In Pakistan, the trade–GDP ratio remained below 50 per cent. In fact, in the early years of this decade there was a decline in openness and poverty was rising. However, openness is not the only factor contributing to decline in poverty. Although the changes in import–GDP ratio are not very significant, the impact on poverty seems to be large. The reason could be a rise in the productive capacity of the economy, resulting in higher growth and lower poverty. The rise in export–GDP ratio is expected to reduce poverty. The linkage is expected to be stronger if economic growth is a result of export expansion and employment generation in the export sector. The two variables seem to be positively linked (see Table 8.2). The inflow of remittances can reduce the incidence of poverty either through consumption smoothening or through a rise in savings. Again, we can say the link between poverty and remittances inflow is negative. Siddiqui and Kemal (2006) also show that a rise in remittances has a larger impact on household welfare and poverty. The average tariff rate shows sharp fluctuations as the tariff rates are reduced and maximum tariff is lowered. However, this indicator of trade liberalisation shows that reduction in restrictions on imports may not result in poverty reduction. This may be a short-term phenomenon, as indicated earlier. The structural indicators also show mixed behaviour. The rise in unemployment rate and inflation are expected to increase poverty.

Results of estimated models

The results of the estimated regression models are reported in Table 8.4. Despite the small sample size, the results are interesting and quite robust. The

Table 8.2 Changes in growth and poverty and internal and external indicators

Indicators	Changes from 1973–80 to					
	1980–5	1985–90	1995	2000	2005	2007
Growth rate of GDP	Decreased from 8.68 to 4.7%	Increased to 9.82%	Decreased to 5.03%	Decreased to 3.91%	Increased to 5.90%	Increased to 6.30%
Poverty	Decreasedfrom 37.97 to 25.87%	Decreased to 20.66%	Increased to 25.49%	Increased to 31.80%	Declined to 30.07%	Declined to 22.30%
Indicators of trade						
Trade–GDP ratio	Increased from 30.72 to 35.54%	Declined to 33.63%	Increased to 36.78%	Declined to 33.98%	Declined to 32.18%	Increased to 37.42%
Exports–GDP ratio	Declined marginally from 11.67 to 11.44%	Increased to 13.78%	Increased to 16.78%	Declined to 15.67%	Constant at 15.68%	Declined to 13.98%
Imports–GDP ratio	Increased from 16.58 to 18.72%	Declined to 17.12%	Constant at 17.81%	Declined to 17.01%	Declined to 16.82%	Increased to 23.17%
Share of primary goods in total exports	Declined from 40.13 to 33.40%	Declined to 28.40%	Declined to 14.80%	Declined to 12.8%	Declined to 11.20%	Constant at 11.00%
Share of capital goods in total imports	Declined from 32.75 to 30.60%	Increased to 36.00%	Increased to 38.00%	Declined to 32.20%	Declined to 31.00%	Increased to 36.00%
Real exchange rate	Increased from 8.89 to 11.13%	Increased to 17.37%	Increased to 26.10%	Increased to 42.82%	Increased to 60.14%	Declined 57.67%
Average duty on imports	Increased from 11.32 to 25.12%	Increased to 32.94%	Declined to 25.78%	Declined to 16.70%	Declined to 9.15%	Declined to 7.61%
Remittances–GDP ratio	Increased from 5.50 to 8.42%	Declined to 5.14%	Declined to 2.84%	Declined to 1.86%	Increased 3.78%	Declined to 2.80%
FDI-GDP ratio	Increased from 0.12 to 0.26%	Increased to 0.47%	Increased to 0.89%	Constant at 0.83%	Increased to 1.07%	Increased to 1.38%

(Continued on next page)

Table 8.2 (continued)

Indicators	Changes from 1973–80 to					
	1980–5	1985–90	1995	2000	2005	2007
	Macroeconomic indicators and human capital					
Inflation	Varied between 1.76 and 1.74%	Increased by 2.31%	Increased by 5.80%	Increased by 5.91%	Increased by 6.33%	Increased by 9.12%
Unemployment rate	Remained constant around 3.63–3.64%	Declined to 3.20%	Increased to 5.42%	Increased to 6.53%	Increased to 7.65%	Declined to 5.66%
Growth rate of employment	Increased from 2.71 to 3.14%	Declined to 2.00%	Declined to 1.24%	Increased to 3.61%	Declined to 3.07%	Declined to 0.37%
Literacy rate	Increased from 24.73 to 27.90%	Increased to 32.08%	Increased to 38.42%	Increased to 45.38%	Increased to 52.62%	Increased to 55.5%
Growth rate of enrolment (H)	Declined from 8.68 to 4.06%	Increased to 4.82%	Increased to 5.87%	Increased to 9.33%	Declined to 2.92%	Increased to 11.85%

Table 8.3 Poverty–growth linkage

	Incidence of poverty	Growth rate	Openness	Employment elasticity	Capability
1973–80	34.58 (2)	5.38	30.72	1.04	8.68
1981–5	27.47 (1)	7.13	35.54	1.38	4.06
1986–90	19.73 (3)	5.30	33.63	4.78	4.82
1991–5	25.49 (3)	5.03	36.73	1.72	5.87
1996–2000	31.80 (2)	3.91	33.98	1.31	9.33
2001–5	30.07 (3)	5.90	32.18	2.13	2.98
2006–7	22.30 (1)	6.30	37.42	0.27	11.85
1973–2007	27.00 (15)	5.49	33.45	1.84	5.37

Note: The numbers of observation on poverty are reported in parentheses. For other indicators all the data are available.

results reported in Siddiqui (2004) support the earlier findings that openness contributes to economic growth significantly. Keeping that result in mind, we examine the trade–growth–poverty linkage. Six indicators of trade/openness – average tariff duty, export–GDP ratio, import–GDP ratio, trade–GDP ratio (openness), remittances–GDP ratio and FDI–GDP ratio – are included in the analysis to capture the direct impact of trade liberalisation on poverty reduction. In all the estimated equations, we retain structural variables, namely unemployment and inflation, with growth as the main contributor to poverty reduction. In addition, trend is included in the model to control for time-related changes and a dummy variable (Dummy-SAP) is included to capture the differences in poverty incidence before and after the adoption of Structural Adjustment Programme. We retain growth as an explanatory variable in each equation, as economic growth may not be a result of trade expansion alone.

The first model shows that economic growth reduces poverty but the impact is not statistically significant. In all the other specifications, the coefficient of growth rate is larger than 1 and it is statistically significant, indicating that marginal impact of rise in GDP growth rate on poverty reduction is either proportionate or more than proportionate. As expected, rise in unemployment rate contributes positively to poverty reduction and it is statistically significant in all specifications. Similarly, rise in inflation rate increases the incidence of poverty and it is statistically significant in most of the specifications. The coefficient of 'trend' is not statistically significant in most cases. The coefficient of 'dummy variable' is not statistically robust. Interestingly, these results are robust as the inclusion of openness indicators does not affect the growth–poverty or other relationships. In all the regressions the coefficients of economic growth, is negative and the coefficients of unemployment rate and inflation rate are positive.

The coefficients of openness indicators show mixed results. Surprisingly, the rise in average tariff rate reduces poverty and the coefficient is statistically significant. The result can be explained in a number of ways. First, this may be a result of a rise in capital intensity of the production structure. With the decline in average tariff, imported machinery becomes relatively cheaper, and

Table 8.4 Results: determinants of poverty

	Equation 1	Equation 2	Equation 3	Equation 4	Equation 5	Equation 6
Constant	5.210	16.594	37.283	70.467	24.155	15.289
	(5.250)	(1.179)	(3.816)	(3.542)	(4.943)	(4.301)
Growth rate	−0.736	−1.207	−1.451	−1.425	−1.299	−1.179
of GDP	(1.593)	(2.102)	(3.032)	(3.370)	(2.645)	(2.099)
Unemployment	2.760	4.750	3.539	1.566	4.828	4.729
rate	(2.270)	(3.967)	(3.079)	(1.044)	(4.648)	(3.938)
Inflation Rate	0.239	0.919	1.224	1.007	0.721	0.921
	(0.484)	(1.718)	(2.669)	(2.573)	(1.509)	(1.626)
Trend	−0.515	−7.616	−7.934	1.494	−11.252	6.612
	(2.591)	(1.047)	(1.791)	(0.297)	(2.064)	(1.221)
Dummy−SAP	−1.202	−0.574	−0.351	−0.345	−0.432	−0.616
	(0.259)	(2.21)	(1.236)	(1.618)	(1.758)	(1.560)
Indicators of trade liberalisation						
Average tariff	−0.278	—	—	—	—	—
	(2.459)					
Export–GDP	—	0.198	—	—	—	—
		(0.199)				
Import–GDP	—	—	−0.945	—	—	—
			(1.989)			
Trade–GDP	—	—	—	−1.290	—	—
(openness)				(2.618)		
Remittances	—	—	—	—	−1.052	—
					(1.639)	
FDI–GDP	—	—	—	—	—	0.547
						(0.030)
Adjusted R−squared	0.792	0.639	0.757	0.804	0.728	0.638
F-statistics	9.887	5.184	8.283	10.582	7.248	5.105
Number of observations	15	15	15	15	15	15

as a result the producer substitutes capital for labour, leading to a rise in unemployment rate and consequently a rise in poverty. A second reason could be the inefficiency of the industrial structure. When tariff protection is lowered, inefficient industries close down, resulting in a loss of employment and a rise in poverty. The third reason could be the loss of revenue due to lower tariff effects affecting economic activity adversely, and as a result poverty rises. This supports the findings of earlier studies by Amjad and Kemal (1997) and Kemal *et al.* (2001). However, the coefficient of export–GDP is not statistically significant, implying that export expansion does not affect poverty. This is not a surprising result as the export–GDP ratio has not increased over time. In fact, Pakistan has lost significant revenue (about US$ 500 million) through the decline in the price of exports in 2005/6 (see Government of Pakistan 2007). Another reason is low competitiveness of Pakistan's exports and low value-added products. However, the rise in the import–GDP ratio reduces poverty. The reduction in poverty due to a rise in the import–GDP ratio may be a result of expansion in productive capacity as the share of capital goods and intermediate goods in total imports increased over time. The increased imports of capital goods may be a reflection of technology transfer, resulting in a rise in the productivity of inputs and improved quality of products. As a result, the economy grows and poverty goes down. The rise in the trade–GDP ratio also leads to a reduction in poverty incidence by 1.29 points and it is statically significant. The rise in remittances is also expected to reduce the incidence of poverty; however, the coefficient is not statistically significant. The direction of the effect supports the findings of Siddiqui and Kemal (2006) that a rise in remittances reduces poverty. The final indicator of trade liberalisation is foreign direct investment as a percentage of GDP. The coefficient is positive but statistically insignificant. This is interesting as both variables indicating resource inflow have a positive but statistically insignificant coefficient, implying that resource inflow does not lead to poverty reduction. However, expansion in productive activities, i.e. imports and total trade, results in poverty reduction.

The elasticity of poverty, with respect to explanatory variables, is reported in Table 8.5. The growth elasticity of poverty incidence varies between -0.15 and -0.30. In most cases it is above -0.25, implying that a 1 per cent increase in economic growth reduces poverty incidence by 0.25 per cent. The poverty elasticity with respect to inflation (changes in consumer price index) varies between 0.11 and 0.19, implying that each percentage increase in consumer prices will increase poverty by 0.11 per cent or more. The elasticity for unemployment rate varies between 0.29 and 0.89. This is a large variation. However, in most cases the elasticity estimate is around 0.8, showing that for each percentage increase in unemployment rate, poverty increases by approximately 0.8 per cent. The poverty elasticity with respect to indicators of openness varies between -0.01 (for FDI–GDP) and -1.591 (openness). Two elasticity estimates corresponding to statistically significant coefficient estimates are -0.616 (import–GDP ratio) and -1.591 (openness). This shows that poverty is responsive to trade liberalisation. Poverty declines more than proportionately with the expansion in total trade, particularly imports. Thus, we cannot say that a trade–poverty nexus does not exist. Trade expansion

Table 8.5 Elasticity estimates

	Output elasticity	Inflation elasticity	Unemployment	Trade
Equation 1 (average tariff rate)	−0.15	0.04	0.51	−0.38
Equation 2 (exports–GDP ratio)	−0.25	0.14	0.87	−0.13
Equation 3 (imports–GDP ratio)	−0.30	0.19	0.65	−0.63
Equation 4 (openness)	0.29	0.15	0.29	−0.56
Equation 5 (remittances–GDP)	0.26	0.11	0.89	−0.25
Equation 6 (FDI–GDP)	0.24	0.14	0.89	−0.01

does lead to a lower incidence of poverty but this is not the case for all indicators of trade. It is important to examine the nexus by looking into various channels of trade liberalisation.

Conclusions and policy recommendations

The results of this chapter show a robust relationship between growth and poverty. Other variables of critical importance are unemployment and inflation rate. Rises in both unemployment and inflation leads to a significant rise in poverty incidence. Therefore, recent rises in prices should be monitored closely to minimise their impact on poverty. Efforts to control unemployment can also be very effective in reducing the incidence of poverty significantly. The linkage between indicators of openness and poverty is not uniform. The rise in imports–GDP and trade–GDP plays an important role in poverty reduction, whereas other indicators, like average tariff rate and export–GDP ratio, indicate that the gains from globalisation depend significantly on the production structure, particularly of the export sector. Another issue is the access of developing countries to markets. Focus on increased market access under the WTO regime will benefit the poor countries if market access is provided for the products produced and exported by developing countries.

This requires a much better grasp of the concept of *pro-poor globalisation* than we presently have. Whichever position one takes in the trade–poverty nexus debate, it is critical to conduct well-focused empirical studies to understand the nexus in a country- or region-specific context, since successful policies for maximising benefits from globalisation while protecting the poor cannot be designed and implemented in isolation. For this purpose, these studies can be extended in a number of directions. Some are outlined below:

1   The micro-foundations of the trade–poverty nexus should be studied to understand the process of poverty reduction and improve the competitiveness of the production sector.
2   Other channels of the linkage, such as the impact of changes in relative prices, resource flows and the role of institutions, should be studied to understand the transmission channels of various policies to reduce poverty.
3   The recent critical challenges faced by the developed and developing countries, such as increased fuel and food prices, the issue of fall-out financial crisis, energy and food security, and the role of institutions in dealing with these crises need to be examined in detail.
4   Another issue of critical importance is distribution of income and assets. As Kanbur (1998: n.p.) notes, the central policy dilemma is 'how to take advantage of the undoubted opportunities that integration into the world economy affords for rapid growth, while managing the attendant risks for domestic income distribution in its different dimensions'. We have not discussed this issue because of lack of estimates of income and asset distribution for the post-reform period.

9 Sri Lanka

Deshal de Mel and Ruwan Jayathilaka

The relationship between trade and poverty has long been debated in academic and policy circles. The purpose of this chapter is to contribute to this debate through an in-depth study of the experience of Sri Lanka, the first country in South Asia to break away from the protectionist past by embarking on a decisive process of economic opening in 1977. During the first decade after independence in 1948, Sri Lanka continued with a liberal trade regime, until growing balance of payments problems induced a policy shift towards protectionist import substitution policies from the early 1960s. By the mid-1970s the Sri Lankan economy had become one of the most inward-oriented and regulated outside the group of centrally planned economies. In 1977, Sri Lanka responded to the dismal economic outcome of the closed-economy era by embarking on an extensive economic liberalisation process, becoming the first country in the South Asian region to do so. Despite major macroeconomic problems and political turmoil, market-oriented reforms have been sustained over the ensuing years. Sri Lanka is now classified as one of the few developing countries outside East Asia that have achieved a clear policy shift from the entrenched import-substitution era. This policy transition has brought about notable structural changes in the economy (Athukorala and Rajapatirana 2000; World Bank 2005b; Kelegama 2006). However, the impact of liberalisation reforms on the incidence of poverty and poverty reduction has not yet been systematically studied. Therefore, the main objective of this chapter is to systematically examine the link between trade liberalisation and poverty reduction through employment channels.

The chapter is arranged as follows: Section 2 provides an overview of trade policy shifts and the role of trade in the economy. Section 3 surveys the incidence and patterns of poverty. Section 4 examines key channels through which trade policy impacts on poverty. Section 5 examines some cross-cutting issues. Section 6 reports the results of an econometric analysis undertaken to examine the determinant of poverty at the household level with emphasis on the impact of trade policy. The chapter ends with a summary of key findings and policy inferences.

Policy context

After gaining independence in 1948, Sri Lanka initially continued with the economic structures inherited from the colonial era, characterised by dependence on the export-oriented plantation sector. However, the United National Party (UNP) government of the day fell out of favour as fiscal imbalances forced it to cut down on welfare expenditure, resulting in political unrest in the form of a general strike (*hartal*) in 1953, leading to the election in 1956 of a centre-left coalition government led by the Sri Lanka Freedom Party (SLFP). The government responded to the widening trade deficit by imposing exchange controls and limiting imports. In the early 1960s controls of foreign exchange expanded; there was a complete ban on the import of 49 products and most other imports were subject to licensing (Athukorala and Jayasuriya 1994). There were also restrictions on overseas travel and repatriation of profits. While ideological factors contributed to these changes, the protective policies were also influenced by the comparative ease of addressing the balance of payments problems by import controls as opposed to tackling the underlying fiscal excesses through spending cuts.

In 1965 a new UNP government was sworn into power. It made a tentative attempt at liberalisation which lacked the momentum and drive to carry on in a sustained manner. A standby arrangement with the IMF in 1965 generated greater confidence in the economy from the developed world. A moratorium on repatriation of profits was reversed and moves to encourage exports such as the bonus voucher scheme for non-traditional exports were introduced. In May 1968 there was a partial attempt at liberalisation with a dual exchange rate operating, with essential imports and major exports operating within the official exchange rate and non-essential items operating at a depreciated rate based on Foreign Exchange Entitlement Certificates. The latter exchange rate was to be determined by proxy (through prices of certificates) by market forces. This early step at liberalisation could not be pursued as the UNP government lost the election in 1970 as a result of high (particularly youth) unemployment, inflation, concerns about foreign debt and, tellingly, the reduction of the subsidised rice ration in an attempt to improve prices for farmers.

The first attempt at liberalisation was reversed when the 1970 election brought to power a left-wing coalition of the SLFP, the Lanka Sama Samaja Party (LSSP) and the Communist Party. The economy was under stress given deteriorating terms of trade, weak productivity of domestic agriculture, the first oil shock and a youth uprising led by the Marxist Janatha Vimukthi Peramuna (JVP) in 1971. This was addressed by increasing state control over the economy. Import licensing was required for all imports, and quantitative restrictions and exchange controls were reintroduced. Most of the plantations were taken over by the state; a Business Undertakings Acquisition Act allowed the government to take over any business firm if it was deemed to be in the national interest. High imported food prices resulted in rations being introduced for sugar and wheat, while rice rations were reduced and became more expensive. Overall expenditure on welfare and subsidies had to be curtailed. At the same time, prices of bus and rail fares and postal charges increased. An economic downturn coupled with authoritarian political actions resulted in government popularity plummeting and a massive victory for the opposition in the 1977 elections.

Liberalisation of the economy in 1977

The UNP won a massive majority and enjoyed a substantial political mandate for reform and liberalisation. Within the first three months of coming into power, several reforms were made to trade and economic policy with broad-based dismantling of state controls over the economy (Cuthbertson and Athukorala 1991; Athukorala and Rajapatirana 2000).

Quantitative restrictions were largely replaced by tariffs which offered less protection to import-substituting industries. A number of measures were introduced to promote FDI, including tax incentives and EPZs. Price controls were also by and large removed and universal food subsidies were replaced by food stamps which indicated low-income families (though in practice the scheme covered half the population). A unified exchange rate was implemented, the Sri Lankan rupee (LKR) was devalued by 45.5 per cent and a managed float came into practice. Some relaxation of capital controls occurred but the LKR was still not fully convertible. Repatriation of proceeds from sale of Sri Lankan shares was permitted and restrictions on release of foreign exchange for travel and education were eased. Foreign banks were allowed to set up branches in Sri Lanka and local commercial banks could operate Foreign Currency Banking Units (FCBU).

Export development became a policy priority and the Export Development Board (EDB) was set up in 1979. The EDB was engaged in direct cash transfers to certain export products, duty rebate schemes and medium- to long-term credit schemes, among others. The GCEC (Greater Colombo Economic Commission) was set up to organise and operate EPZs to attract FDI. Incentives included ten-year tax holidays on salaries and dividends, 100 per cent foreign ownership and duty exemption on machinery and certain production inputs.

However, the reform process lost momentum by 1982 as other concerns forced the government to cut back on the liberalisation agenda. Along with liberalisation the government was engaged in a large public investment programme, with the Accelerated Mahaweli Development Project (AMDP), a housing project and an urban development project being the key projects which accounted for approximately 75 per cent of public investment. The AMDP, a large-scale irrigation project that would provide hydroelectric power and boost agricultural activity in the dry zones, was the biggest of these and accounted for about 45 per cent of public investment. In this context, government finances were weakened as these projects had little or no short-term revenue-enhancing effect. Overall public expenditure was estimated at 35 per cent of GDP (Lakshman and Sri Lanka Association of Economists 1997). Much of this public expenditure was in part an attempt to provide a safety net for those sectors and individuals whose interests were undermined by the adverse impacts of trade liberalisation (sectors such as handloom weaving) by providing employment (AMDP, for instance, was to provide employment opportunities in its construction and in the agricultural jobs that would result from it) or direct income support for the poor (the Janasaviya poverty alleviation scheme) (Kelegama 2006).

The widening budget deficits forced the government to slow down the pace of tariff reduction and a Presidential Tariff Commission (PTC) was appointed to look into appeals on trade policy changes. While some tariffs were reduced based on the needs of reducing costs of imported inputs, the majority of cases resulted in tariffs being increased in response to calls for protection, which were readily accommodated given the revenue imperatives faced by the government. There was a surcharge of 10 per cent on all imports that had a tariff of over 50 per cent, which was intended to fund export development but had a protective element as well, indirectly undermining exports by forming a bias towards the import substitution sector.

Economic conditions deteriorated as the fiscal situation was undermined, inflation increased and between 1978 and 1983 there was a 62.3 per cent deterioration in the terms of trade. Economic growth stagnated and the current account deficit expanded, as shown in Table 9.1 below. Furthermore, in 1983, ethnic tensions that had been simmering over the past decade blew into a bloody civil war which would last 26 years. The war expenditure put further pressure on the fiscal situation and the weak investment climate undermined the ability of the private sector to fully exploit the opportunities provided by trade liberalisation.

The liberalisation process that took place between 1977 and 1982 was to a great extent incomplete. The weak macroeconomic conditions, coupled with conflict and deteriorating external conditions (global economic downturn in 1982, the second oil shock and adverse terms of trade for Sri Lanka), undermined the growth performance in Sri Lanka and true potential for trade liberalisation to have a substantial impact on growth and poverty was not fulfilled.

Contemporary trade policy

Over the past three decades Sri Lanka has become increasingly open to trade – undertaking unilateral, multilateral and regional trade liberalisation. Sri Lanka's applied tariffs are relatively low by the developing country standards. The simple average applied tariff as of 2006 was 11.2 per cent, while that of manufactured goods was 9.2 per cent and of agricultural goods was 23.8 per cent. Prior to 2005 applied rates were even lower, with the average applied rate between 2000 and 2004 being 9.5 per cent. Sri Lanka nonetheless

Table 9.1 Poverty headcount index (percentage) by district

District	Poverty headcount index (percentage) by survey period			
	1990/1	*1995/6*	*2002*	*2006/7*
Sri Lanka	26.1	28.8	22.7	15.2
Urban	16.3	14.0	7.9	6.7
Rural	29.5	30.9	24.7	15.7
Estate	20.5	38.4	30.0	32.0
District				
Colombo	16.2	12.0	6.4	5.4
Gampaha	14.7	14.1	10.7	8.7
Kalutara	32.3	29.5	20.0	13.0
Kandy	35.9	36.7	24.9	17.0
Matale	28.7	41.9	29.6	18.9
Nuwara Eliya	20.1	32.1	22.6	33.8
Galle	29.7	31.6	25.8	13.7
Matara	29.2	35.0	27.5	14.7
Hambantota	32.4	31.0	32.2	12.7
Batticaloa				10.7
Ampara				10.9
Kurunegala	27.2	26.2	25.4	15.4
Puttalam	22.3	31.1	31.3	13.1
Anuradhapura	24.4	27.0	20.4	14.9
Polonnaruwa	24.9	20.1	23.7	12.7
Badulla	31.0	41.0	37.3	23.7
Monaragala	33.7	56.2	37.2	33.2
Ratnapura	30.8	46.4	34.4	26.6
Kegalle	31.2	36.3	32.5	21.1

Source: DCS (2008).

maintains the lowest applied MFN tariffs in South Asia. Sri Lanka maintains a five-band tariff structure with rates of 0 to 2.5 per cent, 6 per cent, 15 per cent and 28 per cent in 2005. Agricultural products and finished manufactured goods receive higher levels of protection while raw materials and inputs into production receive lower levels of protection. Despite Sri Lanka's relative low applied tariff rates, since the year 2000 there has been an increasing tendency towards the imposition of *ad hoc* levies and surcharges on various items in response to calls for domestic protection, government policy changes on domestic production (dairy products being one example) where new government policy is towards encouraging domestic production and thereby levies on competing imports have increased. The special commodity levy on imported milk was increased from LKR 5 per kg to LKR 15 per kg 'with a view to encouraging local dairy production' (Ministry of Finance 2008) and revenue considerations. In more recent years Sri Lanka has implemented Free Trade Agreements with India and Pakistan and is party to the South Asian Free Trade Agreement, along with many other regional trade agreements including BIMSTEC and APTA. However, the impact of these initiatives on trade opening has so far been small compared to that of the process of unilateral liberalisation initiated in 1977 (World Bank 2005b).

Sri Lanka has experienced rapid growth of both exports and imports in recent years. Annual average import growth between 2003 and 2007 was 13.9 per cent, while annual average export growth was 10.6 per cent. Imports have increased at a faster rate than exports resulting in a widening trade deficit. A major cause for the faster rate of import growth is the increase in price and consumption of oil. In 2007, expenditure on petroleum imports accounted for 40 per cent of growth in import expenditure (CBSL 2007). Exports have grown rapidly as well, led by apparel exports and a resurgence of export earnings from agricultural commodities such as tea, buoyed by commodity price booms in 2007. A major concern in trade patterns in Sri Lanka is limited export diversification both geographically and in terms of products. As of 2007, 62 per cent of Sri Lanka's exports were destined for the USA and the EU. While this is an improvement from the past (in 2002, 82 per cent of exports were to these regions), there remains much room for increased diversification. In terms of products, garments made up 43 per cent of Sri Lanka's exports and tea made up 13.2 per cent of total exports. No other export product category contributed over 10 per cent of exports. Such a lack of diversification of products leaves Sri Lanka vulnerable to fluctuations in global market conditions in these product categories.

Trends and patterns of poverty

In this section, we examine recent historic trends in poverty and sectoral and regional disparities in poverty incidences as a backdrop to the discussion in the following section on the relationship between trade liberalisation and poverty.

Poverty in Sri Lanka is predominantly a rural phenomenon (Table 9.1).[1] Several studies have shown that poor households are more likely to be found in rural than in urban areas because of working members being employed in agriculture and other primary production activities (Datt and Gunewardena 1995). The incidence of poverty (as measured by the standard headcount ratio) at national level has shown a steady decline from 26.1 per cent in 1990/1 to 15.2 per cent in 2006/7. At the sectoral level, poverty in the rural sector, where 80 per cent of the population finds livelihood, also declined but at a slower rate, from 24.7 per cent to 15.7 per cent. Poverty in the estate sector[2] which accounts for about 5.5 per cent of the population increased from 30 per cent in 2002 to 32 per cent in 2006/7.

At the district level, Nuwara Eliya and the Monaragala districts, where the estate sector is concentrated, are the poorest. In these two districts the headcount poverty index was above 33 per cent in 2006/7. Nuwara Eliya district is the only district that reported an increase of poverty from 2002 to 2006/7 and the increase is alarming, rising almost 50 per cent from 22.6 per cent in 2002 to 33.8 per cent in 2006/7. Hambantota district, which was among the poorest districts between 1990/1 and 2002, has experienced an unprecedented drop of poverty incidence of over 60 per cent, from 32.2 per cent in 2002 to 12.7 per cent in 2006/7. This achievement has lifted Hambantota district above even Kalutara district of the Western Province, which has always reported the least incidence of poverty. However, Kalutara district has also gained a highly significant continuous reduction in the poverty headcount index from 32.3 per cent in 1990/1 and 20 per cent in 2002 to 13 per cent in 2006/7, and somewhat similar improvements in poverty reduction have been shown by Puttalam and Polonnaruwa districts.

The trade–poverty nexus

As discussed in Chapters 1 and 2 of this volume, the linkage between trade and poverty has been thoroughly examined in both theoretical and empirical research. The primary avenue by which trade affects poverty in the long run is through economic growth. Theory suggests that trade liberalisation results in economic growth and economic growth leads to poverty reduction. However, it has not been possible to completely substantiate this finding in the empirical literature.

Data on per capita income, trade and poverty incidence during the reform period are plotted in Figure 9.1. It can be seen that income and poverty have moved together and poverty has moved in the reverse direction during this period. However, the time period is too short to test econometrically the impact of trade on poverty incidence. What we aim to do in this section is simply to put together and analyse whatever available data relating to the various channels through which trade impacts on poverty in the context of trade policy reforms. In Sri Lankan trade, growth and poverty reduction have all moved in the same direction.

Trade, employment and poverty

A key link between trade and poverty is the impact of trade on employment opportunities because employment is the main, if not the only, source of

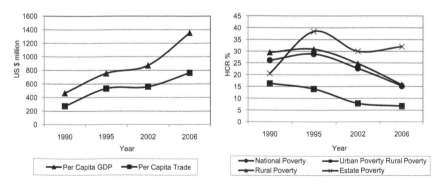

Figure 9.1 Trade, GDP and poverty

income for the poor. Sri Lanka is a useful case study to probe this link. In the period following the liberalisation of the economy in 1977, manufacturing took off substantially compared to the closed economy era. This was primarily due to the emergence of new export-oriented labour-intensive industries, in particular clothing, benefiting from concomitant liberalisation of trade and foreign investment regimes. Also, increased availability of imported inputs helped expansion of domestic-market oriented production with a time lag, following a significant output contraction immediately after the removal of import controls.

Between 1978 and 2003, manufacturing output grew at 8.2 per cent compared to 4.8 per cent in the period preceding reforms. The contribution of manufacturing to total exports in 1974 was 4 per cent and in 1977 was 6 per cent, but by 1984, seven years after liberalisation, this figure had reached 42 per cent, though it was dominated by the garment sector. The importance of export-oriented manufacture also increased substantially. The ratio of exports to gross manufacturing output increased from 12 per cent in 1976 to 24 per cent in 1981 (Athukorala 2006). In the post-liberalisation period, manufacturing in general and export-oriented manufacturing in particular also contributed significantly to employment creation. The manufacturing sector accounted for 36 per cent of employment creation between 1990 and 2001 and export-oriented manufacturing accounted for the bulk of this. Total local employment in export-oriented BoI firms increased from around 10,000 in the early 1980s to 416,000 in 2002 – 40 per cent of total manufacturing employment (Athukorala 2006). These figures need to be considered in the context of an incomplete reform process, with a weak investment climate resulting from conflict and macroeconomic stresses.

While sectors such as apparel and leather thrived through liberalisation, (apparel and leather sectors accounted for 44 per cent of employment creation in manufacturing between 1977 and 1980), there were sectors where employment declined while at the same time imports of these products had increased following liberalisation (Cuthbertson and Athukorala 1991). Examples include glass production, footwear and metal furniture. However, absolute declines had been relatively low. In the textile sector, trade liberalisation is estimated to have resulted in the loss of 40,000 jobs and the closure of some 30,000 small establishments. While there was job creation in other sectors such as garments, it has been argued that there is a mismatch between the industrial and geographic sectors where jobs have been lost and jobs have been created. Kelegama (2006) argues that job losses occurred largely in the rural sectors such as small handloom establishments while job creation occurred largely in the FTZs near Colombo. This mismatch could have contributed to exacerbating regional discrepancies in development.

Along with the positive impact of job creation through trade liberalisation, there were also employment opportunities created through the public investment by the government (AMDP and others) and the increase in employment opportunities abroad through external migration. Unemployment in 1971 was

18.7 per cent; in 1975 it was 19.8 per cent, in 1978/9 it was 14.8 per cent and in 1981/2 it was 11.7 per cent (Athukorala and Rajapatirana 2000). It should also be noted that the different unemployment figures are from different surveys and therefore variance in methodology undermines comparability over time.

Given the importance of livelihood creation for sustainable poverty reduction, the trade liberalisation episode had an important impact on long-term poverty reduction in Sri Lanka. The major examples of the trade–employment–poverty nexus in Sri Lanka's three decades as an open economy are tea, garments, tourism and export of labour (low-skill labour, movement of natural persons) particularly to the Middle East. The success of these has, however, been mixed.

Garment sector

This sector emerged almost entirely through the Multi-Fibre Arrangement (MFA), which ensured quotas for garment exports to developed markets from countries such as Sri Lanka. Since the 1970s, the garment sector has grown and as of 2007 made up 40.6 per cent of total exports from Sri Lanka. According to the latest census of industries in 2004, the garment sector provides employment to 382,000 workers, making up 37 per cent of total industrial employment in Sri Lanka. Of these workers, 87 per cent are women, and experiences with Grameen Bank in Bangladesh showed that income in the hands of women has a better impact on poverty reduction, since a greater proportion of the income is used for household consumption, health and education. Jenkins (2004) provides a similar example from Vietnam. The government of Sri Lanka undertook complementary policies, such as the 200 Garment Factory Programme of 1992, to ensure that investment in the garment sector was spread beyond the Western province, providing employment opportunities in rural areas to maximise the poverty impacts of such investments (Weerakoon and Thennakoon 2006). However, 72 per cent of garment industry firms and 65 per cent of employment in such firms has been within the Western province (World Bank 2005b). This is mainly due to easy access to the port, the higher standard of infrastructure and more reliable access to electricity in this region. Nonetheless, it should be noted that many of the workers migrate from rural areas to the Western Province to work in the garment sector – particularly to avoid stigmas associated with the sector (Rupasinghe 1985).

The same broad sector is often cited as an example of the negative side of trade reform. In Sri Lanka, the import of textiles was completely liberalised in 1997 to provide cheap inputs for production of garments (Yatawara and Handel 2007). As a result, much of the local textile industry was unable to compete with imported textiles. In 1993, there were 414 textile establishments with 25 or more people engaged, employing a total of 52,980 people. By 2002, the number of establishments of 25 or more people had fallen to 149, but 55,057 found employment in this sector (DCS 1994 and 2004b). Trade creates winners and losers: just as trade provides markets for export, import competition can undermine previously protected local industries, resulting in short- to medium-term unemployment. Computable General Equilibrium (CGE) model simulations by Naranpanawa (2005) suggest that import-competing industries catering to the domestic market, such as the food and beverage industry, paper and paper products and chemical industries, face contractions in output and employment in the face of trade liberalisation due to competition from imports. There is limited empirical work on trade related transitional unemployment and less so on the incidence of this among the poor. However, the work of Matusz and Tarr (1999)[3] on the adjustment costs resulting from trade liberalisation in the manufacturing sector suggests that transitional unemployment is limited and durations are relatively short. Nonetheless, safety nets and temporary income transfer schemes are critical in enabling the poor, who lack the financial assets to support themselves, to get through temporary unemployment that could result from trade liberalisation.

Tea

Tea has been Sri Lanka's major traditional export product between independence and the rise of the garment industry in the 1990s. However, this has been less of a success story given poverty rates in the estate sector. Even though significant employment is generated, the bulk of it is very low-skilled employment which yields low incomes. Wages in the tea sector were increased following industrial action in 2006. As of 2007, the average daily wage earned in the sector is Rs 378 for men and Rs 261 for women.[4] To be above the national poverty line requires expenditure of above Rs 2,924[5] per person per month as of April 2008. Thus, a female-headed household in the estate sector with four members including just one provider, who works a full 30 days, would have a per capita income of Rs 1,958, clearly below the poverty line.

There are several reasons for the high poverty in the region, including weak connective infrastructure, particularly transport and communications. A World Bank study[6] showed that even though 77 per cent of sampled estate households lived within 10 km of a road, 42 per cent of the sample households could not use the road year round. However, the study goes on to point out that the organisational structure in the estate sector – including the employment structure – is one of 'resident labour'. Given this dependent relationship, a normal employer–employee wage-bargaining relationship does not prevail. The study suggests that this has been compounded by unrepresentative and self-serving union leaders. Limited educational opportunities have historically provided few alternatives for employment in this sector. Furthermore, historical social exclusion of estate workers has left them marginalised. For instance, according to the World Bank Poverty Assessment only 13 per cent of the sampled estate population received Samurdhi benefits, while the Samurdhi coverage for the entire country is 40 per cent. The estate sector in Sri Lanka shows that trade will not yield results in terms of poverty reduction without human resource development through education and when the labour market does not function through normal market forces.

Trade and stability

A potential negative impact of trade on poverty operates through volatility in trade flows. The poor are less able to respond to shocks created by trade through the lack of financial resources and access to credit to smooth consumption. However, trade does not in its own right increase exposure to shocks. In fact, trade can allow smoother consumption by mitigating domestic shocks – and in theory global supply should be smoother than domestic supply. In Sri Lanka, for instance, rice imports are liberalised whenever domestic production shocks (such as drought) cause increases in domestic price (Jayanetti and Tillekeratne 2005). Trade can also result in changes in the consumption basket, and the poor can thus be exposed to volatility in prices of imported goods. While the wealthy can absorb temporary shocks in prices, the poor are less able to do so. An example of this is the consumption of milk food in Sri Lanka. The bulk of milk consumed is imported milk powder, while consumption of domestically produced liquid milk has declined. In 2007, the price of milk powder increased globally in the wake of supply shocks in major producers such as Australia. This had significant impacts on the poor since much reliance is placed on milk powder, particularly for consumption by infants. Attempts at price controls have failed in such instances, as hoarding and black market formation have been impossible to curb. In this context, the role of safety nets and temporary income transfers become more relevant given the lack of access to credit for the poor.

Trade and government revenue

In many developing countries, Sri Lanka included, tariff revenue plays an important role in government revenue. Tariff revenue, Rs 56.3 billion, made up 9.6 per cent of total government revenue in 2007. This figure excludes miscellaneous levies on imported products such as various cess charges and the Port and Airport Development Levy. Government revenue is in turn used to fund state programmes aimed at poverty reduction and income distribution. In 2007, Rs 110.9 billion was spent on current transfers to households and other transfers (including subsidies such as those for kerosene and fertiliser, used extensively by the poor, particularly farmers and fishermen). The Samurdhi scheme is the major income transfer scheme aimed at supporting poor households directly, and in 2007 Rs 7.2 billion was spent on the Samurdhi programme.

The impact of trade liberalisation on tariff revenue is an empirical question. The outcomes depend greatly on the relevant position on the Laffer curves and the average elasticities of products being liberalised. Greenway and Milner (1991) showed that in the post Structural Adjustment Policy (SAP) economies of Mauritius, Kenya and Jamaica, revenues increased through changes in export/import bases following liberalisation of trade. Ebril *et al.* (1999) showed that, between 1980 and 1992, countries that did not reduce tariffs did not suffer significantly lower revenue as a proportion of GDP compared to those that did.

In Sri Lanka, average Most Favoured Nation (MFN) tariffs have increased in recent years, effectively a reverse of trade liberalisation. Between 2000 and 2004, the average MFN tariff was 9.5 per cent, continuing a trend of falling tariffs where between 1995 and 1999 the average MFN tariff was 19.5 per cent.[7] See Figure 9.2.

In the immediate aftermath of significant tariff reductions in the late 1990s, tariff revenue did fall to an extent. However, this does not necessitate a negative impact on poverty as other forms of levies can be imposed to maintain overall government revenue at a stable level. In Sri Lanka, it can be seen that overall government revenue did fall as a proportion of GDP[8] but later stabilised and increased latterly. Various *ad hoc* levies have been imposed on imports at different stages. For instance, in the year 2000 an across-the-board 40 per cent surcharge on imports was imposed; this was later brought down to 20 per cent. Today, there are several duties such as the Port and Airport Development Levy, cesses and the Regional Infrastructure Development Levy, among others. These have helped shore up government revenue even if tariffs have declined. For instance, between 2003 and 2006, average tariffs fell from 5.3 per cent to 4.5 per cent, while total government revenue increased from 15.7 per cent to 17 per cent in the same period. Furthermore, even if total revenue were to fall, the impact on poverty could be minimised if a government could reduce expenditure in other unnecessary areas and maintain expenditure on the poor.

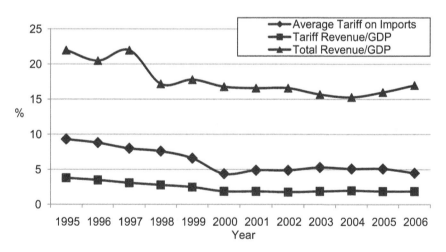

Figure 9.2 Government revenue and tariffs
Source: Produced using Central Bank of Sri Lanka data

Cross-cutting issues

Transaction costs

The actual effects of trade on poverty are contingent on certain conditions. The two main conditions are the transmission of price shocks that arise from trade and the ability of the poor to respond to these shocks. Transmission of price shocks refers to the possibility of a change of price at the border, resulting from trade being not completely transmitted to the poor household. This could occur through high transaction costs – where, for instance, the benefit of a cheaper imported price may be nullified by high transport costs, or an increase in imported price could be magnified by high transaction costs. This could also undermine the cost advantage that a rural producer may have, since high transaction costs could negate the competitiveness of her exports in the international market. This is certainly a problem in Sri Lanka, where the gateway to the international market is in Colombo, through the major port and airport. Naturally, the best infrastructure has developed around this gateway, in terms of financial markets, transport networks and major business services. As a result, Colombo (poverty headcount of 5.4 per cent), and the surrounding Western province, has developed substantially and has succeeded in reducing poverty. However, provinces like Uva and Sabaragamuwa have not been able to reduce poverty to the same extent, influenced by lack of quality transport infrastructure connecting them to the more developed parts of the country such as the Western province.

While it is not essential for all rural regions to have access to international markets, it is important for rural regions to at least have access to local markets that have benefited from international markets. Sri Lanka is a prime example of this. In Figure 9.3, driving distance to Colombo is correlated with

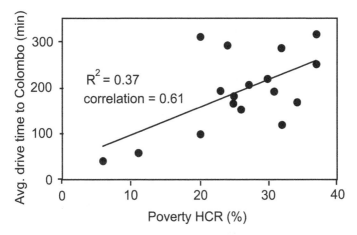

Figure 9.3 Relationship between poverty and driving distance to Colombo
Source: *Sri Lanka Poverty Assessment* (World Bank 2007c)

poverty headcounts, showing that the probability of a household being poor falls by almost 3 per cent with a unit increase in accessibility index of that district, while controlling for factors that affect the probability of the household being poor. Other transaction costs, such as delays in customs clearance and bureaucratic costs, have potential impacts on poverty and need to be addressed in this regard. See Figure 9.4.

Responding to price shocks

As mentioned earlier, trade creates winners and losers, but if the poor lack the resources to respond to price shocks, potential winners will not be able to gain from trade and losers could slip further into poverty. In order to benefit from a positive price shock, an exporter needs to be able to increase production accordingly – therefore requiring access to factors of production. Imperfections in credit markets and land markets and lack of information undermine the ability of poor exporters to do so. As mentioned earlier, access to information by the poor in Sri Lanka has improved significantly, led by mobile telephony. A study by De Silva and Zainudeen (2007) showed that 94 per cent of Bottom of the Pyramid (BoP) users in Sri Lanka had some access to telephony, regardless of ownership of a phone. While this has benefited many users at the BoP, such as trishaw drivers (in getting hires), farmers and fishermen (in obtaining price information) and, in general, reduction of transaction costs (making a call instead of taking a bus to get information), there remains untapped potential for the use of telecom in business transactions. The study suggests that one reason for this is the maintenance of incoming call charges in Sri Lanka, which increase the cost of mobile phone usage.

Access to land is also a problem in Sri Lanka because of state controls on land usage, particularly rice in the interest of domestic food security. According to Jenkins (2004), in Vietnam exports of rice increased following liberalisation, greatly benefiting poor farmers. The result was that, of the poorest households in 1992, 98 per cent had higher incomes six years later and poverty dropped from 75 per cent in 1988 to 37 per cent in 1998. In Vietnam, trade opened up markets for the products of the poor. In the case of Sri Lanka, the poor working in agriculture face rigidities in markets for land. The Land Development Ordinance (1935) governs most land used for agriculture and stipulates in most cases the type of crop that can be cultivated; it also limits usage of land as collateral and prevents the user from selling the land if he wants to shift to a different sector. This limits the ability of farmers to change production in order to respond to market signals. Furthermore, stringent agricultural protection in Sri Lanka also limits incentives to move beyond supplying the domestic market. Such perverse incentives steer farmers away from potential export agriculture, keeping them in the production of rice for the domestic market.

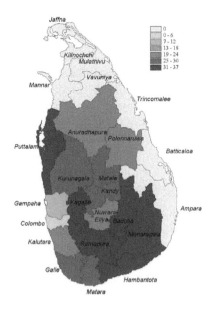

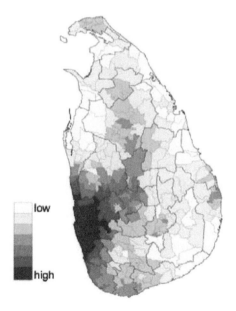

Figure 9.4 Poverty headcount index and accessibility by province and district, 2002
Source: Authors' illustration using Department of Census and Statistics data and World
Bank *Development Policy Review* (World Bank 2006b)

Access to credit has also been cited as a problem in rural Sri Lanka. Credit is essential to be able to respond to market shocks by increasing production. According to an ADB and World Bank (2005b) study, 59 per cent of entrepreneurs identified access to credit as a severe constraint or a constraint to enterprise performance and growth. A previous ADB (2003) survey found that 64 per cent of SMEs felt that availability of credit was a major constraint in expanding their business. Rural firms very rarely obtain finance from private commercial banks – mainly because of collateral requirements. Limited access to formal credit inhibits ability of firms to respond effectively to trade-related shocks by making the necessary investments to increase production.

The trade–poverty nexus: econometric analysis

Although there are different channels through which trade liberalisation affects poverty, as discussed in the previous section the employment channel has been prominent in Sri Lanka. Therefore, the purpose of this section is to undertake an econometric analysis of the impact of trade policy on poverty, with emphasis on the employment–income–poverty nexus.

Methodology

In order to examine the link between trade and poverty, we estimate a simultaneous-equation model, consisting of a poverty equation and an income determination equation, using a panel dataset extracted from the unpublished returns to the household income surveys of 1995, 2002 and 2005 conducted by the Department of Statistics, Sri Lanka Household Income and Expenditure Survey (HIES) 1995/6, 2002 and 2005. The model is estimated using the generalised method of moments (GMM) introduced by Hansen (1982) and further developed by Arellano and Bond (1991), Blundell and Bond (1998) and Hansen (2002). This estimation method has a number of advantages over other econometric techniques: (1) it permits exploiting time-series variation in data, accounting for unobserved individual specific effects, allowing for the inclusion of lagged dependent variables as repressors and, therefore, providing better control for endogeneity of all explanatory variables (Beck *et al.* 2000); (2) it brings efficiency gains in the presence of hetero-scedasticity; and (3) it provides a straightforward test of the appropriateness of the specification of the proposed model.

The formal structure of the simultaneous equations system is as follows:
Equation 1. Poverty:

$$POV = \alpha_0 + \alpha_1 COMM_{i,t} + \alpha_2 TRAN_{i,t} + \alpha_3 INCOME_{i,t} + \mu_i + \varepsilon_{i,t}$$

Equation 2. Income:

$$INCOME_{i,t} = \beta_0 + \beta_1 EDU_{i,t} + \beta_2 DEP_{i,t} + \beta_3 UNEMP_{i,t} + \beta_4 EXPINDU + \nu_i + \xi$$

where *POV* is a poverty incidence variable which was calculated as follows.

$$POV = \frac{Expenditure_{i,t} - Poverty\ line_t}{sd(Expenditure_t)}$$

To calculate poverty incidence (POV), the study uses the official poverty lines which were calculated by the Department of Census and Statistics (DCS). In the POV index *i* represents the households and *t* represents the years 1995, 2002 and 2005. In Sri Lanka, people living in households whose real per capita monthly total consumption expenditure is below Rs 1,817 in year 2005, Rs 1,423 in year 2002 and Rs 833 in year 95/6 are considered poor.[9] This poverty incidence variable produces positive numbers to non-poor households and negative numbers to poor households which are based on the standard deviation of per capita household monthly expenditure. This index is more logical to measure the poverty depth of the household, rather than taking the dichotomous variable to indicate the poverty status. As for the explanatory variables, after controlling for each year's poverty line, the variable of export adjusted per capita income *(INCOME)* is included, because income growth is an important driving force for alleviation of poverty (Dollar and Kraay 2002; World Bank 2002a). This *INCOME* variable is measured by the ratio of total exports to total number of households of each year and multiplied by the household's per capita income, to work as a proxy for the export earnings of the households.

In addition, a number of poverty-related control variables are used to delineate the hypothesised line between employment, income and poverty incidence. The variable communication expenditure *(COMM)* is introduced and measured by the ratio of communication expenditure to total household expenditure. The variable transport expenditure *(TRAN)* is also introduced, measured by the ratio of transport expenditure to total household expenditure, and export-adjusted per capita income *(INCOME)* is calculated and introduced, to minimise the omitted variables of the poverty channel.

The benefit of education in improving the quality of life of people, increasing the productivity of their labour, enhancing earnings, reducing mortality and morbidity, raising fertility control and leading to higher overall welfare has been central to the literature on eradicating poverty (Haveman and Wolfe 1894; Psacharopoulos and Woodhall 1985). Most of the households' main decision-maker would be the person who has the highest education level. In addition, if the proportion of dependency or the proportion of unemployment in a household is high, a relatively small number of income earners will be supporting a large number of dependants. Therefore, there is a stronger likelihood that such a household may become poor. Based on this logic, the study used the variables of highest education level in the household *(EDU)*, proportion of dependency of the household *(DEP)* and unemployment rate of the household *(UNEMP)* as controlling the poverty channel of the model.

Using the simultaneous equations system here, Equation (1) models the determinants of poverty, in which the *POV* is the dependent variable. As for the explanatory variables, the variables of *COMM, TRAN* and *INCOME* are introduced to control the situation of poverty. After controlling for the initial level of export earning, a variable for *EDU* is introduced to capture the education effects of export earnings, and *DEP* and *UNEMP* are included in the regression to capture the impact of changing dependency ratios and unemployment ratios on Sri Lanka's poor. The number of household members engaged in export-oriented manufacturing people *(EXPINDU)* were calculated and introduced to measure the impact of poverty by the export-oriented manufacturing employment. Equation (2) models the determinants of household income, in which the export earning *(INCOME)* is used as the dependent variable. After controlling for the initial level of export earning, a variable for *EDU* is introduced to capture the education effects of export earnings, and *DEP, UNEMP* and *EXPINDU* are included in the regression to capture the impact of changing dependency ratios, unemployment ratios and export-oriented manufacturing employment.

For each regression of GMM, the specification of equation is tested with the Hansen test of over-identifying restrictions, and then with the Arellano–Bond test for the second-order serial correlation. The test results show that all the GMM regressions satisfy the specification tests, which indicates that the instruments are valid and there exists no evidence of second-order serial correlation in the GMM regressions.

Data

To implement the model presented in the above section, data from three micro-level large household surveys in Sri Lanka – the Household Income and Expenditure Survey (HIES) for the years 1995/6, 2002 and 2005 – are used in this study. An HIES is conducted every five years by the DCS. The HIES of 1995/6 was the fourth series and was conducted during the period from November 1995 to October 1996, and the HIES of 2001/2 was conducted during the period from January 2002 to December 2002. The 2005 HIES survey was a special survey which was conducted to take into account income and expenditure patterns of the country after the tsunami disaster of December 2004. This HIES of 2005 was conducted within the three-month period from September to November 2005. These three surveys covered all provinces in the country excluding the Northern and Eastern provinces, which were omitted because of the unavailability of a proper sampling frame and because the civil disturbances in those areas prevented data collection. However, the 1995/6 survey covered 21,220 housing units (19,682 households), the 2002 survey covered 20,100 housing units (16,924 households) and the 2005 survey covered 5,380 housing units (4,576 households).

Results

In this section, results obtained from the model described in the previous section are used to examine the effect on poverty, particularly via the trade–employment–poverty channel. The estimated results of the poverty determinant model and income-earning model related to sectoral and income group differences are provided in Tables 9.2 and 9.3, respectively. As expected, income is negatively related to poverty in both sets of equations related to sectoral differences. The results indicate that the sectoral difference in poverty impact depends on communication and general access to international markets.

However, the result shown in Table 9.2, that manufacturing employment has a positive impact on income in the urban sector, is consistent with the descriptive narrative presented in the background section. This suggests that employment seems pro-poor through generation of income, but the impact is concentrated largely in the urban sector.

In addition to the expansion of export-oriented manufacturing, there are other variables which play some significant role in reducing poverty according to the results presented in Table 9.2. These results demonstrate that the communication expenditure plays a significant role in reducing poverty in urban and estate sectors. In relation to the rural sector, the results show that transport expenditure is a significant determinant of rural poverty.

It seems that in the case of the urban and estate sector, communication expenditure is a significant factor in determining poverty, and for the rural sector transport expenditure is the significant factor in determining rural poverty. The results of the income-earning equation suggest that industrial employment is a significant determinant of household income in the urban sector. Therefore, it is clear that trade creates employment and employment generation reduces poverty in the urban sector.

Table 9.3 reports the estimated results for the poorest 40 per cent and richest 20 per cent of the poverty-determinant and income-earning models. These results also suggest that industrial employment is a significant determinant of household income in the poorest 40 per cent decile. The empirical results are in line with the narrative discussed in earlier sections and suggest that industrial employment contributes to poverty reduction through the generation of income, but this impact is concentrated largely in the urban sector.

Overall, the results of the econometric estimations presented in this section are consistent.

Policy implications and conclusion

Several policy implications can be drawn from the outcomes of this study from a Sri Lankan perspective. An important finding of the econometric analysis and broader observation of the outcomes of trade liberalisation on industrial employment in Sri Lanka is that trade liberalisation has resulted in significant employment creation and, accordingly contributed to poverty reduction, since industrial employment is a significant determinant of household income in the poorest decile. However, this relationship holds primarily

Table 9.2 Determinants of poverty and household income

(Dependent variable = POV)

	Sri Lanka		Urban		Rural		Estate	
COMM	-0.021	-0.28	0.572 a 0.210a	5.15	-0.58	-1.02	-0.19 c	-1.80
TRAN	0.003	0.07	-0.058	-0.91	-0.19 b	1.77	-0.04	-0.56
INCOME	1.7E-04	3.34	-1.4E-05	-0.59	-1.4E-04 a	3.03	6.0E-05 b	2.17
Year_2002	-0.022	-0.27	-0.213 a	-2.90	-0.03	-0.46	0.03	0.53
Year_2005	-1.575 a	-5.41	0.104	0.10	-1.40 a	-4.17	-0.19	-0.58
Constant	0.485 a	3.85	0.538 a	5.41	0.25 b	1.81	0.41 a	3.19
Observations	1,500		1,374		1,500		1,113	
Centred R^2	0.6485		0.4459		0.1029		0.2232	
Uncentred R^2	0.4684		0.0928		0.7750		0.1830	
Hansen test of over–identifying restrictions	χ^2=7.773 Probability χ^2=1.000		χ^2=37.099 Probability χ^2=1.000		χ^2=21.541 Probability χ^2=1.000		χ^2=4.021 Probability χ^2=1.000	
Arellano–Bond test for second order serial correlation	Z= -0.26 Probability>Z=0.719		Z= -0.21 Probability>Z=0.715		Z= -0.29 Probability>Z=0.728		Z= -0.26 Probability>Z=0.721	

Table 9.2 (continued)

(Dependent variable = INCOME)

	Sri Lanka		Urban		Rural		Estate	
EDU	2.284 [a]	5.81	1.122	1.46	1.956 [a]	3.03	1.826 [a]	2.60
DEP	-0.020	-1.15	0.132 [a]	3.87	-0.074 [a]	-2.87	-0.003	-0.07
UNEMP	-0.167	-1.13	0.056	0.68	0.136	1.07	-0.130	-1.03
EXPINDU	0.470	0.91	6.070 [b]	2.54	-0.283	-0.34	5.111	0.80
Year_2002	-0.809	-0.13	-0.097	-0.03	-0.725	-0.41	-2.337	-0.54
Year_2005	8.244 [a]	8.08	46.287 [a]	13.55	12.013 [a]	7.42	7.711	1.58
Constant	24.240 [a]	-4.92	21.247 [b]	-2.17	-17.776 [b]	-2.22	-13.961 [b]	-1.99
Observations	1500		1368		1500		1113	
Centred R^2	0.3979		0.4600		0.0735		0.4124	
Uncentred R^2	0.4305		0.4092		0.1007		0.4140	
Hansen test of over-identifying restrictions	χ^2=9.289 Probability χ^2=1.000		χ^2=22.285 Probability χ^2=1.000		χ^2=16.945 Probability χ^2=1.000		χ^2=11.637 Probability χ^2=1.000	
Arellano–Bond test for second order serial correlation	Z= -0.32 Probability>Z=0.638		Z= -0.24 Probability>Z=0.708		Z= -0.40 Probability>Z=0.337		Z= -0.16 Probability>Z=0.654	

Notes

For all regressions, *t*–statistics values are presented in parentheses.

a, b and c represent significance at the 1 per cent, 5 per cent and 10 per cent levels, respectively.

Table 9.3 Estimated equations – poorest 40 per cent and richest 20 per cent

	(Dependent variable = POV)			
	Poorest 40%t		*Richest 20%*	
COMM	0.005 [a]	0.52	−1.31	−0.86
TRAN	0.002	0.55	1.10	0.80
INCOME	−5.3E−04 [a]	−1.537	3.2E−04	1.25
Year_2002	0.097 [a]	7.93	0.764	0.63
Year_2005	0.288 [a]	7.15	−5.90	−1.34
Constant	−0.108 [a]	−9.62	0.541	0.30
Observations		600		300
Centred R^2		0.1354		0.3237
Uncentred R^2		0.1251		0.1178
Hansen test of over−identifying restrictions		χ^2=12.836		χ^2=9.376
Arellano–Bond test for second order serial correlation		Z= −0.72		Z= −0.76

	(Dependent variable = INCOME)			
	Poorest 40 percent		*Richest 20 percent*	
EDU	0.383 [b]	2.26	1.886	1.01
DEP	0.017 [a]	3.32	−0.106	−1.26
UNEMP	−0.003	−0.10	−0.031	−0.10
EXPINDU	0.295 [c]	1.87	2.379	1.14
Year_2002	0.185	0.06	−3.109	−0.68
Year_2005	1.364 [a]	4.50	23.110 [a]	5.84
Constant	−5.433 [a]	−2.79	−21.264	−0.87
Observations		600		300
Centred R^2		0.5267		0.1528
Uncentred R^2		0.5162		0.2153
Hansen test of over−identifying restrictions		χ^2=12.624		χ^2=8.657
Arellano–Bond test for second order serial correlation		Z= −0.70		Z= −0.72

Notes
For all regressions, t−statistics values are presented in parentheses.
a, b and c represent significance at the 1 per cent, 5 per cent and 10 per cent levels, respectively.

in the urban sector. This finding is consistent with the uneven growth between regions under liberalisation reforms. As has been stressed throughout the chapter, Colombo and the surrounding Western province have developed rapidly due in part to access to international markets through the port and airport. Poverty in the Western province has fallen sharply, while more rural regions have not had as much success in reducing poverty. This example stresses the importance of improving access to international markets in order to benefit from trade. Transport infrastructure in particular is essential to enable the poor to access international gateways without encountering substantial transaction costs. The districts bordering Colombo have benefited from this – particularly Kalutara, Kurunegala, Puttalam and Gampaha, all of which have substantially reduced poverty. However, districts such as Nuwara-Eliya, Badulla, Monaragala and Ratnapura have not been able to do so.

The role of safety nets is also important in the Sri Lankan case. The necessity for safety nets is derived primarily from two sources – first, the possibility of losing employment through frictions in output caused by trade liberalisation (the textile sector in Sri Lanka) and the negative consumption shocks that can occur because of imported food (milk powder in Sri Lanka). The first best solution would naturally be for the poor to have greater access to credit in order to smooth consumption in the event of such negative shocks. It is important for such safety nets to be of a temporary nature for the duration of the relevant trade-related shock. In Sri Lanka, there is much room for improvement in terms of performance of safety-net schemes. The Samurdhi programme, the major welfare scheme in the country, covers 45 per cent of the total population. However, 40 per cent of the population in the poorest consumption quintile is excluded and 44 per cent of Samurdhi expenditure is spent on the richest three quintiles. It is clear that targeting is weak and the benefits are spread too thinly. For instance, it was found that 'The average monthly Samurdhi grant in 2005 was Rs 393 per family, which translated to less than $1 per capita per month for a typical family of four'.[10]

Furthermore, access to credit is important in terms of taking advantage of the opportunities presented by trade. For instance, increasing production to meet an increase in export prices would require greater expenditure on inputs, which may often require credit. Development of the financial sector should therefore take into account the need for credit among the poor. Access to information is equally important in terms of taking advantage of opportunities provided through international trade. The role of international trade in telecommunications services is important in terms of enabling the poor to have access to telecommunications services and at an affordable rate.

Given the importance of the trade–employment–poverty nexus, it is clear that there is a need for synergy between trade and investment policy. Trade liberalisation alone will not create the necessary conditions to boost investment and industrial production. Domestic firms may not have the required capacity and buyer linkages to fulfil potential for exploiting export opportunities created through trade liberalisation. In Sri Lanka's trade liberalisation experience, a large proportion of export value arose from foreign firms established in the country. In fact, over 80 per cent of the total increment in export value between 1980 and 1995 came from foreign firms.[11] Encouraging FDI can therefore support trade policy in terms of helping create employment opportunities.

All in all, the Sri Lankan case study provides several useful insights which add to the literature on the trade–poverty nexus. The positive relationship between trade, industrial employment and poverty reduction is an important finding, and equally important is the fact that this relationship holds primarily in urban areas. This stresses the importance of connectivity to key markets for this relationship between trade and poverty to hold. The contrasting impact of trade on poverty in two of Sri Lanka's major export sectors, garments and tea, is particularly revealing. The continued poverty in the estate sector provides a useful case of how trade does not necessarily lead to poverty reduction without necessary conditions in the relevant labour markets. The rise of the garment sector highlights the importance of complementary FDI policy in making trade work for the poor. The Sri Lankan case also highlights the importance of other complementary policies, including the role of safety nets, human resource development, access to credit and communications infrastructure, in order to maximise the impact of trade liberalisation on poverty reduction.

Notes

1 Residential areas, which do not belong to urban sector or estate sector, are considered as rural sector.
2 Plantation areas which are more than 20 acres in extent and have no fewer than ten residential labourers are considered as estate sector.
3 This involved a survey of over 50 studies on adjustment costs resulting from trade liberalisation in the manufacturing sector.
4 Central Bank *Annual Report* (CBSL 2007).
5 While this is the national poverty line, the poverty lines for estate areas such as Nuwara Eliya (Rs 2,953) and Badulla (Rs 2,807) are not significantly lower.
6 *Sri Lanka Poverty Assessment* (World Bank 2007).
7 *Sri Lanka Trade at a Glance* (World Bank 2007).
8 The fall in government revenue was not primarily due to a fall in tariff revenue. During this period the entire domestic tax regime was also reformed with a shift from BTT to GST, with the latter being lower than was required to maintain revenue neutrality. Furthermore, other levies such as the Defence Levy, National Security Levy and so on were dispensed with.
9 The official poverty line for June 2009 is Rs 2,957 at current prices and now it has increased to more than Rs 2,957.
10 *Sri Lanka Poverty Assessment* (World Bank 2007: Box 2–2, p. 20).
11 Athukorala (2006).

Appendix 1
Estimates of the labour demand function

	Constant	LY	LW	LXO	LMO
Food manufacturing	2.06 (1.48)	0.78*** (0.17)	−0.73*** (0.12)	−0.11 (0.15)	
	1.48* (0.51)	0.65*** (0.06)	−0.74*** (0.11)		0.08 (0.15)
Beverage industry	1.22 (1.62)	0.74*** (0.13)	−0.59* (0.21)	0.15 (0.09)	
	−1.22 (0.85)	0.80*** (0.12)	−.85*** (0.14)		−0.02 (0.02)
Tobacco manufacturing	0.68 (1.08)	0.31*** (0.13)	−1.21*** (0.11)	−0.09 (0.06)	
	1.02 (1.16)	0.40*** (0.13)	−1.12 (0.09)		0.009 (0.03)
Textile manufacturing	3.25* (1.57)	0.63*** (0.16)	−0.69*** (0.07)	**0.31* (0.09)**	
	3.19 (2.11)	0.65** (0.21)	−0.72*** (0.09)		−0.001 (0.01)
Wearing apparel	−1.21*** (0.45)	0.99*** (0.02)	−0.82*** (0.08)	**0.03*** (0.01)**	
	1.61** (0.51)	0.99*** (0.02)	−0.87*** (0.11)		−0.002 (0.02)
Leather and its products	−7.85*** (1.64)	0.91*** (0.18)	−1.96*** (0.21)	0.08 (0.18)	
	−6.71*** (1.05)	0.83*** (0.14)	−1.90*** (0.16)		**0.04* (0.02)**
Footwear except rubber	0.22 (0.49)	0.85*** (0.06)	−0.79*** (0.11)	**0.16*** (0.02)**	
	−1.88*** (0.61)	1.03*** (0.08)	−0.82*** (0.18)		0.004 (0.03)
Wood and cork products	−2.46*** (1.09)	0.75*** (0.18)	−1.41*** (0.31)	0.03 (0.07)	
	−2.51*** (0.83)	0.88*** (0.17)	−1.29*** (0.24)		**0.07** (0.03)**
Furniture manufacturing	1.31** (0.70)	0.36*** (0.08)	−0.94*** (0.16)	0.005 (0.03)	
	1.29* (0.68)	0.36*** (0.07)	−0.95*** (0.16)		0.01 (0.02)
Paper and its products	2.58** (1.25)	0.74*** (0.14)	−0.25** (0.10)	**−0.03** (0.01)**	
	1.69 (1.38)	0.83*** (0.15)	−0.34** (0.11)		−0.006 (0.016)
Printing and publishing	−0.50 (0.59)	0.90*** (0.06)	−0.86*** (0.11)	−0.02 (0.03)	
	−0.42 (0.59)	0.93*** (0.04)	−0.82*** (0.11)		−0.007 (0.01)
Drugs and pharmaceuticals and other chemicals	−1.29 (1.01)	1.08*** (0.09)	−0.46** (0.19)	0.006 (0.01)	
	0.85 (0.93)	0.74*** (0.12)	−0.49** (0.14)		**−0.72*** (0.18)**

(Continued on next page)

(continued)

	Constant	LY	LW	LXO	LMO
Industrial chemicals	1.58 (1.05)	0.69*** (0.13)	−0.77*** (0.21)	0.07 (0.06)	0.02 (0.016)
	2.26* (1.12)	0.52*** (0.12)	−0.87*** (0.19)		
Petroleum refining	7.17*** (0.23)	−0.08*** (0.02)	0.03 (0.04)	**0.02*(0.01)**	−0.015 (0.02)
	7.34*** (0.23)	−0.12*** (0.02)	0.02 (0.03)		
Miscellaneous petroleum products	−5.36*** (1.85)	0.47 (0.26)	−1.81*** (0.21)	0.09 (0.06)	**−0.10** (0.04)**
	−4.39** (1.83)	0.23 (0.26)	−1.66 (0.20)		
Rubber products	0.53 (0.59)	0.79*** (0.08)	−0.69*** (0.06)	0.03 (0.02)	0.02 (0.01)
	0.79 (0.61)	0.73*** (0.08)	−0.67*** (0.07)		
Plastic products	0.99 (1.34)	0.58*** (0.05)	−0.78*** (0.25)	**0.06** (0.03)**	0.02 (0.02)
	−1.26* (0.73)	0.59*** (0.05)	−1.16*** (0.17)		
Pottery and chinaware	2.98** (1.22)	1.01*** (0.12)	0.048 (0.21)	0.0003 (0.03)	0.02 (0.03)
	2.86** (1.03)	1.02*** (0.07)	0.02 (0.22)		
Glass and its products	2.78*** (1.12)	0.64*** (0.13)	−0.40** (0.14)	0.04 (0.03)	−0.007 (0.02)
	2.35** (1.14)	0.64*** (0.14)	−0.43** (0.15)		
Non-metallic mineral products	−2.77*** (1.20)	0.99*** (0.19)	−1.05*** (0.17)	0.027 (0.07)	−0.02 (0.04)
	−3.05** (1.23)	0.99*** (0.18)	−1.07*** (0.17)		
Iron and steel basic industries	5.71*** (0.94)	0.17 (0.12)	−0.50*** (0.09)	−0.01 (0.027)	0.03 (0.19)
	5.63*** (0.97)	0.21 (0.13)	−0.49*** (0.09)		
Non-ferrous metal industry	4.34*** (1.12)	0.52*** (0.12)	−0.49 (0.23)	0.05 (0.06)	−0.002 (0.02)
	3.59*** (0.72)	0.49*** (0.12)	−0.63*** (0.16)		
Fabricated metal products	9.69*** (1.14)	−0.25* (0.14)	−0.15 (0.11)	0.02 (0.03)	**−0.014* (0.02)**
	8.89*** (0.99)	−0.18 (0.14)	−0.19 (0.10)		
Non-electrical machinery	5.88*** (1.99)	−0.21 (0.22)	−0.99*** (0.21)	−0.03 (0.08)	**−1.18*** (0.358)**
	5.17*** (1.58)	−0.11 (0.17)	−0.88*** (0.17)		
Electrical machinery	0.28 (1.04)	0.41** (0.17)	−1.27*** (0.19)	−0.04 (0.05)	**−0.92*** (0.18)**
	1.96(0.74)	0.50*** (0.11)	−0.65*** (0.18)		
Transport equipment	1.11 (1.92)	0.44 (0.31)	−0.31** (0.17)	−0.03 (0.04)	−0.005 (0.04)
	0.82 (2.08)	0.51 (0.33)	−0.26** (0.13)		
Scientific, precision, etc., plus photographic and optical goods	2.52 (2.34)	0.15 (0.36)	−1.02*** (0.06)	0.053 (0.035)	0.02 (0.02)
	2.31 (2.44)	0.14 (0.38)	−1.03*** (0.06)		

Source: Census of manufacturing industries in Bangladesh (1978–2000).

Appendix 2
Trade in relation to GDP growth, composition and revenue

Item		GDP growth % 2006–7	Trade as % of GDP 2007	Main export items share % 1990	Main export items share % 2007	Government revenue (Rs million) 2007
GDP Growth	Real GDP	2.6				
	Agriculture	0.9				
	Non-agriculture	4.1				
Trade	Total trade		35.1			
	Exports		8.5			
	Imports		26.6			
	Trade balance		–18.2			
Trade composition	Woollen carpets			45.0	9.2	
	Ready-made garments			27.1	8.6	
	Pashminas			0.0	1.6	
	Vegetable ghee			0.0	6.8	
	Pulses			4.1	1.3	
	Thread			0.0	6.7	
	Textiles			0.0	5.0	
	Zinc sheet			0.0	5.9	
Government revenue	Total revenue					87,712
	Tax revenue					71,168
	Trade taxes					38,829
	Trade/total revenue (%)					44.3
	Trade/tax revenue (%)					54.6

Appendix 3

Descriptive statistics of indicators of economic growth, employment, openness and human capital

	1973–80	1981–5	1986–90	1991–5	1996–2000	2001–5	2006–7	1973–2007
N Economic growth rate	8.68 (8)	4.06 (5)	9.82(5)	5.03 (5)	3.91 (5)	5.90 (5)	6.30 (2)	5.38 (35)
Indicators of openness of economy								
Exports–GDP ratio	11.67 (8)	11.44 (5)	13.78 (5)	16.73 (5)	15.67 (5)	15.68 (5)	13.98 (2)	13.94 (35)
Imports–GDP ratio	16.56 (8)	18.72 (5)	17.12 (5)	17.81 (5)	17.01 (5)	16.82 (5)	23.17 (2)	17.60 (35)
Trade–GDP ratio (openness)	30.72 (8)	35.54 (5)	33.63 (5)	36.73 (5)	33.98 (5)	32.18 (5)	37.42 (2)	33.45 (35)
Share of primary goods in total exports	40.13 (8)	33.40 (5)	28.40 (5)	14.80 (5)	12.80 (5)	11.20 (5)	11.00 (2)	24.17 (35)
Share of capital goods in total imports	32.75 (8)	30.60 (5)	36.00 (5)	38.00 (5)	32.20 (5)	31.00 (5)	36.00 (2)	33.51 (35)
Real exchange rate	8.89 (8)	11.13 (5)	17.37 (5)	26.10 (5)	42.84 (5)	60.14 (5)	57.67 (2)	27.84 (35)
Average duty on imports	8.89 (8)	11.13 (5)	17.37 (5)	25.78 (5)	16.70 (5)	9.15 (5)	7.61 (2)	27.84 (35)
Remittances–GDP ratio	5.50 (3)	8.42 (5)	5.14 (5)	2.84 (5)	1.86 (5)	3.78 (5)	2.80 (2)	4.41 (30)
FDI–GDP ratio	0.12 (8)	0.26 (5)	0.47 (5)	0.89 (5)	0.83 (5)	1.07 (5)	1.38 (2)	0.61 (35)

(continued)

	1973–80	1981–5	1986–90	1991–5	1996–2000	2001–5	2006–7	1973–2007
Other macro-economic indicators								
Inflation rate	1.76 (8)	1.74 (5)	2.31 (5)	5.80 (5)	5.91 (5)	6.33 (5)	9.12 (2)	4.08 (35)
Unemployment rate	3.63 (8)	3.64 (5)	3.20 (5)	5.42 (5)	6.53 (5)	7.65 (5)	5.66 (2)	4.93 (35)
Growth rate of labour force	1.44 (5)	3.22 (5)	2.17 (5)	2.17 (3)	1.43 (5)	3.04 (5)	2.05 (2)	1.43 (35)
Growth rate of employment	2.71 (8)	3.14 (5)	2.00 (5)	1.24 (5)	3.61 (5)	3.07 (5)	0.39 (2)	2.51 (35)
Indicators of human capital								
Literacy rate	24.73 (3)	27.90 (2)	32.08 (5)	38.42 (5)	45.38 (5)	52.62 (5)	55.50 (2)	40.13 (27)
Growth rate of enrolment at higher level	8.68 (8)	4.06 (5)	4.82 (5)	5.87 (5)	9.33 (5)	2.98 (5)	11.85 (2)	5.37 (35)
Indicators of poverty and income distribution								
Poverty	37.97 (2)	25.87 (1)	20.66 (3)	25.49 (3)	31.80 (2)	30.07 (3)	22.30 (1)	27.0 (15)
Rural poverty	37.97 (2)	25.87 (1)	20.66 (3)	27.71 (3)	33.40 (2)	35.35 (3)	27.00 (1)	29.78 (15)
Urban poverty	29.79 (2)	21.17 (1)	17.59 (3)	20.27 (3)	26.45 (2)	20.01 (3)	13.10 (1)	21.36 (15)
Gini coefficient	35.50 (2)	37.00 (1)	34.67 (3)	40.67 (3)	40.50 (2)	—	—	37.37 (11)
Income share of the lowest 20 percent of the population	7.65 (2)	7.30 (1)	7.83 (3)	6.13 (3)	7.10 (2)	—	—	7.11 (11)
Income share of the highest 20 percent of the population	44.00 (2)	45.00 (1)	43.77 (3)	48.23 (3)	45.85 (2)	—	—	45.52 (11)

Note: The number of observations is reported in parentheses.

Bibliography

Abrego, L. and Whalley, J. (2000) 'The Choice of Structural Model in Trade–Wages Decomposition', *Review of International Economics*, 8(3): 462–77.

Acharya, M., Khatiwada, Y.R., Satyal, B. and Aryal, S. (2004) *Structural Adjustment Policies and Poverty*, Kathmandu: IIDS.

Acharya, R. (2006) *Trade Liberalization, Poverty, and Income Inequality in India*, INRM Policy Brief No. 10, Manila: ADB.

Ackerman, F. (2005) 'The Shrinking Gains from Trade: A Critical Assessment of Doha Round Projections, Global Development and Environment Institute', Working Paper No. 05–01, Global Development and Environment Institute, Tufts University.

Adams, P.D. (2005) 'Interpretation of Results from CGE Models such as GTAP', *Journal of Economic Modelling*, 27: 941–59.

ADB (Asian Development Bank) (1999) *Key Indicators of Developing Asia and Pacific Countries 1999, Vol. XXX*, Manila: ADB.

——(2000) *Key Indicators of Developing Asia and Pacific Countries 2000, XXXI*, Manila: ADB.

——(2001) *Poverty Reduction in the Maldives: Issues, Findings, and Approaches*, Manila: ADB.

——(2002) *Poverty Reduction in Nepal: Issues, Findings and Approaches*, Manila: ADB.

——(2003) *Key Indicators of Developing Asian and Pacific Countries 2003*, Manila: ADB.

——(2006) *Country Water Action: Maldives Recovering the Full Cost of Delivering Clean and Safe Water*, Manila: ADB.

——(2007) *Maldives: Poverty Assessment*, Manila: ADB.

ADB and World Bank (2005) *Sri Lanka: Improving the Rural and Urban Investment Climate*, Colombo, Sri Lanka: World Bank.

Agenor, P.R. (2004) 'Does Globalization Hurt the Poor?' *International Economics and Economic Policy*, 1(1): 21–51.

Ahluwalia, M.S. (2002) 'State Level Performance under Economic Reforms in India', in Anne O. Krueger (ed.) *Economic Policy Reforms and the Indian Economy*, Chicago: University of Chicago Press.

Ahmed, N. (2001) *Trade Liberalization in Bangladesh*, Dhaka: University Press.

Ahmed, S. and Ghani, E. (2007) *South Asia: Growth and Regional Integration*, Delhi: Macmillan India.

Ahmed, S. and Sattar, Z. (2004) *Trade Liberalization, Growth and Poverty Reduction: The Case of Bangladesh*, Report No. 34204, PREM Working Paper Series, South Asian Region, Washington, DC: World Bank.

Ahmed, V. and Amjad, R. (1984) *The Management of Pakistan's Economy: 1947–82*, UGC Monograph Series in Economics, Karachi: Oxford University Press.

Aisbett, E. (2007) 'Why are the Critics So Convinced that Globalization is Bad for the Poor?', in A. Harrison (ed.) *Globalization and Poverty*, Chicago: University of Chicago Press.

Akramov, K.T. (2008) *Reducing Poverty and Hunger in Asia: Decentralization and Public Service Delivery to the Rural Poor*, Focus 15, Brief 14 of 15, March, Washington, DC: IFPRI 2020 Vision.

Amjad, R. and Kemal, A.R. (1997) 'Macro Economic Policies and Their Impact on Poverty Alleviation in Pakistan', *Pakistan Development Review*, 36(1) (Spring): 39–68.

Anderson, K., Martin, W. and Van der Mensbruggehe, D. (2006) 'Long Run, Global Impacts of Doha Scenario on Poverty', in T. Hertel and A. Winters (eds) *Poverty and the WTO: Impacts of the Doha Development Agenda*, Washington, DC: World Bank and Palgrave Macmillan.

Annabi, N., Khondker, B., Raihan, S., Cockburn, J. and Decaluwé, B. (2006) 'WTO Agreements and Domestic Policy Reforms – Implications for Poverty in Bangladesh: A Study in a Dynamic Sequential CGE Framework', in T. Hertel and A. Winters (eds) *Poverty and the WTO: Impacts of the Doha Development Agenda*, Washington, DC: World Bank and Palgrave Macmillan.

——(2005) 'Implications of WTO Agreements and Domestic Trade Policy Reforms for Poverty in Bangladesh: Short vs Long Run', in T. Hertel and A. Winters (eds) *PEP-MPIA*. Online. Available at: http://portal.pep-net.org/documents/download/id/7116 (accessed 15 April 2008).

Arellano, M. and Bond, S. (1991) 'Some Test of Specification for Panel Data: Monte Carlo Evidence and Application to Employment Equations', *Review of Economic Studies*, 58: 277–97.

Arif, G.M., Nazli, H, and Haq, R. (2000) 'Rural Non-agriculture Employment and Poverty in Pakistan', *Pakistan Development Review* 39(4): 1089–110.

Arndt, C., Dorosh, P., Fontana, M., Zohir, S., El-Said, M. and Lungren, C. (2002) 'Opportunities and Challenges in Agriculture and Garments: A General Equilibrium Analysis of the Bangladesh Economy', TMD Discussion Paper No. 107, IFPRI, Washington DC.

Athukorala, P. (2002) 'Introduction', in P. Athukorala (ed.) *The Economic Development of South Asia*, vol. 1, Cheltenham: Edward Elgar, pp. viii–xxxi.

——(2004) 'Trade policy Making in a Small Island Economy: The 2003 WTO Review of Maldives', *World Economy*, 27(9): 1321–498.

——(2006) 'Outward Oriented Policy Reforms and Industrialisation: The Sri Lankan Experience', *Journal of South Asian Development*, 1(1): 19–49.

——(2011) 'Trade Liberalization and the Poverty of Nations: A Review Article', *Journal of Development Studies*, 47(3), 533–543.

Athukorala, P. and Jayasuriya, S. (1994) *Macroeconomic Policies, Crises and Growth in Sri Lanka, 1969–1990*, Washington, DC: World Bank.

——(2000) 'Trade Policy and Industrial Growth: Sri Lanka', *World Economy*, 23(3): 387–404.

Athukorala, P. and Rajapatirana, S. (2000) *Liberalization and Industrial Transformation: Sri Lanka in International Perspective*, Oxford and Delhi: Oxford University Press.

Attanasio, O., Goldberg, P. and Pavcnik, N. (2004) 'Trade Reforms and Wage Inequality in Colombia', *Journal of Development Economics*, 74: 331–66.

Balassa, B. (1971) 'Trade Policies in Developing Countries', *American Economic Review*, 61(2): 178–87.

——(1982) *Development Strategies in Semi-Industrialized Economies*, New York: Oxford University Press.

Balat, J. and Porto, G. (2005) *Globalization and Complementary Policies: Poverty Impacts in Rural Zambia*, NBER Working Paper No. 11175, Cambridge, MA: National Bureau of Economic Research.

——(2007) 'Globalization and Complementary Policies', in A. Harrison (ed.) *Globalization and Poverty*, Chicago: University of Chicago Press.

Baldwin, R.E. and Venables, A.J. (1995) 'Regional Economic Integration', in G.M. Grossman and K. Rogoff (eds) *Handbook of International Economics*, Volume III, Amsterdam: Elsevier.

Bandara, J.S. (2004) 'What Do Quantitative Evaluations Tell Us about Regionalism in South Asia? A Survey', *Asian Studies Review*, 28(1): 57–74.

——(2010) 'Playing with Numbers: Critical Evaluation of Quantitative Assessments of South Asian Regional Integration', *Economic and Political Weekly*, XLIV(48): 67–75.

Bandara, J.S. and McGillivray, M. (1998) 'Trade Policy Reforms in South Asia', *The World Economy*, 21(7): 881–96.

Bandara, J.S. and Yu, W. (2003) 'How Desirable is the South Asian Free Trade Area? A Quantitative Ecoonomic Assessment', *The World Economy*, 26(9): 1293–322.

Banga, R. (2005a) 'Foreign Investment, Technological Progress and Labour Productivity: A Case Study of Manufacturing in India', in H. Kehal (ed.), *Foreign Investment, Globalisation and Digitalisation: Concerns and Opportunities*, New York: Palgrave Macmillan.

——(2005b) 'Impact of Liberalization on Wages and Employment in Indian Manufacturing Industries', Working Paper No. 153, Indian Council for Research on International Economic Relations, 4th floor, India Habitat Centre, Lodi Road, New Delhi-110 003.

Bannister, J. and Thugge, K. (2001) *International Trade and Poverty Alleviation*, IMF Working Paper No. WP/01/54, Washington, DC: IMF.

Bardhan, P. (2004) 'The Impact of Globalization on the Poor', in S.M. Collins and C. Graham (eds) *Brookings Trade Forum 2004 – Globalization Poverty, and Inequality*, Washington, DC: Brookings Institution Press.

——(2007) 'Globalization and Rural Poverty', in M. Nissanke and E. Thorbecke (eds) *The Impact of Globalization on the World's Poor*, New York: Palgrave Macmillan in association with UNU-WIDER.

Bayes, A., Hussain, I. and Rahman, M. (1995) 'Trends in the External Sector: Trade and Aid', in R. Sobhan (ed.) *Experiences with Economic Reforms: A Review of Bangladesh's Development 1995*, Dhaka: Centre for Policy Dialogue and University Press, Chapter 8, pp. 243–97.

Beck, T., Levine, R. and Loayza, N. (2000) 'Finance and the Sources of Growth', *Journal of Financial Economics*, 58: 261–310.

Begum, S. and Shamsuddin, A.F.M. (1998) 'Exports and Economic Growth in Bangladesh', *Journal of Development Studies*, 35: 89–114.

Berg, A. and Krueger, A.O. (2003) 'Trade, Growth and Poverty: A Selected Survey', IMF Working Paper No. WP/03/30, Washington, DC: IMF.

Bhagwati, J. (1978) *Foreign Trade Regimes and Economic Development: Anatomy and Consequences of Exchange Control Regimes*, Cambridge, MA: Ballinger.

——(2004) *In Defence of Globalization*, New York: Oxford University Press.

Bhagwati, J. and Srinivasan, T.N. (2002) 'Trade and Poverty in Poor Countries', *American Economic Review*, 92(2): 180–3.

Bhatti, M.A., Haq, R., and Javed, T. (1999) 'A Sectoral Analysis of Poverty in Pakistan', *Pakistan Development Review*, 38(4): 859–72.

Bhuyan, A.R. and Rashid, M.A. (1993) *Trade Regimes and Industrial Growth: A Case Study of Bangladesh*, Dhaka: Bureau of Economic Research, University of Dhaka.

Blundell, R. and Bond, S. (1998) 'Initial Conditions and Moment Restrictions in Dynamic Panel Data Models', *Journal of Econometrics*, 87: 115–43.

Bruce, E.H. and Kenneth, D.W. (2002) 'Generalized Method of Moments and Macroeconomics', *Journal of Business and Economic Statistics*, 20(4): 460.

Bussolo, M. and Round, J.I. (2006) *Globalisation and Poverty – Channels and Policy Responses*, London: Routledge.

Bussolo, M. and Whalley, J. (2006) 'Globalisation in Developing Countries – The Role of Tansaction Costs in Explaining Economic Performance in India',in M. Bussolo and I.J. Round (eds) *Globalisation and Poverty – Channels and Policy Responses*, London: Routledge.

Butt, M.S. and Bandara, J.S. (2009) *Trade Liberalization and Regional Disparities in Pakistan*, London: Routledge.

CBS (1997) *Nepal Living Standard Survey*, Kathmandu: Central Bureau of Statistics.

——(1998) *Census of Manufacturing Establishments*, Kathmandu: Central Bureau of Statistics.

——(2003) *Census of Manufacturing Establishments*, Kathmandu: Central Bureau of Statistics.

——(2003) *Population Census of Nepal 2001*, Kathmandu: National Planning Commission.

——(2004) *Nepal Living Standard Survey*, Volumes I and II, Kathmandu: Central Bureau of Statistics.

——(2005) 'Poverty Assessment Results', briefing notes presented at a national workshop on NLSS results held in May 2005.

CBSL (Central Bank of Sri Lanka) (2007) *Annual Report*, Colombo: CBSL.

——(n.d.) *Annual Reports*, various issues, Colombo: CBSL.

Charlton, A.H. and Stiglitz, J.E. (2005) 'A Development-Friendly Prioritisation of Doha Round Proposals', *The World Economy*, 28(3): 293–312.

Chen, S. and Ravallion, M. (2004a) 'How Have the World's Poorest Fared since the Early 1980s?', *The World Bank Research Observer*, 19(2): 141–69.

——(2004b) 'Welfare Impacts of China's Accession to the World Trade Organization', *The World Bank Economic Review*, 18(1): 29–57.

——(2007) *Absolute Poverty Measures for the Developing World, 1981–2004*, World Bank Policy Research Working Paper 4211, Washington, DC: World Bank.

——(2008) 'The Developing World is Poorer than We Thought, but No Less Successful in the Fight against Poverty', World Bank Policy Research Working Paper 4703, Washington, DC: World Bank.

CIA (1996) *The World Factbook*, Washington, DC: CIA.

Cockburn, J. (2001) *Trade Liberalization and Poverty in Nepal: A Computable General Equilibrium Micro Simulation Analysis*, Quebec: Centre for the Study of African Economies, Nuffield College and CREFA.

——(2006) 'A Computable General Equilibrium Micro-simulation Analysis', in M. Bussolo and I.J. Round (eds) *Globalisation and Poverty – Channels and Policy Responses*, London: Routledge.

Coe, D., Helpman, T.E. and Hoffmaister, A.W. (1997) 'North–South R& D Spillovers', *Economic Journal*, 107(440): 134–49.

Collins, S. and Graham, C. (eds) (2004) *Brookings Trade Forum 2004 – Globalization, Poverty, and Inequality*, Washington, DC: Brookings Institution Press.

Commonwealth Secretariat (1997) *A Future for Small States: Overcoming Vulnerability*, London: Commonwealth Advisory Group.

Coxhead, I. (2003) 'Trade Liberalization and Rural Poverty', *American Journal of Agricultural Economics*, 85(5): 1307–8.

CRPRID/Planning Commission (2003) *Economic Survey*, Islamabad: Government of Pakistan.

Cuthbertson, A and Athukorala, P. (1991) 'Liberalising Foreign Trade: Sri Lanka' in D. Papageorgiou, A.M. Choksi and M. Michaely (eds) *Liberalizing Foreign Trade: Indonesia, Pakistan and Sri Lanka*, Oxford: Basil Blackwell, 283–411.

Datt, G. and Gunewardena, D. (1995) 'Some Aspects of Poverty in Sri Lanka: 1985–90', *Sri Lanka Economic Journal*, 10(2): 45–76; originally published as World Bank Policy Research Working Paper, No. 1738.

Datt, G. and Ravallion, M. (2002) 'Is India's Economic Growth Leaving the Poor behind?', *Journal of Economic Perspectives*, 16(2): 89–108.

Davidson, R. and MacKinnon, J. (2004) *Econometric Theory and Methods*, Oxford: Oxford University Press.

DCS (1994) *Survey of Manufacturing*, Colombo: Department of Census and Statistics.

——(1995) *Poverty Indicators, Household Income and Expenditure Survey 1995*, Colombo: Department of Census and Statistics, Ministry of Finance and Planning.

——(2004a) *Poverty Indicators, Household Income and Expenditure Survey 2004*, Colombo: Department of Census and Statistics, Ministry of Finance and Planning.

——(2004b) *Survey of Manufacturing*, Colombo: Department of Census and Statistics.

——(2008) *Poverty Indicators, Household Income and Expenditure Survey 2006/07*, Colombo: Department of Census and Statistics, Ministry of Finance and Planning.

——(n.d.) *Food Balance Sheet*, various editions, Colombo: Department of Census and Statistics, Ministry of Finance and Planning.

De Silva, H. and Zainudeen, A. (2007) *Poverty Reduction through Telecom Access at the Bottom of the Pyramid*, Colombo: LirneAsia.

Dean, J.M., Desai, S. and Riedel, J. (1994) *Trade Policy Reform in Developing Countries since 1985: A Review of the Evidence*, World Bank Discussion Paper 267, Washington, DC: World Bank.

Deaton, A. (2001) 'Counting the World's Poor: Problems and Possible Solutions', *World Bank Research Observer*, 16(2): 125–47.

Deaton, A. and Dreze, J. (2002) 'Poverty and Inequality in India: A Re-Examination', Working Papers 184, Princeton University, Woodrow Wilson School of Public and International Affairs, Research Program in Development Studies.

Deaton, A. and Tarozzi, A. (2000) 'Prices and Poverty in India', unpublished manuscript. Online. Available at: www.wws.princeton.edu/~rpds/working.htm (accessed 15 April 2008).

Del Ninno, C. and Dorosh, P.A. (2001) 'Averting a Food Crisis: Private Imports and Public Targeted Distribution in Bangladesh after the 1998 Flood', *Agriculture Economics*, 25(3): 337–46.

Del Ninno, C., Vecchi, G. and Hussain, N (2006) 'Poverty, Risk and Vulnerability in Pakistan', CRPRID, Islamabad, mimeo.

Diaz-Alejandro, C.F. (1975) 'Trade Policies and Economic Development', in P. Kenen (ed.) *International Trade and Finance: Frontiers for Research*, Cambridge: Cambridge University Press.

Dixon, P.B. (2009) 'Comments on the Productivity Commission's Modelling of the Economy-Wide Effects of Future Automotive Assistance', *Economic Papers*, 28(1): 11–18.

Dollar, D. (1992) 'Outward-Oriented Developing Economies Really Do Grow More Rapidly: Evidence from 95 LDCs 1976–85', *Economic Development and Cultural Change*, 40(3): 52344.

Dollar, D. and Kraay, A. (2000) *Growth is Good for the Poor*, Washington, DC: World Bank.

——(2002) 'Growth is Good for the Poor', *Journal of Economic Growth*, 7: 195–255.

——(2004) 'Trade, Growth and Poverty', *The Economic Journal*, 114(493): 22–49.

Donges, J.B. (1976) 'Comparative Survey of Industrialization Policies in Fifteen Semi-Industrial Countries', *Weltwirtschaftliches Archiv*, 112: 626–57.

Dorosh, P. and Valdes, A. (1990) *Effects of Exchange Rate and Trade Policies in Agriculture in Pakistan*, IFPRI Research Report 82, Washington, DC: IFPRI.

Dowlah, C.A.F. (1999) 'Agriculture and the New Trade Agenda in the WTO 2000 Negotiations: Economic Analysis of Interests and Options for Bangladesh', draft paper, World Bank Office, Dhaka.

Ebril, L., Stotsky, J. and Gropp, R. (1999) *Revenue Implications of Trade Liberalization*, Occasional Paper 42, Washington, DC: IMF.

eStandardsForum (2008) 'Country Brief: Maldives', *Econometrica*, 50: 1029–54.

FAO (2003) *Nepal: Agricultural Policy and Strategies for Poverty Alleviation and Food Security*, Main Report, Kathmandu: FAO and UNDP.

Foster, J.E., Greer, J. and Thorbecke, E. (1984) 'A Class of Decomposable Poverty Measures', *Econometrica*, 52: 761–76.

Francois, J. and Shiells, C.R. (1994) *Modeling Trade Policy: Applied General Equilibrium Assessments of North American Free Trade*, Cambridge: Cambridge University Press.

Ghosh, R.N. and Siddique, M.A.B. (2000) 'Labour Market in the Maldives: The Case for Institutional Reforms', in D. Dutta (ed.), *Economic Liberalization and Institutional Reforms in South Asia: Recent Experiences and Future Prospects*, Delhi: Atlantic.

Gisselquist, D. and Grether, J.M. (2000) 'An Argument for Deregulating the Transfer of Agricultural Technologies to Developing Countries', *World Bank Economic Review*, 14(1): 111–27.

Goldar, B. (2002) *Trade Liberalization and Manufacturing Employment: The Case of India*, Employment Paper No. 2002/34, Geneva: International Labour Office.

——(2004) 'Indian Manufacturing: Productivity Trends in Pre- and Post-Reform Periods', *Economic and Political Weekly*, 39(46/47, 20–26 November): 5033–43.

——(2005) 'Impact on India of Tariff and Quantitative Restrictions Under WTO', ICRIER Working Paper 172.

Goldberg, P.K. and Pavcnik, N. (2004) 'Trade, Inequality and Poverty: What Do We Know? Evidence from Recent Trade Liberalization Episodes in Developing Countries', in S.M. Collins and C. Graham (eds) *Brookings Trade Forum 2004 – Globalization Poverty, and Inequality*, Washington, DC: Brookings Institution Press.

——(2007) 'Distributional Effects of Globalisation in Developing Countries', *Journal of Economic Literature*, XLV(1): 39–82.

Government of India (2006) *Economic Survey 2005–6*, Delhi: Government of India.

——(2008) *Economic Survey 2007–8*, Delhi: Government of India. Online. Available at: http://indiabudget.nic.in/es2007-08/seconomy.htm (accessed 15 April 2008).

Government of Pakistan (2003) *Pakistan Economic Survey 2002–3*, Islamabad: Ministry of Finance, Economic Adviser's Wing.

——(2007) *Pakistan Economic Survey 2006–7*, Islamabad: Ministry of Finance, Economic Adviser's Wing.

Green, W.H. (2003) *Econometric Analysis*, fifth edition, Upper Saddle River, NJ: Prentice Education.

Greenway, D. and Milner, C. (1991) 'Fiscal Dependence on Trade Taxes and Trade Policy Reform', *Journal of Development Studies*, 27: 95–132.

Greenway, D., Hine, B. and Wright, P. (1999). 'Further Evidence on the Effect of Foreign Competition on Industry Level Wages', *Weltwirtliftshaftliches Archiv*, 136: 41–51.

Guisinger, S. and Scully, G. (1991) 'Pakistan', in D. Papageorgiou, M. Michaely and A.M. Choksy (eds) *Liberalizing Foreign Trade: Indonesia, Pakistan and Sri Lanka*, vol. 5: Oxford: Basil Blackwell.

Gulati, A. and Narayanan, S.(2002) *Rice Trade Liberalization and Poverty*, MSSD Discussion Paper No. 51, Washington, DC: International Food Policy Research Institute.

Hall, A. (2005) *Generalized Method of Moments*, Oxford: Oxford University Press.

Hamilton, J.D. (1994) *Time Series Analysis*, Princeton: Princeton University Press.

Hansen, L.P. (1982) 'Large Sample Properties of Generalized Method of Moments' *Econometrica*, 50: 1029–54.

——(2002) 'Method of Moment', in N.J. Smelser and P.B. Bates (eds) *International Encyclopedia of Social and Behavioural Sciences*, Oxford: Pergamon.

Harrison, A. (ed.) (2007a) *Globalization and Poverty*, Chicago: University of Chicago Press.

——(2007b) 'Globalization and Poverty: An Introduction', in A. Harrison (ed.) *Globalization and Poverty*, Chicago: University of Chicago Press.

Harrison, A. and Currie, J. (1997) 'Sharing the Costs: The Impact of Trade Reform on Capital and Labour in Morocco', *Journal of Labour Economics,* 153: S44–71.

Haveman, R.L. and Wolfe, B.H. (1894) 'Schooling and Economic Well-being: The Role of Non-Market Effects', *Journal of Human Resources*, 19(3): 377–407.

Hertel, T. and Reimer, J. (2002) *Predicting the Poverty Impacts of Trade Reform*, Working Paper No. 20, West Lafayette, IN: GTAP.

——(2005) 'Predicting the Poverty Impacts of Trade Reform', *Journal of International Trade and Economic Development*, 14(4): 377–405.

Hertel, T. and Winters, A. (2006) Poverty and the WTO: Impacts of the Doha Development Agenda, Washington, DC: World Bank and Palgrave Macmillan.

——(2005) 'Estimating the Poverty Impacts of a Prospective Doha Development Agenda', *World Economy*, 28(8):1057–71.

Hertel, T., Ivanic, W.M., Preckel, Paul V. and Granfield, John A.L. (2004) 'The Earning Effects of Multilateral Trade Liberalization: Implications for Poverty', *The World Bank Economic Review*, 18(2): 205–36.

Hertel, T., Ivanic, M., Preckel, P.V., Carnfield, J.A.L. and Martin, W. (2003) 'Short-versus Long-Run Implications of Trade Liberalization for Poverty in Three Developing Countries', *American Journal of Agricultural Economics*, 85(5): 1299–306.

Heshmati, A. (2007) 'The Relationship between Income Inequality, Poverty and Globalization', in M. Nissanke and E. Thorbecke (eds) *The Impact of Globalization on the World's Poor*, New York: Palgrave Macmillan in Association with UNU-WIDER.

Hoque, M.S. (2006) 'A Computable General Equilibrium Model of Bangladesh for Analysis of Policy Reforms', PhD thesis submitted to Monash University, Monash University, Clayton Campus, Melbourne, Australia. Online. Available at: www.adb.org/ water/actions/MLD/paying-the-price.asp (accessed 15 April 2008).

IMF (2009) 'Maldives: 2008', Article IV Consultation – Staff Report; Staff Statement; Public Information Notice on the Executive Board Discussion; and Statement by the Executive Director for the Maldives, Washington, DC: IMF.

IPS (2010) *Sri Lanka: MDG Country Report 2008/2009*, Sri Lanka: Institute of Policy Studies of Sri Lanka.

Iqbal, Z. and Siddiqui, R. (2001) *Critical Review of Literature on Computable General Equilibrium Models*, MIMAP Technical Paper Series No. 3, Islamabad: Pakistan Institute of Development Economics.

Irwin, D.A. (2005) 'Trade Liberalization', in M. Weinstein (ed.) *Globalization: What's New?* New York: Colombia University Press.

Islam, R. and Zanini, G. (2008) World Trade Indicators 2008: Benchmarking Policy and Performance, Washington, DC: World Bank.

Jafri, S.M.Y (1999) *Assessing Poverty in Pakistan: In a Profile of Poverty in Pakistan.* Islamabad: MHCHD/UNDP.

Jayanetti, S. and Tillekeratne, G. (2005) 'Impact of Trade Liberalization on Poverty and Household Welfare in Sri Lanka', Poverty and Social Welfare Series No. 6, Institute of Policy Studies of Sri Lanka.

Jenkins, R. (2004) 'Vietnam in the Global Economy: Trade, Employment and Poverty', *Journal of International Development*, 16(1):13–28.

——(2007) 'Globalization, Production and Poverty', in M. Nissanke, and E. Thorbecke (eds) *The Impact of Globalization on the World's Poor*, New York: Palgrave Macmillan in Association with UNU-WIDER.

Jha, R. (2000) 'Rising Income Inequality and Poverty Reduction: Are They Compatible?' paper prepared for the WIDER project.

Joshi, V. and Little, I.M.D. (1996) *India's Economic Reforms 1991–2001*, Oxford: Clarendon Press.

Josling, T. (1998) 'Trade Policy in Small Island Economies: Agricultural Dilemmas for the OECS', paper prepared for the IICA/NCFAP Workshop on Small Economies in the Global Economy, Grenada. Online. Available at: http://docs.google.com/gview?a=v&q=cache:HJcDr0JLK (accessed 15 April 2008).

Kabeer, N. (2000) *The Power to Choose: Bangladesh Women and Labour Market Decisions in London and Dhaka*, New York: Verso.

Kalwij, A. and Verschoor, A. (2007) 'Globalization and Poverty Trends across Regions: The Role of Variation in the Income and Inequality Elasticities of Poverty', in M. Nissanke and E. Thorbecke (eds) *The Impact of Globalization on the World's Poor*, New York: Palgrave Macmillan in Association with UNU-WIDER.

Kanbur, R. (1998) 'Income Distribution: Implications of Globalization and Liberalization in Africa', Cornell University, mimeo.

Kaplinsky, R. (2005) *Globalization, Poverty and Inequality: between a Rock and a Hard Place*, Cambridge: Policy Press.

Kelegama, S. (1996) 'SAPTA and its Future', *South Asia Survey*, 3(1 and 2): 156–7.

——(1999) 'India–Sri Lanka Trade and the Bilateral FTA: A Sri Lankan Perspective', *Asia Pacific Development Journal*, 6(2): 87–106.

——(2006) *Development under Stress: Sri Lankan Economy in Transition*, New Delhi: Sage, Chapter 3.

Kelegama, S. and Wijayasiri, J. (2004) 'Overview of the Garments Industry in Sri Lanka', in S. Kelegama (ed.) *The Ready-Made Garment Industry in Sri Lanka: Facing the Global Challenge*, Colombo: Institute of Policy Studies.

Kemal, A.R. (2002) 'Globalization and Poverty', unpublished paper, Pakistan Institute of Development Economics.

——(2003) 'Poverty in Pakistan: Trends and Causes', paper presented at a Symposium on Pro-Poor Growth Policies, organised by UNDP and PIDE, Islamabad, Pakistan (March).

Kemal, A.R. and Amjad, R. (1997) 'Macro Economic Policies and their Impact on Poverty Alleviation in Pakistan', *Pakistan Development Review*, 36(1): 39–69.

Kemal, A.R., Siddiqui, R. and Siddiqui, R. (2001) *Tariff Reduction and Income Distribution: A CGE Based Analysis for Urban and Rural House Holds in Pakistan* MIMAP Technical Paper Series No. 11 (January), Islamabad: Pakistan Institute of Development Economics.

Kemal, A.R, Siddiqui, R., Siddiqui, R. and Kemal, M. Ali (2003) *An Assessment of the Impact of Trade Liberalization on Welfare in Pakistan: A General Equilibrium Analysis* MIMAP Technical Paper Series No. 16 (December), Islamabad: Pakistan Institute of Development Economics.

Khan, M.H. (2000) 'Rural Poverty in Developing Countries: Issues and Policies', IMF Working Paper WP/00/78.

Khondker, B.H. and Mujeri, M.K. (2006) 'Globalisation–Poverty Interaction in Bangladesh', in M. Bussolo and I.J. Round (eds) *Globalisation and Poverty: Channels and Policy Responses*, London: Routledge.

Khondker, B.H. and Raihan, S. (2004) 'Welfare and Poverty Impacts of Policy Reforms in Bangladesh: A General Equilibrium Approach', paper presented at the Seventh Annual Global Economic Conference (GTAP), World Bank, Washington, DC, 17–19 June.

Krishna, A. (2004) 'Escaping Poverty and Becoming Poor: Who Gains, Who Loses, and Why?', *World Development*, 32(1): 121–36.

Krueger, A.O. (1978) *Foreign Trade Regimes and Economic Development: Liberalization Attempts and Consequences*, Cambridge: Ballinger Publishing.

——(1983) *Trade and Employment in Developing Countries, Vol. 3: Synthesis and Conclusions*, New York: NBER.

——(1995) *Trade Policies and Developing Nations*, Washington, DC: Brookings Institution.

——(1997) 'Trade Policy and Economic Development: How We Learn', *American Economic Review*, 87(1): 1–22.

Kurzweil, M. (2002) 'The Need for a Complete Labour Market in CGE Modelling', paper presented at the 5th Annual Conference on Global Economic Analysis, Taipei, Taiwan, 5–7 June.

Lakshman, W.D. and Sri Lanka Association of Economists (eds) (1997) *Dilemmas of Development: Fifty Years of Economic Change in Sri Lanka*, Colombo: Sri Lanka Economic Association.

Lal, D. (2005) *The Hindu Equilibrium: India c.1500 BC – 2000 AD*, Oxford: Oxford University Press.

Lal, D. and Mynt, H. (1996) *The Political Economy of Poverty, Equity and Growth: A Comparative Study*, Oxford: Clarendon Press.

Lall, S. (1999) *The Technological Response to Import Liberalization in Sub-Saharan Africa*, London: Macmillan.

Levine, R. and Renelt, D. (1992) 'A Sensitivity Analysis of Cross-Country Growth Regressions', *American Economic Review*, 82(3): 942–63.

Lewis, S. (1971) *Pakistan: Industrialization and Trade Policies*, OECD: Paris.

Liang, Z. (2007) 'Trade Liberalization, Economic Restructuring and Urban Poverty: The Case of China', *Asian Economic Journal,* 21(3): 239–59.

Little, I.M.D. (1994) 'Trade and Industry Revisited', *Pakistan Development Review,* 33 (4), 359–89.

Little, I.M.D., Scitovsky, T. and Scott, M. (1970) *Development and Trade in Some Developing Countries: A Comparative Study*, Oxford: Oxford University Press for OECD.

Lopez, J.H. (2004) 'Pro Growth, Pro Poor: Is There a Trade Off?' World Bank Policy Research Working Paper 3378 (August).

Lopez, R., Nash, J. and Stanton, J. (1995) 'Adjustment and Poverty in Mexican Agriculture: How Farmers, Wealth Affects Supply Response', World Bank Policy Research Work Paper 1494.

McCulloch, N. and Ota, M. (2002) 'Export Horticulture and Poverty in Kenya', Working Paper No. 174, Brighton: Institute of Development Studies at the University of Sussex.

Mahmud, W. (1998) 'Bangladesh: Structural Adjustment and Beyond', paper presented at the International Conference on 'Adjustment and Beyond: The Reform Experience in South Asia', Jointly organised by the Bangladesh Economic Association and the International Economic Association, Dhaka, 30 March–1 April.

Maldives Monetary Authority (MMA), *Annual Report* (2007 and various years), Malé: MMA.

Matusz, S.J. and Tarr, D. (1999) 'Adjusting to Trade Policy Reform', World Bank Policy Research Work Paper 2142.

Mengistae, T. and Pattillo, C. (2002) Export Orientation and Productivity in Sub-Saharan Africa, IMF Working Paper WP/02/89, May.

Ministry of Finance (2004) *Bangladesh Economic Review*, Dhaka: Government of Bangladesh.

Ministry of Finance (2008) Budget Speech 2008, Colombo: Government of Sri Lanka.

Ministry of Finance (various years) *Economic Survey*, Kathmandu: Ministry of Finance, Government of Nepal.

Ministry of Tourism, (2001) *Tourism Statistics 2001*, Malé: Ministry of Tourism.

MPND (Ministry of Planning and National Development) (2005) *Maldives – Key Indicators 2005*, Malé: MPND.

——(2006) *Population and Housing Census*, Malé: MPND.

——(2008) *Consumer Price Index – National (January)*, Malé: MPND.

MPND/UNDP (2004) *Vulnerability and Poverty Assessment II*, Malé: MPND.

Mujeri, M. and Khondker, B. (2002) 'Decomposing Wage Inequality Change in Bangladesh: An Application of the Double Calibration Technique', DFID Project Paper. Online. Available at: www.gapresearch.org/production/MusafaDecomp.pdf (accessed 15 April 2008).

Naranpanawa, A. (2005) 'Trade Liberalization and Poverty in a Computable General Equilibrium (CGE) Model: The Sri Lankan Case', unpublished PhD thesis, Department of Accounting, Finance and Economics, Griffith Business School, Griffith University, Brisbane, Australia. Online. Available at: http://www4.gu.edu. au:8080/adt-root/public/adt-QGU20070130.165943/index.html (accessed 15 April 2008).

Naranpanawa, A. and Bandara, J.S. (forthcoming) *A Sri Lankan General Equilibrium Model with Income Distribution*, IPS Working Paper, Colombo: IPS.

National Statistics Bureau of the Royal Government of Bhutan (2000) *Household Income and Expenditure Survey*, Thimphu: Royal Government of Bhutan.

——(2004) *Poverty Analysis Report*, Thimpu: Royal Government of Bhutan.

——(2007a) *Poverty Analysis Report*, Thimpu: Royal Government of Bhutan.

——(2007b) *Living Standard Survey*, Thimpu: Royal Government of Bhutan.

Nicita, A., Olarreaga, M. and Porto, G. (2003) 'Designing a Pro-Poor Tariff Reform: The Case of Ethiopia', unpublished manuscript, World Bank.

Ninno, C., Dorosh, P.A., Smith, L.C. and Roy, D.K. (2001) 'The 1998 Floods in Bangladesh: Disaster Impacts, Household Coping Strategies, and Responses', Research Report 122, International Food Policy Research Institute (IFPRI).

Nissanke, M. and Thorbecke, E. (eds) (2007) *The Impact of Globalization on the World's Poor*, New York: Palgrave Macmillan in Association with UNU-WIDER.

Nordstrom, H., Ben-David, D. and Winters, L.A. (1999) *Trade, Income Disparity and Poverty*, Special Studies 5, Geneva: WTO.

NRB (various years) *Quarterly Economic Bulletin*, Kathmandu: Nepal Rastra Bank.

Osmani, S.R. (2002) 'Growth Strategies and Poverty Reduction', paper presented at the Asia and Pacific Forum on Poverty, 'Reforming Policies and Institutions for Poverty Reduction', organised by the Asian Development Bank, Manila, 5–9 February.

Osmani, S.R., Bajyacharya, B.B., Wangyel, Tashi and Tenzin, Sonam (2007) *Macroeconomics of Poverty Reductions: The Case Study for Bhutan*, Asia Pacific Regional Programme on the Macroeconomics of Poverty Reduction, United Nations Development Programme, Thimpu: UNDP.

Palanivel, T. (2005) *Trade Liberalization, Macroeconomic Performance and Poverty Reduction*, Colombo: UNDP.

Panagariya, A. (2002) 'Trade Liberalization in Asia', in J. Bhagwati (ed.) *Going Alone*, Cambridge, MA: MIT Press, pp. 219–302.

Parikh, K.S. (2006) *Explaining Growth in South Asia*, New Delhi: Oxford University Press.

Planning Commission (2006) 'Rapid Rural Urban Development Assessment', RGOB.

——(2006) *Bhutan Millennium Development Goals, Needs Assessment and Costing Report*, Thimpu: RGOB.

Porto, G.G. (2007) 'Globalization and Poverty in Latin America: Some Channels and Some Evidence', *The World Economy*, 30(3): 1430–56.

Pradhan, B. (2002) 'Debating the Effects of Trade Liberalization on Poverty: How Experiment Specificity Determines the Conclusions', DFID project paper. Online. Available at: www.gapresearch.org/production/BasantaPov.pdf (accessed 15 April 2008).

Psacharopoulos, G. and Woodhall, M. (1985) *Education for Development: An Analysis of Investment Choices*, Oxford: Oxford University Press for the World Bank.

Qadir, U., Kemal, A. and Hasan, M.M. (2000) 'Impact of Trade Reforms on Poverty', *The Pakistan Development Review,* 39(4): 1127–37.

Qureshi, S.K. and Arif, G.M. (2001) *Profile of Poverty in Pakistan, 1998–99*, MIMAP Technical Paper No. 5. Islamabad: PIDE.

Radhakrishna, R. and Ray, S. (eds) (2005) *Handbook of Poverty in India – Perspective, Policies, and Programmes*, New Delhi: Oxford University Press.

Rahman, M. (2001) 'Bangladesh's External Sector in FY2001: Review of Performance and Emerging Concerns', in Rehman Sobhan (ed.) *Bangladesh Facing the Challenges of Globalisation*, Dhaka: Centre for Policy Dialogue.

Raihan, S. (2007) *Dynamics of Trade Liberalization in Bangladesh: Analysis of Policies and Practices*, Dhaka: Pathak Shamabesh.

Rajan, R. (2006) 'From Paternalistic to Enabling', *Finance and Development*, 43(3): 54–6.

Ramesh, C. (1999) 'Effects of Trade Liberalization on Agriculture in India: Commodity Aspects', Regional Co-ordination Centre for Research and Development of Coarse Grains, Pulses, Roots and Tuber Crops in the Humid Tropics of Asia and the Pacific (CGPRT Centre).

Ravallion, M. (1990) 'Rural Welfare Effects of Food Price Changes under Induced Wage Responses: Theory and Evidence for Bangladesh', *Oxford Economics Papers*, 42(2): 574–85.

——(1997) 'Can High-Inequality Developing Countries Escape Absolute Poverty?' *Economic Letters*, 56: 51–7.

——(2001) 'Growth, Inequality and Poverty: Looking Beyond Averages', *World Development*, 29(11): 1803–15.

——(2004) 'Competing Concepts of Inequality in the Globalization Debate', in S.M. Collins and C. Graham (eds) *Brookings Trade Forum 2004 – Globalization, Poverty and Inequality*, Washington, DC: Brookings Institution Press.

——(2007) 'Looking Beyond Averages in the Trade and Poverty Debate', in M. Nissanke and E. Thorbecke (eds) *The Impact of Globalization on the World's Poor*, New York: Palgrave Macmillan in Association with UNU-WIDER.

Ravallion, M. and Chen, S. (2004) *China's (Uneven) Progress against Poverty*, Policy Research Working Paper Series 3408, Washington, DC: World Bank.

——(2009) *Weakly Relative Poverty*, Policy Research Working Paper Series 4844, Washington, DC: World Bank.

Ravallion, M., Chen, S. and Sangraula, P. (2007) *New Evidence on the Urbanization of Global Poverty*, Policy Research Working Paper No. 4199, Washington, DC: World Bank.

Ravenga, A. (1997) 'Employment and Wage Effects of Trade Liberalization: The Case of Mexican Manufacturing', *Journal of Labour Economics,* 15(3), part 2: S2CS43.

Razzaque, A., Khondker, B.H., Ahmed, N. and Mujeri, M.K. (2003a) 'Export–Growth Nexus and Trade Liberalization', Chapter 3 in *Trade Liberalization and Economic Growth: Empirical Evidence on Bangladesh*, MAP Technical Paper, Bangladesh Institute of Development Studies, Dhaka: MAP.

——(2003b) 'Liberalization and Growth', Chapter 2 in *Trade Liberalization and Economic Growth: Empirical Evidence on Bangladesh*, MAP Technical Paper, Bangladesh Institute of Development Studies, Dhaka: MAP.

Reserve Bank of India (2006) Reserve Bank of India Bulletin, August, Delhi: Reserve Bank of India. Online. Available at: http://rbidocs.rbi.org.in/rdocs/Bulletin/ (accessed 15 April 2008).

RMA (2000) *Annual Report*, Thimpu: Royal Monetary Authority of Bhutan.

——(2004) *Annual Report*, Thimpu: Royal Monetary Authority of Bhutan.

——(2005) *Annual Report*, Thimpu: Royal Monetary Authority of Bhutan.

——(2006) *Annual Report*, Thimpu: Royal Monetary Authority of Bhutan.

——(2007) *Annual Report*, Thimpu: Royal Monetary Authority of Bhutan.

Rodriguez, F. and Rodrik, D. (2001), 'Trade Policy and Economic Growth: A Skeptic's Guide to the Cross-National Evidence', *NBER Macroeconomics Annual 2000*, Cambridge, MA: MIT Press, pp. 261–324.

Rodrik, D. (1997) *Has Globalization Gone Too Far?*, Washington, DC: Institute for International Economics.

——(2000) 'Comments on *Trade, Growth and Poverty*, by David Dollar and Art Kraay'. Online. Available at: http://kgshome.harvard.edu/~.drodrik.academic.ksg/papers.html (accessed 15 April 2008).

Round, J.I and Whalley, J. (2006) 'Globalisation and Poverty: Implications of South Asian Experience for the Wider Debate', in M. Bussolo and I.J. Round (eds) *Globalisation and Poverty – Channels and Policy Responses*, London: Routledge.

Royal Government of Bhutan (2000) *Poverty Assessment and Analysis Report*, Thimpu: Royal Government of Bhutan and ADB.

Rupasinghe, K. (1985) 'Women Workers in Garment Factories in FTZs: Sri Lanka', International Peace Research Institute, Oslo, mimeo.

Ruud, P.A. (2000) *An Introduction to Classical Econometric Theory*, Oxford: Oxford University Press.

SAARC (2007) *Country Paper – Regional Poverty Profile, 2006–7*, Kathmandu: SAARC Secretariat.

Sachs, J.D. and Warner, A. (1995) 'Economic Convergence and Economic Policies', *Brookings Papers on Economic Activity*, 1: 1–95.

Salvatore, D. (2007) 'Growth, International Inequalities, and Poverty in a Globalized World', *Journal of Policy Modelling*, 29: 635–41.

Sargan, J. (1958) 'The Estimation of Economic Relationships Using Instrumental Variables', *Econometrica*, 26(3): 393–415.

SAWTEE (2005) 'Trade, Development and Poverty in Nepal', South Asia Watch on Trade, Economics, and Environment, Kathmandu, mimeo.

——(2007) *Human Development Impact Assessment in the Post ATC Period: The Case of Nepal*, Kathmandu: South Asia Watch on Trade, Economics and Environment (SAWTEE) and Action Aid International Nepal.

Sen, A. (1998) *Development as Freedom*, New York: Knopf.

Sharma, K. (2006) 'Food Security in the South Pacific Island Countries with Special Reference to the Fiji Islands', United Nations University, Research Paper No. 2006/68.

Sharma, K., Jayasuriya, S. and Oczkowski, E. (2000) 'Liberalization and Productivity Growth: The Case of Manufacturing Industry in Nepal', *Oxford Development Studies*, 28(2): 205–22.

Siddiqui, R. (2004) 'Energy and Economic Growth in Pakistan', *Pakistan Development Review*, 43(2): 175–200.

Siddiqui, R. and Akhtar, N. (2000) 'The Impact of Changes in Exchange Rate on Prices: A Case Study of Pakistan', *Pakistan Development Review*, 38(4): 1059–66.

Siddiqui, R. and Kemal, A.R. (2002a) 'Remittances, Trade Liberalization and Poverty in Pakistan: The Role of Excluded Variables in Poverty Change Analysis', DFID project paper. Online. Available at: www.gapresearch.org/production/RizwanaRemittR2.pdf (accessed 15 April 2008).

——(2002b) 'Poverty Inducing or Poverty Reducing? A CGE-Based Analysis of Foreign Capital Inflows in Pakistan', DFID project paper. Online. Available at: www.gapresearch.org/production/RizwanaFKI2.pdf (accessed 15 April 2008).

——(2006) 'Remittances, Trade Liberalization and Poverty in Pakistan: The Role of Excluded Variables in Poverty Change Analysis', *Pakistan Development Review*, 45 (3): 383–415.

Siddiqui, R. and Zafar, I. (2001) *Tariff Reduction and Functional Income Distribution in Pakistan: A CGE Model*, MIMAP Technical Paper Series No. 10 (January), Islamabad: Pakistan Institute of Development Economics.

Srinivasan, T.N. and Bhagwati, J. (2001) 'Outward-Orientation and Development: Are the Revisionists Right?' in D. Lal and R.H. Snape (eds) *Trade, Development and Political Economy: Essays in Honour of Anne Krueger*, London: Palgrave Macmillan, pp. 3–26.

Stryker, J.D. and Pandolfi, S. (1997) 'Impact of Outward Looking, Market Oriented Policy Reforms on Economic Growth and Poverty', Technical Paper, CAER II, Discussion Paper Number 7, HIID, USA.

Taslim, A. (2004) 'Trade Policy of Bangladesh: 1990–2003', article published in the Souvenir of the Dhaka University Economics Department Alumni Association (DUEDAA) Meeting.

Taylor, L, and von Arnim, R. (2007) 'Modeling the Impact of Trade Liberalization: A Critique of Computable General Equilibrium Models', OXFAM International Research Report.

Thirlwall, A.P. and Pacheco-Lopez, P.P. (2009) *Trade Liberalization and the Poverty of Nations*, Cheltenham: Edward Elgar.

Thomas, V. and Nash, J. (1991) *Best Practices in Trade Policy Reform*, Washington: World Bank and Oxford University Press.

Topalova, P. (2004) *Trade Liberalization and Firm Productivity: The Case of India*, IMF Working Paper No. WP/04/28, Washington, DC: IMF.

——(2005) 'Trade Liberalization, Poverty and Inequality: Evidence from Indian Districts', Working Paper 11614.

——(2007) 'Trade Liberalization, Poverty, and Inequality: Evidence from Indian Districts', in A. Harrison (ed.) *Globalization and Poverty*, Chicago: University of Chicago Press.

Uddin, F. and Swati, A.A. (2006) *Pakistan's Economic Journey: Need for a New Paradigm*, Islamabad: Institute of Policy Studies.

UNCTAD (2004) *The Least Developed Countries Report 2004 – Linking International Trade with Poverty Reduction*, New York: UN.

——(2008) *World Investment Report 2008*. Online. Available at: www.unctad.org/fdis-tatistics (accessed 15 April 2008).

UNDP (2004a) *Nepal Human Development Report*, Kathmandu: UNDP/NPC.

——(2004b) *Macroeconomics of Poverty Reduction: The Case of Nepal*, Asia Pacific Regional Programme on the Macroeconomics of Poverty Reduction, Kathmandu: UNDP.

——(2005a) *Tsunami Impact Assessment 2005*, New York: UNDP.

——(2005b) *Voices of the Least Developed Countries of the Asia and Pacific Region in Achieving MDGs*, New York: UNDP/UNESCAP.

——(2007) *Public Finance Implications of Trade Related Policy Reforms in Least Developed Countries*, Nepal Case Study, Colombo: UNDP Asia-Pacific Regional Centre.

UNESCAP (2000) *Reducing Disparities: Balanced Development of Urban and Rural Areas and Regions within the Countries of Asia and the Pacific*, New York: UN.

——(2001) *Promoting Complementarities and Investment in Selected Manufacturing Sectors: Resources-Based Industries and Poverty Alleviation*, New York: UNES-CAP.

——(2008) *Economic and Social Survey of Asia and the Pacific*, New York: UN.

Virmani, A., Goldar, B.N. Veeramani, C. (2004) 'Impact of Tariff Reforms on Indian Industry: Assessment Based on a Multi-Sector Econometric Model', Working Paper, ICRIER.

Wade, R. (2004) 'Is Globalization Reducing Poverty and Inequality?', *World Development*, 34 (4): 567–89.

Wagle, U.R. (2007) 'Are Economic Liberalization and Equality Compatible? Evidence from South Asia', *World Development*, 35(11): 1836–57.

Weerahewa, J. (2002) 'Assessing the Impacts of Globalisation using Decomposition Methods', DFID project paper. Online. Available at: www.gapresearch.org/production/JeevikaPov.pdf (accessed 15 April 2008).

——(2006) 'Rice Market Liberalization and Household Welfare in Sri Lanka: A General Equilibrium Analysis', CATPRN Working Paper 2006–1, Department of Food, Agricultural and Resource Economics, University of Guelph, Ontario.

Weerakoon, D. and Thennakoon, J. (2006) 'Sri Lanka in the WTO Doha Round Negotiations: Issues and Concerns', *South Asian Journal*, 12: 39–49.

White, H. and Anderson, E. (2001) 'Growth versus Distribution: Does the Pattern of Growth Matter?' *Development Policy Review*, 19(3): 267–89.

Wijayasiri, J. (2007) 'Maldives in the WTO', in S. Kelegama (ed.) South Asia in the WTO, New Delhi: Sage Publications, 183–206.

Winters, L.A. (2000) 'Trade Liberalization and Poverty', a paper presented for DFID, UK.

——(2000a) 'Trade and Poverty: Is There a Connection', in D. Ben David, H. Nordstrom and L.A. Winters (eds) *Trade, Income Disparity and Poverty, Special Study No. 5*, Geneva: World Trade Organization.

——(2000b) 'Trade Liberalization and Poverty', Discussion Paper 7, Poverty Research Unit, University of Sussex.

——(2002) 'Trade Liberalization and Poverty: What are the Links?' *The World Economy*, 25(9): 1339–67.

Winters, L.A., McCulloch, N. and McKay, A. (2004) 'Trade Liberalization and Poverty: The Evidence So Far', *Journal of Economic Literature*, XLII: 72–115.

Wooldridge, J.M. (2002) *Econometric Analysis of Cross Section and Panel Data*, Cambridge, MA: MIT Press.

World Bank (1990) *World Development Report*, Washington, DC: World Bank.

——(1999) 'Bangladesh Trade Liberalization: Its Pace and Impacts', Report No. 19591BD, mimeo.

——(2001) *World Development Report 2000/01: Attacking Poverty*, Washington, DC: World Bank.

——(2002a) *Globalization, Growth and Poverty*, Washington, DC: World Bank.

——(2002b) *Pakistan Poverty Assessment – Poverty in Pakistan: Vulnerabilities, Social Groups, and Rural Dynamics*. Washington DC: World Bank.

——(2004a) *Nepal Trade and Competitiveness Study*, Kathmandu: World Bank.

——(2004b) *Trade Policies in South Asia: An Overview*, Report No. 29949, Volume II, Poverty Reduction and Economic Management Sector Unit South Asia Region, New Delhi: World Bank.

——(2005a) *Nepal Development Policy Review: Restarting Growth and Poverty Reduction*, Poverty Reduction and Economic Management South Asia Region, New Delhi: World Bank.

——(2005b) *Sri Lanka Development Policy Review*, Washington, DC: World Bank.

——(2006a) *Can South Asia End Poverty in a Generation?* Washington, DC: World Bank.

——(2006b) *Sri Lanka: Development Policy Review*, Washington, DC: World Bank.

——(2007a) *A Chance to Eliminate Poverty: Scaling Up Development Assistance in South Asia, Strategy Update, South Asia Region*, Washington, DC: World Bank.

——(2007b) *Sri Lanka Development Forum: The Economy, Regional Disparities and Global Opportunities*, South Asian Region, Washington, DC: World Bank.

——(2007c) *Sri Lanka Poverty Assessment*, Washington, DC: World Bank.

——(2007d) *Sri Lanka Trade at a Glance*, Washington, DC: World Bank.

——(2008) *The Maldives: Trade Brief*. Online. Available at: http://info.worldbank.org/ etools/ wti2008/docs/brief118.pdf (accessed 15 April 2008).

——(2010) *World Trade Indicators 2009–10*, Washington, DC: World Bank.

WTO (World Trade Organisation) (1998) *Trade Policy Review: India*, Geneva: WTO.

——(2000a) *Trade Policy Review: Bangladesh*, Geneva: WTO.

——(2000b) *Trade Policy Review: India*, Geneva: WTO.

——(2002) *Trade Policy Review: India*, Geneva: WTO.

——(2003) *Trade Policy Review: Maldives*. Online. Available at: www.wto.org/english/ tratop_e/tpr_e/tp209_e.htm (accessed 15 April 2008).

——(2007) *World Tariff Profiles*. Online. Available at: www.wto.org

——(2008) *World Tariff Profiles*. Online. Available at: www.wto.org

——(2009) *Trade Policy Review, Maldives*. Online. Available at: www.wto.org/english/ tratop_e/tpr_e/tp321_e.htm (accessed 15 April 2008).

Yatawara, R and Handel, D. (2007) 'Gender Related Transition Issues Resulting from the Expiration of the Agreement on Textiles and Clothing', unpublished report, Institute of Policy Studies of Sri Lanka.

Yilmaz, K. and Varma, S. (1995) *Trade Policy Reforms in Bangladesh*, Industrial Sector Study Working Paper No. 28, South Asia Country Department, Washington, DC: World Bank.

Index